Better Lucky Than Good

LOUISVILLE STORY PROGRAM

Louisville Story Program
851 South 4th Street
Louisville, KY 40203
www.louisvillestoryprogram.org

ISBN 978-0-9914765-5-8
Library of Congress Control Number 2019948264

Edited by Joe Manning
Book design by Shellee Marie Jones
Cover photo courtesy of Paul Goffner

Contents

Introduction

*I*f we're lucky, the first week in May is the most intoxicatingly beautiful week of the year in the Commonwealth of Kentucky. If we're not, it's cold and wet, but the magnolia blossoms still smell great, folks get gussied up anyway, and Louisville may be the only place on earth where school kids get a district-sanctioned holiday in honor of a horse race. Like Carnival or Mardi Gras, The Kentucky Derby is Louisville's spring festival. It's our party, and we make a big time of it. We have picnics, a big parade, an increased incidence of corn dogs and Derby Pie, weird hats and weird celebrities. We drink a special drink, we sing an old song, and in the middle of it all, we shake our tickets in the air and holler at the horses as they run.

But the track has been right there at 4th and Central every single day of the year, in one form or another, for the last 145 years. Outside of Derby season, though, many Louisvillians don't have a meaningful awareness of Churchill Downs or the neighborhoods that support the most famous racetrack in the world. When the reporters have filed their stories of grit and glory, when the cameras have been carted off, and when the roses have been dried for keepsakes, there's still work to do in the shedrow, stalls to muck, horses to walk and bathe and feed and shoe. The track surface needs to be maintained, and the folks who come to work behind the scenes on the backside, every day, rely on one another to put on another race. There's always another race to run somewhere.

The backside of Churchill Downs is a complete community hiding in plain sight. It's a literal village—with housing, health care and social service providers, a chaplaincy, food services, a bustling economy of vets, farriers, pony people, exercise riders, hay and straw men, a security detail, rules, a rich, shared history, traditions, stories, heroes, villains, and superstitions (Never bring peanuts into the barn. See: p. 134)—of upwards of 1,000 people who work and sometimes live there, and who sustain the most iconic institution in the city, one that has made Louisville famous the world over. Nevertheless, many Louisville residents never have even a glancing encounter with the backside community or the South End neighborhoods that have provided Churchill Downs with a workforce for generations.

Our mission at Louisville Story Program is to amplify the voices and stories of folks in Louisville who we don't hear from often enough. We knew the backside was the perfect place to dig in and develop a book that would offer the rest of us a clearer picture of a community that is seldom seen, but one which is so rich and so valuable to the city as a whole.

So we started showing up on the backside of the track, introducing ourselves at Wagner's Pharmacy, listening to the scuttlebutt at the Kentucky Thoroughbred Association office, asking racetrackers (that's what track folks call themselves) to show us the lay of the land and make introductions. By and by, they were happy to help, and, slowly, we made new friends.

We showed up repeatedly and did a lot of listening before we ever turned on the tape recorder for one of the many, many interviews we conducted over the course of three years. It took a long time to convince folks that *we* were not writing a book about the track. That, on the contrary, *they* were to be the authors. They would tell their stories in their own words. Over the course of three years, we sat down with these participants in recursive, in-depth interviews. We listened closely as they talked about their lives and encouraged them to describe their experiences as fully as they cared to. As they elaborated on their stories, revealing greater detail and specificity, and as they collaborated with us throughout the editing process, the chapters hewed closer and closer to the narratives they wanted to tell, and which they have chosen to share with the world.

The type of mindful community building required to carry off a deep-dive project like this takes patience and immense resources. But this rigorous, time consuming, and fruitful process of deep listening and collaboration, one which gives real authorship to the participants, is the key ingredient to documenting a community from the inside out. We don't tell people's stories for them. These chapters were authored by a representative cross section of 32 backside workers and South End residents, and you're reading the first book in the history of American thoroughbred racing in which equine workers have documented their industry and their lives in their own words.

Like most of the non-racetracker world, we didn't know squat about horses or racing, and had to ask a lot of very dumb questions in order to elicit very simple answers. So, reader, you're welcome for that. As a result, you'll find within these pages, straight talk from grooms, assistant trainers, a shedrow foreman, an outrider, a pony person, a member of the gate crew, and many others, about what it takes to put on a race. You'll get a finer understanding of the outsized influence and importance that African Americans from South Louisville have had on the backstretch through the ages. You'll read about how the entire American thoroughbred racing industry relies on a workforce of dedicated horsemen and women who have migrated here from Mexico and Central America. You'll hear from home-grown South End residents who knew, straight out of the gate, that there was no life for them but a life on the track. Several authors were born and raised within spitting distance of the backside. One can see the track's enormous video screen from his front yard. Alternately, three authors came to work at Churchill from the same county in Guatemala, 2,700 miles away from 4th and Central. All of the authors took a different path onto the track and into this book. But each of them came to this project with a willingness to share the types of real, three-dimensional stories—of joy, work, love, loss, and victory—that are so valuable to those of us who want to know our neighbors with a little more clarity, and who appreciate a good story.

I'll never forget one day when I was sitting in Neil Huffman's tack room—two TVs going, one for racing and the other for daytime talk shows—as he was fussing with one of the beloved barn cats he named after some of his favorite beer joints: Fern, Moody, and Jim Porter. Neil's been retired from racing for years, but still comes to the track every day to take care of the cats and to keep his office hours as the emeritus storyteller-in-residence on the backside. Neil can spin a tale like no one I've ever met, and I spent many good hours listening to him over the years, marveling at his craft. Neil's also a fount of important institutional knowledge about the track, has the clinical understanding of horse physiology and pathology of a veterinarian, and an unrivaled historical understanding of South Louisville. Neil shares freely of his wisdom and seemingly bottomless well of stories, but only up to a point. There were more than a few times when he told me, "Now you're gonna have to turn your recorder off before I tell you this next one." But on this particular day, he was asking the questions. Neil, who just could not believe it when I told him it was my actual job, wanted to know why I kept coming around listening to a bunch of racetrackers. "I don't see why anyone would care about my life. Who the hell is going to read any of this?" It's a fair enough question. What is it about the everyday experiences of our neighbors that should be really noteworthy? There's enough spectacle and glitz and noise to entertain and divert all of us for the rest of our lives. Why bother hearing from "regular folks"?

This was one of the only times I've had a leg up on Neil Huffman, though. "You're gonna have to take my word for it, Neil. We've published some books before, and I know for a fact that people are really interested in hearing from folks like you. You've lived a remarkable life and you're a great storyteller. People are going to eat it up. I promise." And it's true. A good yarn, spun well, never goes out of style, even if it pushes against the truth a little. Stories of real adversity, of getting up, dusting off, and getting in the next race never grow old.

So, this book isn't about the Kentucky Derby. It's not even about horses as much as you might expect. This book is about all the living that occurs in South Louisville on the days when most of us aren't watching, and all the work that happens when most of us are still sleeping. You'll not be surprised to discover that these pages are bound together with a strong thread of very common dignity. These stories have dirt under their nails and a heartbeat, and the authors of this book are the real stewards of horse racing in the Derby City. They are the homegrown historians of the South End, the bards of the backside, and we're lucky to have heard from them. /

—Joe Manning, editor

Bob DeSensi

TRAINER

*H*orses are just like humans. You never trust a man who won't look you in the eye when he's talking to you, and it's the same way with horses. When you go to a sale to buy a horse, and that horse won't make eye contact with you, I don't care if he sells for $10 million: he's no count. You can just write him off.

I had a horse, a pretty good filly named My Little Firefly, who could run a lot. One day as we saddled her in the paddock, an old valet named Matty Brown was with the favorite, and these two horses locked eyes. My horse pulls up, and I told my valet, "Back up a minute. This filly's going to do something stupid." She froze, and the other horse froze too. They were just like two boxers in the ring, and finally the other horse walked off. I saddled my horse and old Matty Brown came over and slipped me $10.

"Bet $10 on your horse for me," he said.

I said, "Are you crazy? Your horse is 9-5."

"They locked eyes, and yours won," he said. He'd been around enough horses to know.

Mine went off at 12- or 14-1, and I beat the favorite that day.

You always think you can improve a horse, no matter what anybody says to you. You always think you

can develop him. You feel like you can understand what that horse is trying to tell you. You never get over that. It's not just winning races. The feeling you get—like you can do something no one else can do—is just like teaching school when you take a kid who doesn't have any self-confidence or who is not trying, and you bring him up to be an outstanding student. There's so much pride involved in that. Nothing else matters. It's the same way with horses. You want to improve that horse. You want to get everything you can out of that horse. The more that you feel like you can communicate with that horse, the more satisfaction you get out of it.

Horses are tremendous creatures of habit. When you come back to the barn at 9:00 p.m., you want the horse to be doing the same thing it was doing last night at 9:00. If not, you want to know why. If a horse leaves four oats in his tub, is that a good sign or a bad sign? You become so obsessed with it. You make a training chart, and you might have a 30-day line drawn with exactly what you want to do with that horse for 30 days or 45 days out: This is where this horse is going to run at this time. Now, you might change that 100 times in between, but the horse will tell you if you're going in the right direction. He's going to let you know by his attitude, by the way he handles himself on the racetrack. Most of it's just in the eye contact and the rapport you build with the horse. Sometimes the horse gets beat, gets in trouble, stumbles or something, but the plan is there. When it all comes together it's like a miracle. The horse has to fit into that plan, and very few do. When you can hit it 100%, you're on top of the world because you know you've done everything right that you could possibly do. Those horses win, and you feel like you've really accomplished something.

Whenever a horse got beat, it was always because of something you did wrong. Not because of something the horse did wrong or because the jock did something. It was because of some mistake that you weren't mentally capable of handling. It becomes an obsession. *What did I do wrong? What do I need to change to make sure it doesn't happen next time?* It's like taking dope. You can't get off of that horse. It consumes your whole life. You keep getting those babies in. Two-year-olds keep a trainer young because you always think you can develop them. You just become obsessed with some horses and know they're going to win if you put them in the right place. It was my whole life. I got to where I couldn't stand anything but being around horses. I didn't want to be around people.

Then one day you wake up and you're old. You don't know how it went by that fast—it just passes you up. It's almost impossible how all the years run together; trainers deal with fifths of a second, not years. Somebody will ask you when your daughter's birthday is and you have to think about it for 10 minutes. But somebody asks you about a horse, "What time did he go in?" and you say, "He went three-quarters in a minute and ten," without even thinking about it. That's how people grow old on the racetrack. Very few horsemen ever quit. They die on the racetrack. That's what people don't understand.

I have been blessed with a good family. I have a good wife. I have good kids. Maybe my family suffered because of the attitude I had. You go to bed early, but you wake up 11:00 that night, put your clothes on, and go to the barn to see what this horse is doing. Your family wants to go out to eat, but you look at your watch, it's 8:00 at night, you're getting up at 4:00 in the morning. So they have to sacrifice as much as you do. I didn't even think about it at the time. I never asked. I think there might be some resentment. Maybe there were a lot of things I should have done that I didn't do. Two things I never did, though: I never drank in front of my kids at all, because I grew up living upstairs over a bar. Everybody drank all the time, so if you wanted to be an adult, you had to drink. I started drinking at 13 because I was grown up at 13. So I didn't want my kids to think that's the way people did it. I also never talked about horses. I didn't want my kids around the barn, because I wanted them to live regular lives. Now, my son came to work for me one summer. He wanted to quit school, so I gave him the worst, meanest son of a bitch I had in the barn. And he did a really good job with him, but he decided, *No, this isn't gonna work for me.* I'm glad he didn't follow in my footsteps. I don't know if I had any footsteps for him to follow in, but I didn't want him to be around it. It's a dirty life. It's not something you recommend to somebody. It's not a job. People who are looking for a job don't need to come to the backside of the racetrack. It's a way of life.

The only thing I regret in my life is not spending more time with my children when they were young. I don't know what happened. I stopped training and looked up and my kids had kids. One day you wake up and you're 70 years old saying, "Where the hell has my life gone?" It's gone in that barn. That's where. But everybody was like that, not just me.

———

I worked for Del Carroll as a foreman. The foreman runs the shed, makes sure all the help's there and everything's getting done. Then he made me assistant trainer. You got to make your bones just like anything else. We won the Preakness in '72 with Bee Bee Bee. That was the first time in my life I had a chance to work with really good horses. I'd always been around cheap horses. This may have been the turning point in my life. It was when I could see what made a champion. We had this mare, Deceit. To see the look in her eyes—how she carried herself every day, how the other horses looked at her—made me understand that horses know when they are good. I would spend the rest of my life trying to understand this.

She was either tied or right behind the champion her three year-old year, but when I came she was pretty sore all the time. She had suspensory problems that made it very hard to train her and keep her sound. She would get so sore sometimes that we couldn't hardly walk her. As sore as she was, when she walked on the racetrack she was sound, because she had the mental ability to put pain out. Normal horses don't do that. Mr. Carroll didn't believe in medication, so none of his horses ever got medication of any kind. Deceit ran because she was a racehorse, and that's what made the difference. She ran on heart. I had never been around horses like that before.

I was praying Deceit wouldn't break down in her last race at Hialeah. She hooked up with a horse at the 3/8 pole and would not let the horse go by; she was going to die on the racetrack before she let that horse go by her. I was scared to death she'd break down, and they came to the wire and dead heated in the race. She was a champion and she won. We couldn't cool her out after that. We had to pack her in ice, and we all stayed in the stall with her all night. There was about five of us—the exercise girls, the groom. Everybody loved her, because she was just that kind of horse. She had a heart as big as my dining room table. After she cooled out that night, she was fine, but she didn't race anymore. She went to a broodmare farm and I never saw her again.

I've had horses break down that were perfectly sound. Four of us owned a really good horse. He was the real deal. Not only the best horse I ever trained, but the best I ever put my hands on. He just had what it took to be a good horse. He did everything right. Never did a thing wrong the whole time I had him in training. He let you know he was good. You didn't have to guess. I looked at 200 horses at the Calder sale. He was the last one, and I told the owner I'm not buying anything else. That's the horse I'm going to buy. So I waited and bought him for $22,000.

The first time I ran him, in the fall as a two year-old, he won easy. In his next start, another trainer came to me and said, "I've got a horse in the race with you. I can't beat your horse, but I've got my horse sold for a lot of money. How much will it take for you to scratch your horse?" I said, "I can't scratch my horse. This is a pretty good horse. I need this race to move forward from here, so I can't do it." Later that afternoon he comes to my barn and hands me a check. He says, "Fill it out. Whatever you want. Just put it on there, and scratch your horse." I said, "Listen, I can't scratch my horse. You don't understand. You can't beat my horse. You better scratch yours or leave it alone. I'm not scratching." Well, I knew I was in serious trouble when I got to the paddock. My jockey took off sick, and the stewards had named another rider that I didn't know.

My horse bolted, got beat. The rider came back, looked up at me and said, "You should've taken the check." That was an education. One that taught me to have a lot of acquaintances on the racetrack, but count your friends on one hand and never trust anyone.

I took that horse to Florida, and he came up to the stakes race perfectly. About six lengths in front of a horse who ended up horse of the year. My jock looked back to see where the field was, and my horse switched leads and broke one off. They had to put him down when he broke his leg. We had him planned all the way through his three-year-old year. It would've taken a really good horse to beat him.

I thought I had my heart broken 100 times as a young man from all the beautiful girls that broke up with me, but that horse taught me what it really felt like to have all of your dreams and a lifetime of hopes destroyed. How stupid do you have to be to let a horse change your life? I had developed a relationship with this horse that "normal people" will never understand. I never want to make that connection with a horse again.

They're getting ready to put him down, and he's looking you right in the eye. He wants help. For two years, you've spent every day of your life with this horse. Now he's looking you right in the eye and he says, "What's going on? Help me." You're thinking, *What can I do? I don't want to put him down, but I know I have to.* There's nothing you can do but ruin your life. You're dead in the water. That destroyed me as a trainer. I was through, because I was never going to let myself get that attached to another horse as long as I lived.

Everything he did was perfect. He never made a mistake. If you were doing something wrong, he almost told you, "No, I don't want to do that. Let's do this." It was amazing, the intelligence that horse had. And when we had to put him down I told myself, "I'll never do this again." And I never did. I had a couple of pretty good horses after that, and I liked them. But I wasn't going to put myself in that position again. I wasn't going to get attached.

But it's part of the game. You got to take it. You got to suck it up and go from there, but it never gets easy. You almost have to devoid yourself of most emotions. Because you're going to have a lot of horses break down. You're going to have to destroy some horses you don't ever want to. Everybody likes horses, or they wouldn't be around them. Nobody could work on the racetrack that didn't like horses. You work seven days a week—hot, cold, rain, snow, doesn't make any difference. So you've got to have respect for the animal.

There are two types of people on the racetrack: people that want to be there, and people that have to be there. The people that want to be there love horses, want to do a good job, think nothing about working seven days a week. The people that have to be there, if you close the racetrack, they're going to be in jail or living under a bridge because they can't function in society. But the racetrack gives them structure and they can function on the backside.

I was driving to Latonia one morning in a snow-storm. It's snowing like hell. It's 4:30 in the morning and I can hardly see the road. Here's two white boys hitchhiking. They're on the road to Latonia, so I know they're going to the racetrack. I pull over and say, "What's going on?" They said, "We're looking for a job." I said, "Come on. You got a job." They didn't know anything about horses. Anybody standing out in the snow on a highway looking for a job, they'll learn. Well, they did learn. They stayed with me about two and a half, three years and were excellent help.

One time one of those boys called me on a Sunday morning and said, "Come and get me, I'm in jail. I got a DUI." I said, "Well, it'll be four hours. I'll be down there." I get there and the guy says,

"You can't have him." I said, "What do you mean I can't have him? It's a DUI." I had a real good friend I had some horses for who was a judge, and I called him. I said, "I don't know what's going on. They won't release that boy." He said, "Call Tommy," who was a big shot in the police department. Tommy says, "I'll come down." I'm still at the jail, I've been there two or three hours trying to get this boy out. Tommy comes out laughing and says, "Bob, that boy's wanted for robbing a bank in Cincinnati." That's where Turfway is. Right across the river.

I said, "He's been with me for almost three years!" He said, "Kid just told me the whole story. Here's what happened. He and the other boy robbed a bank. They got $35,000, threw a party with all their friends at a motel with a spinning restaurant or something on top, blew all the money, went on the run, and you've been harboring them for two and a half years." Later on, that red-headed boy got killed in a bar. He was a good groom. He did three years, got released, and got killed in a bar fight in Cincinnati.

The first year I went to Sunshine Park, which was next to Florida Downs, I was working for Jerry Romans. We shipped down there, unloaded the horses, and there was a bar called The Barn right across the street. Racetracks always had a bar to hang out at. You only went to places where there were racetrackers. You didn't go hang out at regular bars. At that time, Tampa, Florida was like nothing around it. We got in the bar—lot of racetackers in there. First thing you know, somebody hits somebody with a cue stick and kills the guy. We stayed there all night waiting for the police to investigate that. Racetracks always had those kind of places. The most horrible place in the world I ever raced was Hazel Park, because every gangster in the world was in Detroit at the time. I knew guys who had horses for Whitey Bulger, Murder Incorporated.

I grew up in West Louisville. There was a bread company at 15th and Broadway near my house that still delivered with horse-drawn carriages when I was a kid, and there were people that collected trash in the neighborhood that also had horses. When we were kids, it was a big deal to wait until they put their horses up and then go ride them or play with them. We would watch those old timers work on them. They'd do different things to keep them sound, like treat harness sores with old-type medications to keep them going. They had to work.

Those guys were good teachers, but I really learned about horses because my dad was a dedicated, every day, two-dollar bettor. My dad loved the game. He taught my older brother and me how to read the racing form, how to figure the odds, how to make a turnaround, when to make a parlay—the basics of becoming addicted to the game.

He owned a tavern called Joe's Little Brown Jug on 15th and Breckinridge. It's not there anymore. Guys would come in on their lunch hour when they had time to kill. They'd eat a sandwich and bet on horses, and those guys followed the horses all over the country. That was going on all over the city. The whole West End. My uncle had a book down there too. There were maybe 10 guys I knew when I was a kid who all had books.

Then a black guy they called the Sheikh wanted to take control of the West End, which was turning from white to black then pretty much. He wanted the control. At that time, you paid off politicians, you paid off the local cop, the captain, everybody that came in. You took care of everybody. He got control of the politicians. One by one he would put these people out of business so he could take over. Dad didn't want to sell. And they said, "Well, here's the deal. You're gonna sell. And here's the price." They came in with axes,

A guy from Detroit offered me an outstanding job training for him, but I couldn't take it. There was no way I could put myself in that situation. Detroit was a bad city. When you went someplace in Detroit, you'd better be packing or you'd better be with somebody who was. About half a dozen of those guys went to prison for fixing races.

———

sledgehammers, broke all the tables, broke the beer cases. Put holes in the walls. Said, "Now you gonna sell?" So Dad sold the place to the Sheikh when I was 12. We lived upstairs over the bar, so we had to move. We didn't have any place to live. Everybody was broke. Busted. So we ended up in the South End. Rented us a house at 4th and Colorado.

My dad, my grandfather, and my uncle were all horse fanatics. They all loved going to the racetrack and loved going to the bookmaker. They brought us to the track in 1950 to see a horse called Your Host who was going to run in the Derby. Once I saw those horses I knew I wanted to get back there. I was a horrible student, and I hated school. I saw racetracking as a way to live. I was going to graduate and start working on horses.

In high school I started spending more time at the track. Me, my brother, and two other guys—Jerry Cahill and Jimmy Humrich—came to the races almost every day. We'd get out of school at 2:10. Post time might have been 2:00. The bus came right down from St. X. at 2nd and Broadway and dropped us off right out on 4th Street. We'd jump that fence where the quarter mile chute is and go right into the grandstand. I wasn't a professional gambler, but I made a little money. I made more money taking bets from others then I did by myself. We would split show bets: The four of us would put up 50 cents apiece, and bet show-bets on horses. Or we'd just watch them run and we wouldn't bet. We all had jobs, so we might be able to stay for two or three races, and then had to go to work. We'd go just about every day that the races were in town.

Miles Park was harder to sneak into. It was tough. It was a small racetrack, and they had night racing. A lot of four-and-a-half furlong races. Matter of fact, a horse called Dear Ethel set the world record for four and half

furlongs at Miles Park. A guy named Mike McGee trained her, and I was walking hots for Mike McGee. I was walking hots down there the summer of '67 or '68. It was like a fair. Like a country fair.

When I was a kid in high school, I'd follow horses all over the country. We would watch them run here and they'd go to Chicago and we'd follow. We'd want to know what they were doing when they came back. We had a connection with the horses, because they got beat and we watched them get beat, or because they won and we won money. I don't think people followed the claiming horses like we followed them—they were our bread and butter.

———————

I went to college reluctantly. I didn't want to go. I was a bad student, a horrible student. I went to St. X, then I went to Bellarmine. It was still a college then and filled with a bunch a priests who had absolutely no business trying to teach. I did my graduate work at Catherine Spalding when it was still a college. They had one or two courses in the education department to get your master's in education. I taught high school one year and grade school maybe three-and-a-half years before I quit. I worked on the racetrack in the summers.

When I went to Bellarmine, it was a very strict school. You had to wear a tie, and you could only get three absences a year. I didn't like it. If it hadn't been for Vietnam I don't know if I'd ever have gone back to school. I got kicked out twice. Once for grades and once for gambling. I got deferred from the draft, but then I was 1A to go the year I graduated. Father Roger White, a teacher there who was a really, really super guy, said, "Do you want to go to Vietnam?" I said, "I'm not anxious to go, but if I gotta go, I gotta go, ain't no big deal." He said, "If you'll teach in a poverty area,

I'll get you deferred for a year." I said, "I got no background in teaching." He said, "Well, you're gonna go to summer school."

I took two courses in summer school, then got a job in Marion County, and that got me deferred for a year. At the end of that year, they called me and said if I would teach in a Catholic grade school and start on my master's, I could get another deferment. So I came back to Louisville. When that deferment was up, I got drafted. I had developed an ulcer from drinking, so when I went to Fort Knox they said, "You can't come in here like this."

After they saw the ulcer they said, "Here's the deal. Because you've got a college education and you've taught school, we'll operate on you, we'll fix your ulcer, and we'll send you to Officer Candidate School and you can come in as an officer." They said it would take four years. I said, "Draft's two. I wanna go for two." He handed me a paper and said, "You have to sign this paper saying that you know you have this physical disability. It won't interfere with your ability to be in the Army, and you hold us not responsible for anything that happens." I said, "I don't think I want to sign that. If anything happens, I want to be treated like something happened." They chewed my ass out.

I said, "Do what you gotta do." He said, "Get your ass out of here. There'll be a bus to pick you up." I didn't wait for any bus. I hitchhiked back to Louisville. Every six months for the next three years, I had to take another physical to see if I was going to go in or not. That's the way they treated you.

I got my education from three great horsemen. Sunny Lower was the best leg man I was ever around. I was green as grass when he took me under his wing and taught me how to watch for problems before they became major problems and what to do to prevent them and then to fix what I missed. Del Carroll was a master of bringing top horses up to a race in perfect condition. He trained hard and

made his horses hard, and he earned the respect of all who ever worked for him. Harry Trotsek was a true horseman. He was a finesse trainer, no medication, and he could make a horse think he was good. I owe everything I ever learned that was good for the game, and more important for the animals, to these three horsemen.

You'll see a lot of people on the backside—especially the old timers—who refer to somebody as a horseman, not as a trainer. If people have a trainer's license, they're a trainer, but that doesn't make them a horseman. A horseman is somebody that knows about horses, cares about horses.

If they look at the next guy and say, "Well, he trains horses," in their eyes, he's not a horseman. Somebody like Neil Huffman, he's a horseman. Neil was more of a farm man, with brood mares and stuff like that. He and his brother ran a lot of horses off of Starlight Training Center. First he went to work for Skip Dunn at Prudential and America Savings and Loan. They went bankrupt and Skip went to prison.

Then he went to work for Dan Lasater, who went to prison. Then he went to work for J.T. Lundy, who also went to prison. Everybody he's worked for has ended up in prison. In spite of this he is respected on the backside as a horseman.

His brother Blackie Huffman was a full-time trainer. They grew up around the corner from Churchill. They went to Holy Name School and hung around the track and really learned the business. Blackie was good. He knew how to take his time and work with horses and develop them. He had good horses, top-stake horses. He got all the run out of them he could get, and he won a lot of races. He was not just a trainer, but a true horseman.

Blackie was also a prolific liar. He'd lie five minutes about the time of day. He could not tell the truth. One time I walked up and Blackie was writing in a notebook. I started talking to him, and he held up his hand. "Hold on," he says, "I just thought of a good lie. I'm writing it down so I don't forget about it."

He was a funny guy. Blackie was as good as there ever was and he was a good friend of mine. Tops. When Blackie was dying I'd go by the hospital to see him early when it would be just him and me. I went to the hospital to see him the day before he died. He had been taking chemo and radiation. He couldn't talk, but he called me over to the bed. Held my hand and said, "I want you to do me a favor."

"What do you need?" I said. "Anything you want."

"I've never asked you to do anything," he said. "I want you to do me one favor now."

"What's that? What do you want? Tell me what you want."

"Put that pillow over my head," he said.

"Blackie, I can't."

"No, you can do it," Blackie says.

"I can't do it, buddy."

Now, my name ends in a vowel, and Blackie says, "Bob DeSensi. *You're Italian.* It's in your blood."

Here I am with tears all up and down my face, and he couldn't stand to miss a chance to get me! What a great guy he was.

There's a book called *Fixed* that's about two fixed races here on Derby Day. It's about these horses Scottish Thorn and Postal Milagro, and I just happened to be in on both races when they ran. That was a big deal on Derby Day, to fix the last race every year. This went on every year for a long time until finally they stopped the last race from being a claiming race. Everybody on the backside knew it. It's the way we got money to go to the next town. It went on everyplace. It wasn't just here. You never asked questions but you could figure out what was going on. You knew the trainers that would be involved, the bets that would be involved. When you went back and started looking at the forms and the horses that were in the races, you'd know who was being played and who wasn't. It was just a question of being smart enough to figure it out. The people that were directly involved with the horses were closed-mouth about all of it. The only way you would be in on it is if you had a horse in the race, or one of the jocks would tell you about it in advance, or one of the grooms that was rubbing the horse would tell you what they'd done with the horse.

A horse that was 15-1 on a program went off at 9-5 on Derby Day. You could imagine how much money had to be bet on Derby Day to bring that horse down when there was no telephone betting or anything. It all had to come through Churchill. The bookmakers were so swamped with the money because they weren't going to get burned when they figured out what was going on. They'd sucked up so much of it, but then they said, "No, no. Not this one." They wanted the odds to come down on the horse, so they didn't have to pay off as much. They brought the money to the track and bet it at the windows. They were protecting themselves too.

When people were gambling to make a living, it was popular to hold horses—get them beat intentionally—and then take them to another racetrack where people didn't know them to bet on them. The trainer can get his horse beat by training methods or something else or running him where he doesn't belong. At one time, there were four different editions of the *Racing Form*. If you ran a horse in Kentucky three or four times, and you sent him up east where there was a different edition, all they would see was the beaten races. They wouldn't see past performances where the horse had been running different. That was the way a lot of gamblers would do it.

The greatest one would be to sprint a horse, take a horse that wants to run long and run him short.

He'd get beat, beat, beat, beat. Then they'd run him long, and he'd win. Everybody at the track, they would see this horse, didn't know what was going on. They wouldn't see that 10 races ago he'd won for twice what he was running for. Now, astute gamblers would be able to look it up and find out, but the average people on the racetrack wouldn't do it. The problem was most of the money had to go through bookmakers because if you bet on the track it lowered your odds.

I bet on a lot of those horses. You had to gamble to make a living when you only had a few claiming horses, and you had to really pick your spots. You had to kind of play the game or be on your own. I didn't play the game. I never got involved with professional gamblers or people who fixed races. I stayed to myself. I wanted to do my thing the best I could do it. If I couldn't succeed, I'd quit. If I didn't think I was doing the right thing, I'd quit. I didn't want my kids to ever disrespect me because of what I'd done. That's what I'd patterned my career on. I didn't think they'd ever be proud of me because I wasn't on top of the game, but I never wanted them to be ashamed of me for something I did wrong or something I was accused of doing wrong. I made a lot of mistakes and may have pushed the rules to the very edge. My problem was I felt that if a rule doesn't apply to everyone in the same way, I didn't consider it a rule, I considered it a guide. So maybe I didn't follow the guidelines the way that they were written, but I never broke a rule.

When I came around, racing was a sport. Then two men changed the game forever. Tom Meeker made the track a corporation with the sole purpose of making money for the owners of the racetrack. In doing this he brought racing to a new level. He added class to the game, changed the racetrack from a dingy place where people came to gamble into a place where people could enjoy the surroundings, get a meal, and have fun. At first he knew nothing about racing, but in his determination to make money for the corporation he created, he learned what a great game this was. I wish Meeker would have stayed around longer. I feel that as his understanding and appreciation for racing grew, he would have made a lot of positive changes.

The other man was D. Wayne Lukas, who made racing a business and created the mega-stable, with control of hundreds of horses at different racetracks around the country. He taught all of those around him to go first class—get the best owners, the best horses, make the most money—as you would in any other business. Mr. Lukas has great respect for the thoroughbred as an athlete, and he demands the absolute best from his employees, his horses, and himself. He's one of the few hands-on trainers who looks at every horse in his care every day. Is he the most successful to have ever trained a race horse? I can't judge that. But if you look at the great horses he has trained, the records he has set, and the success of the people that he has mentored who have become top trainers, you have to admit, he sure changed the game.

Racing horses is not the same as the breeding end. They're different businesses, and the breeding end has changed. Used to be more matching niches, following the bloodlines of families that matched together to produce good horses. When you went to Lexington and you saw all of those old-time farms, those people were in business because they loved the horse, not just the business. Calumet, Mrs. Markey, Bull Hancock—they all wanted the best horses that they could breed, and they didn't want anybody else to have them. It was a select club and you couldn't break into it. The old timers bred horses strictly to run. You don't get that anymore. Now, people breed horses only to sell. They don't care whether they can run or not. If you've got a mare you want to

breed, and you want to pay $150,000, come on up to the stud barn; there's no question about it. When I first came around, no stud was going to breed more than 40 mares in a season. Now horses like Animal Kingdom breed 100 to 200 per season. It weakens the gene pool. You got so many of these horses being bred to bad mares. That's why you don't have horses like Kelso and Gunbow anymore. Yes, one comes along now and then, but he will be the exception, not the norm. Those horses were the best in the country, and they ran until they were five- and six-year-olds. But the gene pool has been diluted only to sell. They're bred for speed. They're hot-housed like tomatoes, and a hot-house tomato is all flash but no substance when you compare it to a homegrown tomato.

I don't know if it's better for the industry or worse for the industry. I can't judge that. I see racetracks that can't fill races. We used to race six days a week; now we do four. We used to have entries close the day before; now they close four or five days out trying to fill races. Are there too many racetracks? I don't think so. Santa Anita had to call off two days of racing because they couldn't fill the races. Their barn area is full, so why can't they fill races? See how many people they get here on Derby Day? On a Monday or Tuesday or Wednesday, there's nobody here. They're having a hell of a time filling the card. We never had that trouble. We had eight races on weekdays and nine on Saturday most of the time. We raced six days a week, every day but Sunday. If you had a horse running in a $5,000 claiming race, it might take you three or four weeks to get him back into a race. That's how full those races would be. I've entered horses in races here where there's been 100 excluded.

In the old days, it was common that we didn't have as many allowances. Probably only one or two allowance races a day. They were all claiming races where anybody can buy your horse after the race. And there were more four-, five-, and six-year-old horses running than there are now. You might run a horse 20 times in a year, and you don't see that anymore. One of the Derby winners ran 28 times as a two-year-old. They were bred to run. They were stronger boned. They were athletes. Some of the farms never put their horses up. They were raised in the snow, in the cold, and they stayed out in the field. They were fed in the field. Now they run once every six weeks, or even less, because of the way they are raised. They don't develop the stamina or the physical and mental strength that horses had back then.

What makes a racehorse is class. You could go spend millions of dollars on horses because of their confirmation, because of their parents. But you can't judge what's inside of them. Anybody can go up there and say this horse is by so-and-so and he's worth a million dollars, and then five people want him because he's worth a million dollars. They paid $13 million for The Green Monkey and he never won a race. Go to Keeneland, and they'll give you a list of horses that were sold for over a million dollars that never made it to the race. It's a high percentage. It's not about measurements. It's about balance. Horses can overcome a crooked leg, but they'd can't ever overcome not being well-balanced. One of the best that ever raced, Seattle Slew, had a crooked leg. He also had bad ankles. The horse has to be mentally intelligent. Dumb horses can't run—we call them pencil-headed horses. When you can look at a horse, and his head isn't wide, you know he doesn't have any brain. Good horses have big, wide heads and eyes focused on you. A horse has to be smart. He has to have that mental attitude. He has to want to win. It's about heart—and no one can measure the heart of a horse. You learn that when he looks you in the eye and says, "Do you want to try me?" /

Cristina Bahena

FOREMAN

I started working with horses when I came to Chicago from Mexico in 1988 when I was 19 years old. My sister worked at Sportsman's Park in Chicago, and I went over there and started working with her and Eddie Reynolds. I didn't like horses. They were huge, and I was scared of them. I thought, *These horses are going to bite me or trample me.* Sometimes they just bite. Sometimes, they stomp on you. One horse bit me and I still have the mark. I didn't think it was going to work. I told myself this was not for me, that it would be better for me to go back to Mexico. But little by little I started to lose my fear. It probably took me one or two months to get comfortable with the horses.

I like horses now because I like working outside. I like being free. In Mexico I worked in a factory, and I'd be trapped in there for eight to twelve hours a day and never see anything. Sure, in the barn we work seven days a week, but you can look at this kind of work like a sport. Walking the horses is a sport. Cleaning the stalls and sweeping the halls is harder. If you learn to do your job with ease, you are going to be fine. That is what you have to do: Make your day easy, do a good job. You have to be positive. If you work just because it is a job and you have to, it's a drag. When you come with a negative attitude, work is going to be hard. But if you come with a positive attitude, the work can be easy.

When I came to work at Churchill Downs later in 1988, Dale Romans was the assistant for his dad, Jerry Romans. I talked with Dale and told him I wanted a job and he said okay. So I started walking the horses and later I started grooming. It was two weeks before I even saw Jerry, and he didn't say anything to me. He just looked at me. He wasn't liked by everyone. He was strict. But I never had problems with him. He never called me out.

I worked as a groom. The groom's job is to clean the stalls, and when the horses go to the track, to put the saddles on them and get them out. When they come back from the track, you walk them for 20 or 30 minutes and put them in the stall again, put out the hay and alfalfa. Then you wait a little bit and bandage their legs. Some horses you wrap four legs, some only two. You wrap them because you have to take care of their legs. Sometimes the horses jump in their stalls or something, and the wrapping protects them from hurting themselves. Some horses have medicine in their wraps, depending on what they need.

When I arrived at Churchill Downs, there were very few Hispanics and only two Hispanic women on the backstretch, and I was the first Latin woman that worked on the block where I worked, and the first to work for Jerry Romans. It was hard to work with it being almost all men here. Especially with this one guy, an American groom who just bothered me every day. He'd tell me I wasn't doing my job right and then he would tell the boss that. So I'd get called into the office by Jerry, but he only did that to not cross this other worker. He'd call me in like he was going to punish me, but then he'd say, "Don't worry, everything is fine." I liked Jerry and he liked me. He wasn't strict with me. It was difficult to work with only men. It was difficult work and I did it. I was doing a man's job—back then, grooming was more for men than women. Women only walked the horses. It is not like that today. Today many women work as grooms.

The majority of the Hispanics that first arrived here came with Wayne Lukas. He was the one who began to bring more Hispanics here from California. What happens is that one person arrives and then they bring their cousin, and their sister, and they start to bring more people. And the people that began coming here, they arrived and they liked it, and they started to stay and the community got bigger. Today it is a majority Hispanic workforce on the backside. There's people on the track from all over. Almost everyone who works here has been here for many years. Five, ten, fifteen years. We work together and live together. Everybody is friends and works well together.

I've been with the Romanses for 30 years, and now I'm one of Dale's foremen. I help the assistant trainers make sets—the schedules—for the riders. I put the saddles in every set, put the horses out. Right now at Churchill, Dale has close to 100 horses. I help other people when they're busy. I'm in charge of more than 30 people. I've been a foreman for about nine years. I never thought I would be here. But I worked very hard and over the years, I was able to get a better job. I don't really like moving around to different bosses, and I think it helped that I stayed here.

Dale's a good boss and I try to do a good job. Whatever problem I have, I can go to him and he listens and is there for me. He is a friend. His family, especially his mother, is so kind. She has always cared for me like I was her own daughter. I have a lot of people close to me that care about me and they love me, and that makes me very happy.

Dale trained a filly that was named after me: Cristina's Journey. One day the owner came to the stable and asked where his horse was, so we introduced ourselves; I told him my name and showed him where his horse was. Dale showed up later and they hadn't named it yet, so they were thinking about the horse's name. The owner wanted to know more about my life. Dale knows my life story and told him about the problems I'd had coming to the U.S. The owner asked if he could give the horse my name. I told them they shouldn't give it my name—why would they do that? He said it was because he liked my name. So I said, "Okay. All right. That's fine."

She came here and ran good, but in the Breeder's Cup she didn't run good. I think her heart was broken. When the horses are racing, if you enter them in a level that is too high for them, the horse gets scared and then they don't want to race. I think that is what happened to this little horse. She ran in the Pocahontas Stakes and won. That is why they took her to the Breeder's Cup, thinking that she would be something she wasn't. After that she didn't want to race anymore.

I'm from Mexico. I was born in Guerrero, and I was really young when we lived on the ranch there. My dad had horses for work, but I don't remember taking care of them. I knew about horses, but I didn't have much interaction. The horses there are much different than the horses here, because these are pure bloods and those were for riding in rodeos and stuff. They were smaller. Later we moved to the state of

CRISTINA BAHENA   21

Morelos in Cuernavaca and didn't have animals. First we went to visit a sister that was living in Cuernavaca. Then my father's wife wasn't doing well; she was sick and we went there for treatment. The doctors there are much better. One year passed, two years, three years, and when my dad wanted us to move back my older brother and I didn't want to move back to the ranch. We didn't want to move away from the city because there were more opportunities there than at the ranch.

Cuernavaca is in the south in Morelos. It's a beautiful city. Not hot, not cold. It's touristy. Lots of Americans, but I never met any of them when I was a kid. My life in Mexico was not very good, not very nice. My mom died when I was 12 years old. My dad had a hard time finding good work. He was a good carpenter and built houses, but there wasn't enough good work. My dad had a house but didn't have any money to provide for us. I have two brothers and five sisters. I'm the seventh. My stepmom had three more, so we were a big family in a little house. As a girl, all of my siblings and I had responsibilities to help out around the house. From a young age, our parents taught us to do our chores. Depending on our age, they gave us chores that we were able to do. I was supposed to help clean the house and take care of my younger siblings.

I stopped going to school in fourth grade. My brother was finishing secondary school and was going to start a school that cost money. There were four of us in school at the time and it was hard for my dad. He had to pay for books, school supplies, uniforms, all that stuff. He didn't have enough money. I saw that he couldn't afford to send me to school, so I told my dad that I didn't want to go to school anymore.

Today, I regret it. At least I could have finished primary school. But I just couldn't. I started working when I was 13 years old. I babysat for somebody who had two little kids, but I didn't make any money.

Then I worked in a ceramics factory for seven years, making cups and plates and everything. The factory was 40 minutes from my house. Sometimes I walked, sometimes I took the bus. We made coffee cups and plates, and I painted the color on them. I'd paint them white, or I'd paint something with little flowers. I liked it. I made a little bit more money, but I didn't want the same life for my daughters and my son.

Back then I didn't have a lot of hopes. I had my children very young, and I don't regret that at all. My mistake was to get married so young. I was 17 years old when I had my first daughter, Tahnia. At 19, I had Norma and was separated from the father of the girls. He came over here to the U.S. and I never saw him again. I was the one that supported my girls. It was difficult for me, but it was my responsibility and I did it. I took care of my daughters. Alone. I had a job, and rented a house, and I had enough to eat, but I always thought about having my own house one day. I started to work more and more but couldn't save any money to buy a house or a piece of land to build a house. It was for my daughters that I made my decision to move over here. I needed some money to provide for my kids. I left Mexico because I wasn't making any money and didn't have a house.

In Mexico, they paint a beautiful picture of the U.S., just lovely: You just come here and make a bunch of money! So I decided that I would go to the U.S. for two years and, in those two years, I'd make enough money to build my house. I asked my sister-in-law, "Can you help me out a little bit?" She said, "What do you need?" I am close to her and she really loves my girls. She adores them even today. I talked with her and asked if she could take care of my girls. She asked me why I was leaving. I told her that I needed to buy a house for my family, that I'd go to the United States to work. She said, "Don't go, you are fine here."

I told her that I wasn't okay, that I needed to do it for my daughters. She took care of my girls for three years. It was a difficult decision to leave a two-and-a-half-year-old girl and another girl just a year old. It wasn't easy. I left my life behind.

The first time I left Mexico I came to Arizona. I came here begging God to let me get in and be okay. I came with two other people. The coyote was an Indian guy. It took two days from Sonorita to Arizona in a car. Then I got on a plane to Chicago where my sister was living and working.

So I came to the United States by myself, and I stayed here for three years. When I moved over here, it was very, very hard for me. I talked to my girls on the phone—not daily or even every week, because back then you had to pay with quarters on the pay phones. I would talk with them every month or two with my quarters.

It was so hard for me. Dale says that I cried every day for three years. He would always say to me, "How are your girls, Cristina?" and I would have to just turn around and walk away because I couldn't answer him without crying. I was never able to talk about my daughters because I would just cry and cry and cry. I wanted to be with them but I couldn't.

That is why today I understand what it is like for those people who are far away from their family, from their wives, or their children. Or the reverse: the mothers who are separated from their children for years. There are women I know who have not seen their children for five or ten years. It is so hard. It was three years before I saw my children. You see many people from many countries that have had to leave their children behind. If we have to leave them behind, it is for a good reason. We have left them behind but

not forgotten them. We have left them behind but we would never abandon them, because we want to secure a better future for them that we could not have for ourselves.

I lost three years of my children's childhood. It is hard, super hard. And it is for that reason that I brought them here. Today I have my whole family here. They have gone to school. Evelyn is in college now. All of this has made it worth it. I am happy to be here and happy that I got out. I had to leave my daughters for a period of time. That is what I had to do, but I think it was the right thing to do.

Many mothers have done it and many fathers, too. Entire families and marriages have been lost trying to provide something better. I'm sorry for all the little kids who have so many dreams and are being deported. Many of these kids want to study but don't have the power to study. My heart aches and I want to help them. There are good people. Most of them want to study, to work, to pay taxes. But everyone is scared. It's bad. Some girls just cry.

Some days are hard because they are thinking about their families, and they can't travel. It affects everybody because all the Hispanics, even though we are from different countries, have families. It affects all of us. Everyone tries to help, and it makes us all a little more united, being so far away from our families. If we see a friend down on his luck and they need us and we can help them, we do it without thinking twice. We are close knit. That is just how we are. Sometimes we don't have enough to give to help. Many people have helped me, and I have helped out too. I am very happy here. I am so grateful to be where I am.

I got my girls when I went back to Mexico. My older sister Martha died in a car accident. She died too young, when she was 33 years old. I tried to make it in time for the funeral but couldn't. I stayed two months to see my kids, my little ones who my ex-sister-in-law had been watching. When I arrived, she said to my daughter, "Look Norma, it's your mama."

Norma says, "No, it's not."

She says, "Yes. See? It's the girl from the picture."

Norma says, "No. That is not my mama!"

I told Norma, "I'm your mama," and she said, "I'm not going anywhere. I'm staying with my other mama." My heart broke. I told my sister-in-law, "Look, I'll take them both. I'll stay one or two months, then I'm taking my kids. I thank you for everything, I know you took care of them, but I'm sorry, I'm taking my kids." And she said, "Can you take Tahnia, and leave Norma?" Norma is the little one. And I told her, "No, I'm taking them both, or I'm not going anywhere," and she started crying because the little ones had stayed with them for three years. I stayed for a couple months over there and then we came back to Kentucky. We lived in an apartment on South 3rd Street, close to the track.

I like living here by Churchill Downs. I like living in Louisville. The city is quiet, everybody's nice, there's no crazy people like Chicago. My neighborhood, it's good, the people are nice. I see my neighbors and say hi, but I don't stay too close because I don't have time. I work seven days a week for my little ones—well, there's no more little ones, Jonathan is the last one. I take Jonathan to school, and I pick him up later.

Norma was five years old, and Tahnia was seven when we came to Louisville. I started work at 5:00 a.m. every day. I had a babysitter for my girls, a good lady. Ms. Norma was like a grandma for my daughters. When they went to school, she put them on the bus and everything. She took care of them for 10 years.

I dropped my kids off at Ms. Norma's around 5:00 a.m. and went to the track where I was a groom. I'd come to the track and take care of five horses. When I finished, I'd go pick up my girls, go home, cook lunch, take a shower. Then I'd come back in the afternoons at 3:30 to feed the horses. Around 5:00 I'd go home, take a shower again, make dinner for my girls, clean the house. I did that seven days a week.

When I arrived in the U.S. in 1988, I was here through amnesty. When it was available, I went to get my permit in Chicago, I had to be really brave—I didn't know if I was going to be able to get it. But I applied for amnesty, and they gave it to me for three months. I applied for a work permit. It was for three months. When I came here to Louisville, I let my work permit expire, and I didn't go back to try and get another one. I didn't go back because everyone told me that I wouldn't qualify for amnesty. I just left it like that.

I was working here for many years and in 1995, unfortunately, Immigration came to the backside. This is where Immigration caught me. They picked up two or three of us. They didn't take me away, but they gave me a notice saying that I had a court date. I went to my court date thinking that I was going to win my case. I had lawyers. Imagine how much it cost. It cost me a lot of money.

I had my case with a judge in Chicago, but he was extremely racist. I took my daughters with me and they begged him to let me stay here in the U.S. He just said I had to leave, and I could not enter the U.S. again for two years. So I made the decision to leave my daughters once again. My two kids stayed here. I sent them to stay with my brother in Florida. I wanted what was best for my daughters and they had better opportunities here.

It was a really difficult time when I was back in Mexico. I had to get through it. I worked in Mexico for two years. I worked in a different ceramics factory.

After two years, I came back. When I was back here, I went to see the lawyer again to let him know that I was back in the country. The lawyer said, "You were punished for two years and you have completed your punishment. Let's fight to get your papers." And we put in my application for papers again. My husband had already submitted his application for citizenship. He became a citizen in 1998. He had to get his citizenship in order to for me to become a citizen. So that was when I submitted my papers here.

I had to pay a fine to Immigration. They gave me the options: I could leave and wait for my papers outside the U.S. or stay here and pay a fine. I didn't want to leave the country so I decided to pay the fine. For the three of us—me, Tahnia, and Norma—I had to pay $3,000 to Immigration. Not to the lawyer but just to Immigration.

Ten years later I put in an application for my citizenship, and now I'm a U.S. citizen. It took 10 years and cost me a lot of money. Twenty-five or thirty thousand dollars. I had many emotions when I got my resident permit.

I took citizenship classes at the Backside Learning Center. One day a week for probably three or four months. They helped a lot. I wasn't able to take many English classes because of work, but I understand English very well. The citizenship test has 100 questions, but only 10 questions count, and you don't know which 10 it will be. One was, "What colors are the flag?" Another one is, "How many stripes are on the flag?" Things like that.

For three months, I got CDs and books to study. I listened to the CDs in my car, and I was thinking and trying. It was hard, and I got nervous when I went to take my test. The officer giving the test scared me. I think he didn't like Mexicans. When I talked to him he was not really nice. But I passed the test four years

ago, and got my citizenship that March. A lot of people were at the ceremony at the courthouse on 6th and Broadway, but all of my friends at the track were gone because there was no racing. All the horses were gone and the track was closed. So, later during the spring meet, my English teacher from the Backside Learning Center said to me one day, "Hey, would you meet me in the track kitchen later and bring something for me?"

I said, "What do you need?'

"Bring this paperwork for me and meet me at 6:00."

I said, "Aw, that's too late, can you come at 4:00?"

"No, I have things to do, I am busy," he said.

"Okay, fine," I said.

So I came at 6:00, and as I parked my car, I noticed that there were a lot of cars. I thought, *Maybe a lot of people are eating or something*. And when I went over there, all my friends were there to surprise me. They all congratulated me and gave me a big American flag. I cried.

I think it is very beautiful. God has given us the opportunity to be here. At times I can't believe it. We are not rich, but we do fine. We have always had work, thank the Lord. That is the most important thing. We have always liked maintaining a stable job. We don't like switching jobs. Thank the Lord we have always had work and are doing good. And we have met great people.

I'm very content and grateful to God. It was a hard way, but I'm here now and I'm all right. I love this country and I'm happy here with my kids. /

CRISTINA BAHENA 27

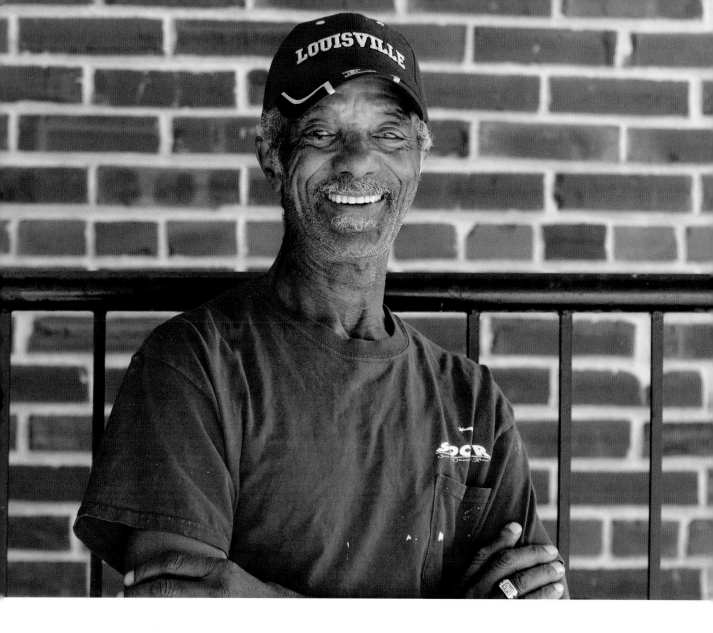

Paul Goffner

RETIRED GROOM

My mother had four boys and four girls. We grew up on Newburg Road at Indian Trail. That was country back then. We ain't have to come to town for nothin' but to buy shoes or clothes because we raised all our food. We had our own garden, had pigs and chickens and colts and hogs. We had our own smokehouse. You want some bacon? Go out in the smokehouse and get you some bacon, sausage, or ham. Want some chicken? Go out there in the chicken coop, wring that sumbitch's neck. Me and my brother used to go next door, steal the next-door neighbor's chickens. We used to take zip guns and go fox hunting. The only place we had to go swimming was those ponds out there. One time I dove in and my head got stuck in the mud. My cousin had to jump in and pull me out.

We had plow horses when I was a kid. They looked like they were big as a building to me. They were named after my father and my uncle: Pete and Its. We'd run them through the dirt to turn it over to plant our corn and peas and carrots and everything. We had a hell of a garden.

Once a friend of mine pushed me up the hill and I stepped on a cornstalk. It went through my foot and I had to go to the hospital. My mother kept that splinter in a little brown bag until she died. But she wasn't scared of nothin'. Not her. She was a country girl, and they ain't scared of shit.

Tommy Long, who was a legend on the backside, was out there in Newburg when I was a kid. We had a guy that lived out there that bought an Edsel in '56 or '57. Tommy Long raced the Edsel on foot one time from Turner's to the park. Outran it. He was a fast dude.

Tommy had a hog farm out in Newburg. One time he sold a hog to Dr. Harthill. He said, "I'mma raise him up for you, Doc. It'll be ready for you come slaughter time." So Doc Harthill paid him to raise the pig. Come slaughter time, Doc come by and said, "Where my pig at, Tommy?" Tommy shook his head and said, "Doc, I'm sorry, but your pig died." He's got a hundred hogs out there, but Doc's died.

When I was 11 years old, my grandmother passed and we moved from Newburg to the West End. My mother was ready to get up out of there. They were still building on to Southwick; they didn't have but four or five buildings down there at the time. That was in '66. They called it Little Africa down there then. It was a hell of a difference moving from the country to the city. We wasn't used to running water and all that. In the country, we were used to the outhouse and catching rainwater to fill them tin tubs. When we got to city we thought, *A bathtub? What the hell is that?* Hell, we thought we was rich!

Miles Park fire, 1964

When I was in sixth grade, the elementary school was too crowded, so I had to go to junior high school. That's when I had to start fighting to keep my lunch money. They were older than me and bigger, but you ain't takin' shit from me, as hard as my mama worked for this quarter. We used to have to fight to go to the store, and fight to come home with our groceries. If somebody got killed at night, they'd just kick him to the curb because the police wasn't comin' down there until the next day.

Southwick was by Miles Park. A friend of mine, Larry Martin, his father worked on the racetrack. I didn't know nothin' about racetracks, but I went over there with him a couple times and I said, *Shit, I like this*. So every morning before school we'd go to Miles Park and walk a few horses. You'd walk them until they

cooled out, water them off, take them to urinate, and that's it. In that day, they'd give you 50 cent a head. I made about three or four dollars in the morning before school. I had all the girls!

Miles Park was like a bull ring, little bitty track. It used to be the Kentucky State Fair Grounds. After the fair left, they made the racetrack. It was just half a mile radius. It was real small. It was hard on the horses to make that turn. You wouldn't make that turn every time.

First trainer I walked horses for was Ham Morris. He was a hell of a trainer. He ran thoroughbreds but he also had a pony called Gay the Wonder Horse; that's the first pony I walked at Miles Park. Ham Morris had taught him all kinds of tricks. He taught him how to drive a convertible Cadillac. Ham would take a razor, put it in that pony's mouth, and the horse would shave his face. The horse could tell you, "Feed me." He had a bucket for urine and another bucket for his bowels and he *would not* piss in the other bucket. Ham had a one legged rooster he'd trained. He'd tell that sumbitch, "Get up there and ride like Arcaro," and he'd get up on Gay and ride him around. This is the honest to God truth. Look it up.

I was there when Miles Park had the fire. That was 1964. I was way downtown when I seen all that smoke. I got off the bus and went back down to Miles Park. Horses all over the place. That was terrible. Horses running all over the place. Tried to let them out, but they run back into the stalls. That's the only thing they know. They in there 23 hours a day. That's home. Ain't no telling how many horses got lost that day. They had a lot of horses burn up. They were standing in there, right by the door. Wouldn't come out.

They closed it after the fire, then opened it up for quarter horse racing and mule races. That's when Tommy Long was riding mules down there. Tommy Long won a big race down there. They swore to God that mule was a thoroughbred!

In the summers, I'd go down to Ellis Park for a few months, and then when school started, I'd go back home. My mother was all right with it as long as I did my school thing. She needed the help anyway. I bought my own school clothes and helped her out because my parents was divorced. There was eight of us kids, so I said, "I'm out of here." I was 16 or 17 and I thought I was a casanova. It was fun. Money in my pocket. Girls staring at me. I got a car down at Ellis. Didn't have no license, but I got a car. I won it in a craps game. I rolled a four—that's one of the hardest ones to make. You got to roll it again. It was a $75 shot. A guy put his car keys up, a 1957 Pontiac. He says, "I bet you don't bar it." If it's a four, you got to bar it. I did, and I won the car.

Tommy Long

I was at Latonia once hanging out at the security gate messing around with Tommy Long. We heard some drums beating and we said, "What the hell is that?" Some guy said, "That's the Klan having a rally. Some of them are on the backside." We said, "The Klan!? What!?" Tommy started crouching down low. It was scary. We got the hell out of there. Tommy and Slug and all of them jumped in that car. We had an old '56 Ford you had to shift with a screwdriver. Man, we come up out of there and come on home and we drove straight through the rally in Florence, Kentucky. They had crosses burning in a big field full of hoods.

Man, I've been through so much stuff in my life. I tell my kids, "Y'all don't know what we went through to get what y'all got today." I remember black and white water fountains. I remember having to go to the back of the bus. If you were sitting on a bus and a white person got on there, you had to get up and give them your seat and go to the back. I never paid no attention—I just did it, just went on. Because we knew what the situation was: Get up or get whooped.

I was working for a guy named Arthur Bender once and when we came back to Louisville one year, R.E. Vance came by and asked how much the guy was paying me. When I told him, he said, "Put that shit down and come on." I went to work for him. He was a bull rider and he'd broken his pelvis. He was in so much pain and he wanted me to take care of the horses, be the groom.

Vance said, "Well, you know how to walk 'em. Now I'm gonna teach you how to rub 'em." He pulled me into the stalls, showed me what he wanted me to do. He taught me about horses. Old Man Vance taught me how to do the figure-eight wrap on their legs. He'd make me take them off and do it right. "It ain't right, Goober! Take it off!"

He called me Goober. He couldn't hear. He wore hearing aids and the first time he cut a check for me he said, "What'd you say your name was?"

"Goffner"

"Goober?

"*Goffner!*"

He wrote my check out for "Paul Goober" for 10 years, and they'd cash it.

If you needed a draw, a little money to last you to your next paycheck, he'd turn that hearing aid off. I'd go to him, I'd say, "Turn that sumbitch on, cause I need some money."

He was a hell of a trainer. Won a lot of races. He always kept a lot of horses at Churchill Downs. He had a whole barn full. He had Barns 7 and 8 full. I was with Mr. Vance for a long time. Eight or ten years. He was good to me. I loved him. He's like a father to me.

I don't mean to be boasting or bragging, but when I got on a job, *everybody* I worked for won plenty of races. I don't know if it was luck or the hands or what. That ain't no lie, *everybody*. Shit, I had a few of them who wanted me to train their horses, but I said, "I don't want to do that. I like peace of mind, man." I've seen trainers, guys younger than me, look like they're 90 years old. When you're a trainer, they'll call you any time of the night: "What's my horse doin'? I wanna run him here. I wanna do this and that."

I learned what to do with bossy owners from Old Man Vance. One day, one of the owners came in. Hawkins was his name. He had car lots in Indiana. He was holding a damn condition book saying, "Look Vance, this is the race I want to run this horse in." Vance didn't say nothing. He just walked up to the track kitchen to use the phone and two hours later, two vans came by. He told the owner, "Don't come in here telling me where to run these horses. You're the owner, not the trainer. *I* do this. You want to train these sons of bitches, you train 'em." He looked at me and said, "Load 'em up, Goober!" And he shipped all that man's horses out. Two days later we had another barn full.

In 1969, he said, "I'm gonna get you a trainer's license and send you to Hot Springs." That was the year I got married, and before we went to Hot Springs we were going to take a trip to New York to visit my mother-in-law. That was the longest visit I ever had in my life: seven years. I loved it. We lived in Queens and had two New York breds and two Kentucky breds: Shaunta, Jude, Jennifer, and Dominic.

Churchill Downs
B.M.Hawkins, Owner

"Jack's Forever"
May 4, 1967

H. Moreno, up
David Vance, Trainer

The first year I went up there, the grooms was on strike. That was '69. Them owners and trainers got tired of catching them horses. I was going out there to look for a job, but I ain't crossing no picket line. They got everything settled down. The strike didn't last long. I worked at Belmont. I've always favored Belmont. Back then, we all thought if you went to New York and California, you'd be on the top of the world. But it wasn't like that. I looked at the bandages they were putting on horses and said, "Why'd you do it like that?" First guy I worked for, Peter Howells told me, "I'll put on my own polo wraps and bandages." He had things wrapped all around the damn coronet band. I just didn't understand it.

I wasn't taught like that. I said, "Well, you're gonna rub the horse then, 'cause if something happens, it's my fault. Where I come from, we do this." Then I put the bandages on and did that figure-eight wrap and he said, "Oh, god. You put on all the bandages now." So when I started showing them how, they'd do it wrong and I'd snatch all the bandages off and say, "It ain't right. Do it over."

In '72 I was working for Sherrill Ward at Belmont. The guy that was rubbing Forego—he was from Jamaica—had to go home for an emergency. He went home and I had to start taking care of Forego. As a two-year-old, he was 17 hands. He couldn't get through the barn door, he was so tall.

About that time is when they turned Forego out to operate on him. He had some bad-ass ankles. When they operated on his ankles, I said, "Y'all better cut him or he won't do shit." They did castrate him, and his Derby run was the next year, '73.

He'd hurt you, man. When you'd go to rub on him, he'd get ornery. He was just so damn big, I guess he knew he could bully us. If you didn't know what you was doing you was in trouble. He never messed with me, though. Every job I had, I always had the toughest sons of guns that we got. But I could handle them. I knew how to rub them.

Eddie Sweat was at that same meet rubbing Secretariat. I knew him well. Shoot, we used to hang out at the bar at nights. We'd all be kickin' it, him and his wife. They were from Holly Hill, South Carolina. You talk about country!

Eddie was a good guy. He was quiet, real quiet. He didn't mess with too many people. Just did his job. He was a good guy, nice guy. We didn't talk work when we went out. Because our secrets are our secrets, you know.

Tommy Long made up his own brace for the horses' legs. It's something you rub on the horses' legs to keep them cool and tighten them up. People would come buy it from him. You think he's gonna tell somebody? I got a brace that Old Man Vance gave me he wouldn't even give his son the ingredients. He told me, "Don't you *never* give this to *nobody*!" And I never did. Smelled like it had a little bit of everything: Bigeloil, Absorbine Jr., a lot of different stuff. But it worked.

Up until I retired eight years ago, I was always on the road. I enjoyed it. Meeting different people, different lifestyles. Everywhere you go, it's something different. We met so many people in our lifetime. New York. California. Jersey. Everywhere there was a race-track, we been there, making friends and enemies. We were big ballers, making money. Racetrackers were the only ones who had money. We'd party hardy. Come in for work with our suits on, catch that horse, then while he's gone to the track, go in the room to change clothes, then go on to work. When we got through working, we'd head right back down.

Back then, it was a party everywhere you went. You'd go out and enjoy yourself. You might get in a fight, somebody might pull out a knife every now and then, but there wasn't no shootings and all that shit. We'd just get a couple gallons of beer and sit around and talk about it. Get with your friends the next day. /

Paul with What It Is, who won the 1981 Derby Trial.

Cristobal Resendiz Trejo

GROOM

I grew up on a farm in Mexico in Zimapán, Hidalgo. It's a couple of hours from Mexico City. We had some land. It's very steep, and very hard. We had to work with what we had. If you wanted to grow corn or some other crop, you had to clean it up first with picks, then you put the animals on the plow and planted. We would plant corn and beans, and we had to help Mom in the garden. The only grown-up in the house was my mom, so we'd have to help with everything. She taught us everything we know. Our house was not very nice: two rooms and a kitchen. We didn't have electricity. Sometimes in the night, when we had a lot of rain, you'd have to move your bed because the roof was leaking. But I loved the farm.

I took care of the animals: goats, pigs, cows, chickens. I was about nine when I started working with the horses. We had saddle horses, not race horses. We'd have to break them and everything. I learned horsemanship by seeing other people do it. When you're interested in doing something, you say, "Teach me how to do it." You watch, and when you grow up, you do it that way.

The horses didn't have names, just "black one" or "red one" or whatever. They lived in the barn and we fed them—even if there was nothing for us to eat, we fed and watered them. We didn't have water in our house, so we had to go about two miles to get the water. We took the animals there, and brought some water back on a wagon. It was really hard work. My job here at the track is easier; I don't mind getting up at 3:00 in the morning.

Every weekend, my mom would pick up all the eggs from the chickens, and I would go with her to the markets they have in little cities in Mexico on the weekends. I'd go with my mom to the market and we'd sell the eggs to buy things for the house, like sugar and flour. It was pretty good money. It was maybe five miles to the market. We walked half the way and took a car half the way because the road didn't go all the way to our house.

Sometimes we sold this drink called pulque. It's not tequila, but it's similar. People like to have their alcohol. We planted the maguey cactus. It's like agave. It takes maybe eight years before it's ready to harvest. We cut the center of the maguey cactus and it has a lot of sweet water. You collect it three times a day: early in the morning, about 12:00 in the daytime, and in the afternoon. You dump it in a bucket, and three days later you already have alcohol. We had maybe 40 magueys and we collected that water and made pulque. We'd go to the market to sell it. It's the way we survived until the next time Dad sent money home.

My mom passed away in September of 2018. She was 99. Salustia was her name. She passed away at the farm where she lived. She probably lived so long because the food she ate was clean. She wasn't sick; she just passed away because she was old. She was a good lady. Good mom. She took care of us kids. She took my daddy's place when he was in the U.S.

When Dad would come home, it was like a stranger coming through the house. He didn't look like my dad because we hadn't seen him very many times. We were scared. He'd stick around maybe a month, and he'd leave again—not because he wanted to, but because we needed the money. Before he had a green card, my dad got caught once. They put him on a boat and took him all the way to Yucatán, Mexico. Dropped him over there so he couldn't come back so easy.

My dad never went to school. He didn't know how to read or write. He wanted everybody to go to school, but how could he afford eight kids going to school? I'm sixth out of eight, six boys and two girls. My sisters are older, so they're the ones who had a chance to go to school.

When I was 14 years old, I decided to come to the States to help the family. It was 1968, and the Olympics were in Mexico, but I missed the Olympics. My dad was in California at that time, working the fields. He said, "I'd like you to stay on the racetrack with horses," because he thought the racetrack would be more of a straight life: no drugs or alcohol or whatever. So I started working in Phoenix at Turf Paradise. I've been working with the horses for 52 years since.

In the winter, my dad and I used to go to Mexico for a couple months and come back. Usually he worked in California. He retired when he was 65 and he was looking very good. But when he retired he only lasted three years in Mexico. After all those years here in the United States, he didn't like life in Mexico.

My dad is the one that got my green card. He was a resident. In that time it was easy, not like right now. Now it's harder. I had a green card for 30 years. After that, I applied to become a U.S. citizen. First, you have to do your income taxes every year. Because when you're applying to be a U.S. citizen, they ask you for the last five years to prove you've paid taxes. If you don't, then you can't become a U.S. citizen.

I took classes on the history of the United States. You had to learn 100 questions—like how many stars are on the flag, who's the first president of the United States, the name of the president right now, things like that. When you go to the court for the test, they pick five questions, and you don't know which ones they're going to ask. Now I'm a U.S. citizen and my daughter is too, even though she and my wife live in Mexico. My wife has a green card and we're going to apply for her citizenship. When I go to Mexico to visit, they might come to the U.S. for a week and we'll all go back together. But I can't afford for them to stay here with me all the time.

I worked in Arizona for a year. When I started working in Phoenix walking hots, I had to walk 10 horses at a time. I had to walk with one in each hand. If one jumped, the other one jumped at the same time. You have to go to the big tracks if you want a different life. Here, inside the shedrow, one horse in your hand is all you get. I tell everybody, "You wanna work with horses? Go to Kentucky." When I came to Kentucky, everything was different. You have to treat the horses more respectfully. I like the way they treat them here.

When I moved to Kentucky, I started working for an old man named D.W. Kelly. I worked for Kelly for eight years, We stayed in the rooms above his barn back in Barn 22. He had nice horses, and he trained horses real good. It's where I learned medicines. He was about 75 years old. He was in the barn every single

CRISTOBAL RESENDIZ-TREJO

day at 5:00 in the morning. He paid close ttention to the horses.

He had a mare named Susan's Girl. She was the first millionaire mare in the country. At that time, the biggest purses were about $50,000. First millionaire mare in the country and I rubbed her. We won a big race at Keeneland and we won the Kentucky Oaks in 1973.

Kelly never bought expensive horses. He bought horses with good blood, but with a crooked leg or something that wasn't right; they sold them cheaper because nobody wanted them. He waited for the horses to mature. He was a smart horseman. He always waited until they were three or four years old. He'd always have a good horse to run with the big expensive horses.

There's a difference between now and years ago. It used to be that you never raced a horse when they were a two-year-old, and horses ran until they were eight or nine years old, and they were still running good. Now, you see good horses, but they don't last. They push them too hard when they're two-year-olds now. A two-year-old is just a baby. Maybe it looks big, but its bones don't have any material.

Racing was better years ago. How you treated the horse was better. People working on the backside cared more about horses. There were more good horses, and you could learn something from them. Now it's hard to teach somebody something, because you don't treat the horses the same way. Now we think about big horses, big money, and there's no love for the horses. Back then, there was no money. It was just a sport. You enjoyed working for the race, and you'd grab the program and see five good horses in the same race and say, "Oh, I wanna see who's gonna win this." You enjoyed it.

When D.W. Kelly hired somebody, he'd give him a room. He'd give him a bed, give some clean sheets, and even if it wasn't new it was clean. He cared about his workers. He'd bring some donuts and everybody would be happy. Now you're on your own. Now nobody cares about you. You want to sleep in the road? That's fine. Sometimes an owner, if he's good, gives a little stake money after a win. Sometimes he gives you nothing. Sometimes he won't even say thank you. My boss is good, though. I've worked for Mike Tomlinson for 16 years, and he's been very good to me.

When I started working at the racetrack, I walked hots for three years. Then they gave me two ponies to rub to learn to be a groom. The assistant showed me what I needed to know. Back then, they used to teach you something if you wanted to know. I learned to put bandages on them. You don't want to put them on too tight, but if it's too loose it can fall on the track and that would be dangerous. I rubbed those ponies for a year. If you qualify, you go rub racehorses. Now, people show up, and they're ready to rub horses with no experience at all because trainers need the help.

There's two kinds of people here on the backside: a few who like the job, and the rest who don't. Some of my partners rotate and take an afternoon off. I don't. I want to be here. I'm here because of the horses. I have horses in my heart, but there's a problem on the racetrack: I could work here 100 years and I'm going to make the same money as somebody who walked in today. Outside, the more years you have on a job, maybe they'll pay you more. Not here. This is the only problem that we have. If I worked outside the track—like construction or whatever—I'd probably make more money. But I don't want to do those jobs. I love horses, and as long as I can work, I want to be with them. I think to myself sometimes, "I can make more money somewhere else," but it's not the point. I need the money, but I care more about the horses.

On the backside there's a large dormitory for workers, and people also stay above the barns. I stayed in the dorms for a month once, but I had to move out of there. Too many people together is no good. I got real sick in my chest. I said, "No, I gotta get out of here." I can't stay away from the horses. They're like friends, like part of my family. I prefer to stay near them. I get along really well with the people working in the barn with me, but I don't have many friends. I never fight, never argue with nobody. I say hi every time someone goes by. They know my name. "Good morning, how are you?" But friends to go out with? No, I never do that. I stay away from drink and drugs. There used to be a lot of parties on the backside. Now, it's more strict. No alcohol. After 9:00, nobody sticks around outside.

Sometimes you get drunk, and you feel bad the next day. You feel sick, but you keep doing it. It's not too smart. Horses don't do that. They're more intelligent. They smell something bad, they don't eat it. The reason I get along with the horses is because you turn the lights off and they go to sleep when it's dark.

I have family that needs me very bad, so I have to take her easy. I have a wife, Olivia, and a daughter, Jazmin, who has a disability. She had a car accident 10 years ago. Her teacher stopped at our house to give her a ride to school and on the way there they had an accident. They rolled over. She broke her spinal cord. Her lungs filled with blood. I stayed with her in the hospital for a month.

At the hospital they said, "I don't think she's gonna make it." My daughter told me, "Tell the doctors I can't breathe." They said, "You're okay. You're just nervous." She said, "I can't breathe." She was going to pass out, and they found out one of her lungs was full of blood. They had to put a tube in her lung to drain it, and then it was the same thing with her other lung. It was painful. They didn't give her a pain killer or anything; she just had to go through with it.

Olivia has to keep an eye on her all the time. It is hard. It's a big job. It's been like that for the last 10 years. She takes care of Jazmin 20 hours a day. Helps her get up, take showers, go to the bathroom, and things like that. She can't feel her legs.

Last year, they came over here because University of Louisville Hospital is qualified to give help. They gave her medication and it was easier for her to move her legs. Big improvement. If we get lucky, we are coming back next year for some experimental treatments they have at the University of Louisville. A lot of patients sign up for it—maybe they call you, maybe they never call you. The hospital called and she came up here to get help. She had big scars on her hip, and bedsores. They saw my daughter, and now we're waiting for her bedsores to heal. As soon as my daughter is okay, she can come back over here for the treatment.

I started reading the Bible five or six years ago. When my daughter was very sick, we started believing in God more. I always have, but we were more interested. My wife and daughter started going to church every Sunday, sometimes twice a week. They convinced me to go too. No matter how good you are, you need help. You get nothing by yourself. I read the Bible every day. When your read the Bible you learn a lot of things. Like how to be a good person, how to see that people are the same whether they are Hispanic or black or whatever. Sometimes we don't understand. When you feel bad, you can read the Bible, then you feel better. You feel relaxed.

We asked God for help when my daughter was sick. She's not okay, but she is still with us. And she's happy, even though she can't walk. She can talk to us, laugh, and we feel okay. Ten years ago already.

Cris and Jazmin

Cris (far right) with his mother and two brothers

When she comes over here to the hospital, she's going to stay for maybe a year. She wants to learn English. From there, we'll see what she can do. When she feels better, she'd like to have a job. I guarantee you, if my daughter was okay she'd be here with me because when she sees the horses, she's always interested. Like my favorite horse, Green Grass Wyoming. Everybody knows I call him my son. When I would talk to Jazmin she'd say, "How is my brother doing?" She has said, "I wish I could work with you so you can teach me what you know."

When my family isn't okay, I'm always thinking about them. I'm always thinking, *Why don't I get another job outside, so I can make more money?* I say, *Well, I like horses.* It's the only reason that keeps me here.

Some people get up in the morning and have to wait for the boss to tell them what to do: "Today, you have to do this. Tomorrow, you have to do that." Here, you don't have to wait for anybody. You get up in the morning and start working with your horses. Every day, same horse, and I love that. I love to have the same horses all the time.

My alarm is set for 2:00 in the morning. I drink coffee, shave, clean up, and I start at 3:00 with horses. Some old timers do the same thing, but not many. Everybody else starts at 5:00 and finishes before I do.

Horses don't like to be in a dirty house. They're very clean animals. As soon as I clean the stall, they're going to lay down for another hour. The reason they're there is because we put them there, not because they want to be there. So you have to treat them the best you can.

When you pull all your feed tubs out, you might find out a horse didn't eat; something's wrong. You have to figure out why it left the feed. You have to watch them very close. You have to find out. Sometimes it's training too hard. Sometimes you put medication in the afternoon feeding and the horse doesn't like it. If your mom gave you big plate and you didn't finish it, you don't want to fill it up again. You have to change it, clean it out. That's the way I do it. You find out if everything is filling up, if the horse is doing good.

After I clean my feed tubs and water buckets, I check temperatures. A two-year-old horse is supposed to have a temperature of 101 degrees; any more than that, it's a temperature. But I have so many years on the racetrack that I don't need a thermometer. A mom knows there's something wrong with her child when they're sick. It's the same thing with horses. You look your horses in their eyes to see if there's something wrong. If that horse eats, it's okay. It feels good. When he's sick, he leaves some of it there.

After that, you start cleaning stalls. You fill up the hay racks. You have to change them at least once a week. They wake up and stand up, wait for you to clean the stalls, then go lay down for another hour. Some lay down completely like people. Then they get up and get ready. You have to have everything ready when the track opens at 6:00. If you do a good job, it maybe takes 15 minutes to clean a stall. But some people take 10 minutes and just pick up half. Shitty job.

You have to like the work. If you don't like it, if you're doing it because you have to, and that's not good. You go to work, and you treat the horses like people; you don't treat them like animals. They'll respect you later. Don't try to scare them. When you're brushing, don't brush them real hard; they don't like that. You have to be gentle with them. When you're rubbing a horse you have a brush in your left hand, and a towel in your right. A lot of horses don't like being brushed too much, so you only use the towel. A lot of horses are ticklish on the belly. For that you have a special rag, like for a shoe-shine. When you give a bath, give a good bath. Don't just make them wet. Rub the horse. I put a little vinegar in my water sometimes; that makes

their hair soft and shiny. Not many people do that. Very few.

Don't expect him to be looking good right away, but mix hay with alfalfa and your horse is going to look good. Feed them the best hay. Not all of it's the same. You want it green and fresh. The best alfalfa comes from Arizona. It's dry. No mold. Even when you see a bale from there, you can smell it. It's good to smell it.

You have to make them happy. Most of my horses run good. They try their best because they're happy. I have a filly who's very nervous. The owner doesn't want anybody else to take care of her. This year when I went to Mexico, she ran third and got claimed. She ran again with the new owner and she ran last. She was a hard filly to take care of. You had to treat her good. You have to think about your horses. I don't make any money, but I like the competition. I want my horses to go over there and do a good race. My boss can give me any horse, and in a month that horse will be perfect: quiet, go to the track, and do a good job. It's just the way you treat them.

When I go back to Mexico, I like my family, I like the weather over there, I like everything. But I'll always have something here. When I'm in Mexico, I'm always thinking of the horses. Especially that horse I love the most: Green Grass Wyoming. I took care of him for six years, since he was a little baby. A couple years ago, we lost him when he got claimed.

He was like a person. A good person. Different from the other horses. Good-looking, happy all the time. Every day at 3:00 in the morning when I threw the lights on, he was excited. *HAA HAAA!* He'd look at me like he was saying, "I'm going to have a good time!" You have to like somebody like that. Horses change, but he didn't change. He was the same happy horse all the time. I called him Bebe because he was always acting like a little kid.

I spent $10 of my own money every week on apples. I gave him two in the morning and one in the afternoon. You had to cut it into pieces for him or he wouldn't eat it. Plus peppermints.

In the winter, we put a blanket on every horse, but he needed two blankets, so I'd sneak him an extra one. A lot of horses don't like wearing blankets, same as us. I don't like wearing a jacket, but you have to wear one when it's cold. He was so smart, though, and he didn't mind. He'd say, "Well, if my friend put it on, it's because I need it."

When he slept, he slept like a person. He laid down with his head against the wall like it was a pillow. Sometimes I'd lay down with him.

As soon as he saw me, he was happy. I'd go inside the stall—they tied him up in the back—and I wouldn't need to call him. He'd go by himself, and wait for me there. We could be 10 people together that are talking, and he would be watching me. He wouldn't be watching nobody else. He was watching me. He could play in the stall, but when you put the tack on him, he got very serious. He'd just start walking, go to the track, and never do anything wrong. He'd say, "It's time to work."

He became a good horse. Nice looking. He won here, he won at Keeneland, he won in Chicago, he won in Miami. Everywhere he went, he won. He didn't make any excuses. He said, "I'm here right now." That horse was like my family. That horse was the most intelligent horse I ever saw.

He won a couple big races, and long races. He ran out all of the conditions he had, and he wasn't allowed to run allowance races, only big races or claiming races. One day my boss put him in a claiming race at $62,000 and he won easy. Mike Maker claimed him. He kept him for less than a year, and he hurt his leg, then he was taken to the Kentucky Horse Park. He's still there.

He was six years old when he got claimed. He'd made half a million. My boss said to me, "Oh, don't worry about it. We can get another one, a good one." I said, "That's not the point. Good one or better one, this horse is special for us. For me."

When he got claimed, I told his new groom, "You treat this horse good, he'll be good for you. If you treat him bad, I don't know what he'll do because I never treated him bad. But if you treat him good, he's a perfect horse."

I'm not ashamed to say it, but I cried for four days. And every day, I still remember him. I have a relationship with all of the horses I work with, but that horse was special for me.

I've thought about going to visit Green Grass Wyoming at the Kentucky Horse Park. I don't know how I'm going to feel, or how he's going to feel—because I guarantee he'll remember me. That's why I felt so bad when I lost him. He trusted me so much. He thought we were going to be together for the rest of our lives. I feel like I did something wrong to him when I lost him, because he didn't think we would ever split up. He didn't decide that. God made him, but he depended on me. /

Greta Kuntzweiler

JOCKEY, ASSISTANT TRAINER

I was 12 or 13 the first time I pushed cattle. I grew up in Boulder, Montana, which has about a thousand people. The whole town is ranchers, so people just say, "Do you wanna help us push cattle?" They were friends of my parents, so I'd say, "Yeah, sure." You'd just ride all day and push them out into the mountains. It was boring as fuck. I hated it, but it was the only riding around. I would do it just to ride.

There was a guy named Brud Smith who brought the cattle back in old-school style, where you rope the cows and castrate, dehorn, and brand them. Most people now have the chutes that they put them through, and they flip them on their side. So you don't have to rope or anything, and it's faster. But he made a big party out of it, with a campfire and lots of drinking and people trying to rope cattle. That was fun, especially on good horses. The branding part was kind of fun, but I always felt bad for the babies because it's pretty traumatic. Pushing cattle out is just so boring, though; all you do is walk behind stinky cows. I wanted to run. That's the only thing I ever wanted to do on a horse: go fast.

I wanted to be a jockey since I was eight when we went to the theatre to see *The Black Stallion*. It's gorgeous. It's about a little kid that gets shipwrecked with his horse. They form this bond, and when they get rescued, they live in New York and meet up with this old guy, Mickey Rooney, who's a trainer. They decide the horse is fast—that he can really run—and they need to come up with this scheme to get him to the races. I read all the books in the *Black Stallion* series.

When I was 12 I got my first horse, Lady. She was about 25 years old when I got her. I took her to a bareback class at the 4-H county fair, and after the class a bunch of people came up to me and said, "I learned how to ride on that horse!" She'd been teaching pretty much the whole Boulder, Montana valley how to ride. She was really sweet and really easy to learn on.

I didn't have a really good background as far as knowing the right way to treat a horse. I didn't know anything about anything, really. It's amazing that I've had to learn so much basic horse care. I taught myself by reading books. I remember reading that horses eat oats, so I had my mom get oatmeal. I fed this poor horse oatmeal. She loved it, but it's not what you feed horses.

There weren't other kids who were into horses like me. I think I'm a loner to begin with. I mostly ended up riding by myself, almost always bareback. I'd take my bike and a duffle bag with my bridle and my brush and I'd go ride in this huge field where we kept the horse, or ride into town and go around the track at the high school and jump in the sprinkler on the football field, or there was a road out to the dump—it was just mountains and forest out there.

I always said I was going to be a jockey. But if you're not from the racetrack, or you don't have family, you don't understand how it works. How do you even get in? There's just no way to get in. It's a mystery. So when I was 19, I went to this jockey school in Indiana. I'd seen this tiny little ad in *Horse Illustrated*, which is like the *Teen Beat* for the horsey set. I thought, *Oh my God. This is a way to do it.*

First, there was a correspondence course you did with this lady in Indiana. Stuff like, "Name the parts of the horse on a diagram, then mail it to me," and you had to send her money. And then when you're ready to come to the school, you sent her a *bunch* of money. So when I was 19, I drove from Montana to Indiana. When I got to the place where she said her school was, there was a guy standing out in the driveway, and he said, "She doesn't live here anymore. She had some tax problems and lost this place a while ago."

I thought, *What do I do?* He said, "Well, there's another girl who came down here with her mom. She's at that cafe down there." So I went down to the cafe, met the girl and her mom, and we called the lady and got her address. When we went over there she said, "Oh yeah. I do it out of my house now." She had about four thoroughbreds in a field. She taught us how to sit on a horse, and we cleaned her stalls and galloped her horses. So what we were doing was paying her money to do her work for her. It was a racket. But if you don't know, you don't know.

She took us to Churchill and we worked horses, and that was the first time I went fast. I had no idea what I was doing. I didn't know where the poles were and I really wasn't ready for it, but she was hard up for people. I screwed up really bad, but I was still really happy. I didn't care that she was yelling at me. The feeling was just exciting. Like swimming, or floating. You're floating.

She got my foot in the door, and I got my license to come on the backside. I finally just left her place. There wasn't a graduation. I just said, "I'm done. I need to work. I need to make money." If you show up to the backside every day and want to learn, someone will teach you and pay you. You don't pay them.

I was there for a couple of months walking hots for Steve Morguelen and then I met Julio Espinoza. He knew that I really wanted to do it, and if you're interested, you work hard, you show up every day, then someone will show you where to go, or the next step that you can take. He took me over to Dale Romans's barn, and Dale let me gallop at his track but said, "She's not good enough. I can't do anything with her."

I didn't understand how hard it is to ride. When you see a jockey ride a horse, they're just sitting, just perched there. It looks easy, and especially at a certain level people make it look really easy. They're all kind of doing the same thing. You have no appreciation for all that work. First of all, just holding yourself in that position is really hard. You have to develop muscles to do that and it takes a long time. Then you have to be strong enough to hold up in your back and your arms, because horses want to go faster. Or they'll want to get out or get in—tugging on the reigns to the left or right. You have to be strong enough to correct that behavior. And then you have to realize what's happening around you. Another horse might be wanting to get out and you have to adjust. Or the rider is stupid and you have to adjust for all that.

It's hard. There's a lot to learn, and I was really bad when I started. I think you're better off taking your time and really learning what you're doing. I basically knew nothing about horse care. Everything I'd learned, I had taught myself. I was so ignorant.

Thoroughbred horses need a completely different level of care than ponies in Montana because they're athletes.

I worked on a farm out in La Grange for a few months and then I got a job exercise riding at the Sports Spectrum, which is Trackside now. I always freelanced—I never worked for one barn or got "on salary." That's what they call it. I just went from barn to barn and made friends. Got on one or two horses here, one or two horses there, and that actually set me up well to be a jockey. I see a lot of girls that come in and work a salary job and get really coddled. They don't get to experience hustling. When you freelance, you get on anything, you learn how to be aggressive, and you try to make money. So it just served me well to be a rider. That's what you have to do. In the morning, you have to go around to all the barns and see if they'll let you ride something. And you have to be connected. It helps to know everybody and say, "I know you. Why don't you let me ride this horse?" or "Do you have anything for me?"

I galloped for four years and broke horses with my boyfriend at the time. Breaking horses taught me more than anything. That's how you learn: by teaching a horse how to be a racehorse. It's one thing to get on a horse that already knows the deal. But to teach a horse

from the first time you get on it to galloping around the track, you have to know what you're doing.

The first horse I ever broke was Chadwick Beach. I broke her and I was her groom. I was totally in love with her. I walked her, I groomed her, I went back and fed her in the afternoon. I did everything for her, except I did not get to ride her in a race. But I galloped her. She was short, she was chestnut, and she used to sit like a dog in the stall. She had some personality.

I learned a lot on Chadwick Beach. I learned how to teach a horse to accept a saddle, then to accept a rider, how to turn, how to go fast, how to slow down— all that stuff. I taught her how to bow for peppermints, which you're not supposed to do. A racehorse is a racehorse, not a trick pony. One day at the Sports Spectrum I got in trouble when I was pulling up on Chadwick Beach and saw a big mess of geese in the middle of the track. I pointed her to them and I said, "Go get 'em!" She trotted over there and we were chasing the geese, and when I came off, I was so proud of myself. It was just fun. But the trainer said, "Don't teach that horse how to do that! You both could get hurt!" You don't take a risk like that. But she loved me. She really loved me.

She was a cheap horse. I think she broke her maiden for $1,750 at Turfway Park, and then she ran at bottom level claimers. She got claimed, and then I lost track of her. I got scared to try to find her again because she could have broke down. She could be dead. I'm hoping she's a mother, but I don't think that's what happened. Maybe she's some girl's little pony. It's what I hope. I got a tattoo on my wrist of the ID number she had tattooed on her inner lip. I just got really attached to her, because she was my first horse.

I'd been galloping for four years when my boyfriend, Mike, saw me working a horse one day and said, "I think you're ready." I knew I wanted to ride races, but I wasn't actually thinking about it.

Mike knew everybody on the track, and I just started asking people I had ridden for. "I think I'm gonna get my license. You wanna put me on something?" One of our good friends, David Stober, said, "Yeah, I'm gonna ride you on something," and he got me some jockey pants that said "Greta" on the back. I got my boots, I got all my gear, and I'd started dieting to lose a lot of weight.

Then I got my bug—my apprentice license—which lasts for one year. When you're a bug, you have to be even smaller than a regular jock. When the horse gets entered into a race, depending on the condition of the race, the horse will weigh in with, say, 125 pounds. That means that the jock and all of the tack has to weigh exactly that amount to make sure that every horse in the race is carrying the same weight. If they are underweight, normally they have to add lead plates in pockets in the saddle pad to get to the right weight. But an apprentice gets a weight allowance. At first you get a 10 pound allowance, meaning that you can be up to 10 pounds underweight and not have to add any lead, giving your horse an advantage over the other horses. That's why the bug is so important, so that people can get their careers started, because if it didn't exist, no one would use someone that's never ridden before. Why would you use an apprentice when you could have someone that knows what they're doing? There's no reason to. You get 10 pounds for the first however many races, and then you get seven pounds until you've won 40 races, and then you get five pounds until your year is up.

I started dieting and trying to find somebody who would ride me on something. That was harder than I thought it was going to be. I would eat two eggs in the morning, a salad for lunch, and a piece of fish and a baked potato for dinner. I started at 115 pounds and eventually got down to 100. I was probably 103 when I started racing. You need to be able to tack 107 pounds to really be competitive, to really sell yourself. Which means, stripped, I have to be 102 or 103 pounds. Your saddle is going to weigh like a pound. They're super tiny saddles. The stirrups are like nothing. They're super light. And your clothes are a pound.

When I started, the other riders respected me because I knew where I was and I didn't do a lot of stupid shit. But I dropped myself this one time. I was in a race and there was a horse in front of me, a horse coming up the outside, and we were getting closer to this horse in front. I thought, *I'll just push him out when we get up to this horse.* Well, he wouldn't let me push him out. He made me stay down in there, so I clipped the horse's heels and he went down. I went down so fast that I didn't have time to be scared at the moment.

The first time I went down, I was fine, but the horse hurt his knee. I don't think they put him down, but I don't think he raced again. After that, I knew how close you could get to another horse before you go down. That's how you have to learn. If their nose is at that horse's tail, that's getting too close.

I did really good with the bug. I did good for two or three years after that, and it was really fun. I felt well-liked and well-respected in the jocks' room. I got a lot of attention. Newspapers did articles on me because I was "the girl rider." People wanted to talk about the girl rider. I won the holiday meet at Turfway. I got the trophy and still have it. It was fun and I made a lot of money. I was really bad with money. One time Mike was going through my laundry and he pulled out a $10,000 check. "What the fuck, Greta? Come on!" I had no idea what to do with it. I just didn't know.

Even when I was doing good, I always thought I could do better. I always thought it was my fault if a horse didn't run good. I thought it was something that I could change, which helped and hurt me.

I started struggling. Me and Mike just weren't getting along, and I felt that something needed to change. I don't know if I was just going through a slow period. It's hard to keep up seven days a week. It's hard to keep your enthusiasm up and to keep the momentum of doing well, and you get beat down.

My first injury was breaking my ankle at Keeneland, and then I broke my back working a horse. Then I separated my shoulder at Ellis Park. My problem was that when I got injured, it was always a struggle to get my business back. That was a bummer, and I never bounced back like I thought I should have. It's just a hustle, walking around, trying to get a shot. Asking people for help is the worst part of the job. People are supportive when you're doing good. When you're not doing good, it sucks.

I was ready to change everything. So I broke up with Mike and fired my agent. I started dating Bob, my new agent, and we moved to Chicago. We were just trying to make it there. Bob was a musician, but he was done with music. He'd just been a gambler, but he's really smart, and he did better than anybody else walking off the street to be an agent. He knew all the horses, and people liked him.

Still, I didn't realize how good my previous agent was until I fired him and realized how connected agents have to be. It was hard for a new agent to come in and do it. Bob did great, but he wasn't connected like agents typically are. So we decided to try Chicago. We tried really hard every morning, beating the doors, trying to get something. I was getting tired of it. I was getting frustrated and my business was going down the tubes.

It was the early 2000s. Chicago is a really cool town to do touristy stuff. We did all the museums and the music shows—stuff like that—but I did not like the people or the town. A bunch of meatheads. Bob said they had Italian sausages in their skulls instead of brains—just meaty sausages inside. But the jockey colony up there was really cool. Really tight. They were all really supportive of each other. It was just a good feeling in the jocks' room. Everyone was really close.

We stayed up there almost a whole year. I was doing so bad in Chicago. But Bob got me on a horse named Freeforinternet. I don't even know how he did it, but Bob sent me out of town to go ride Freeforinternet at Mountaineer, and he won. His next race was in Chicago, at the Hawthorne Gold Cup, and he won that too. That was a $750,000 graded stakes race. It was a big deal. The biggest that I've ever won. It felt like a no-big-deal race while I was winning it. This could be any race. We broke from the gate at the start and I was like, *He's not gonna run at all.* He was coming out of the gate so slow. I said, "What the hell is wrong with you?" I got mad and spanked him a few times and then he took off, and I ended up winning the race. He was this grouchy old horse, his feet were bad, but he could run.

There was this guy standing at the backside later and he told me, "I saw you come by the first time and I thought, *Man. Poor Greta. She's all the way in the back. She's got no shot.* Then I saw you come in on the turning end and you were in front and I thought to myself, *The field broke down.*" He thought every horse in the field broke down but me.

I don't know if it was a shock reaction, but I just remember not really feeling it, not being super excited. I came back to the Winner's Circle and I was just smiling and riding. They're walking me around and there's a bunch of photographers there, and they're all yelling, "Hey! Give a thumbs up or something!" I thought, *This is so dumb. Why are you making me do this?* I think I'd been doing so bad for so long and struggling so hard in Chicago that maybe I was already half broken. I was just beat down by riding and by struggling.

The Hawthorne Gold Cup was the last good race Freeforinternet ran. The next race was the Breeder's Cup Classic six weeks later. The track was super hard and, since the horse had bad feet, he hated it and he was pretty much over it. There was zero pressure on me at the Breeder's Cup because the horse was a longshot at 50-1.

We were in between the two favorites, and he came out of the gate and bumped both of them. He did his typical thing where he feels like he's going to pull up and jog into the first turn, and I was super behind the field. I tried to get into him like I had every other time so he would take off. I tried it, but I almost knew he wasn't going to respond. So I didn't have that same panic that I had before. I asked him, but I asked him knowing it was all for naught. So we just galloped behind the field. I might have caught the last horse. I don't remember where I finished, but it was nowhere.

After the race, the trainer wouldn't talk to me. The owner wouldn't talk to me. I went back to the barn, and nobody was there. No one would even talk to me. You couldn't even talk to me? Why? You won't answer my call? Because everybody has that hope. You go into it with that hope. It was disappointing. That's horse racing—highs and lows.

My parents had come down to watch me in the race, and at dinner, they told me they were divorcing after 35 years. My parents getting divorced was really bad, and it was really hard on my mom. It was just weird and really sad that we weren't going to be a family again. My mom was crushed and full of rage and hate. I was shaken by that whole thing.

After the Breeder's Cup I decided to stop riding and just gallop for a while. Then I came back to Louisville. I left Bob. I said, "I can't do it anymore. I'm going home." I was frustrated with the business. I was sick of it. I had worked through my 20s super hard every day and thought it was a normal routine. I missed the whole college experience of just screwing off for a while. Nobody really knew I was having a hard time. It was just ripe for something bad to happen. I sought it out. I wanted to escape. Doing drugs was perfect. I had a lot of fun being by myself, getting high.

The first time I took meth, I was crashing on the floor at this girl's place. I was just lying there, in the dark, and I had a big smile on my face. I was euphoric. It felt so good, and I fell in love with it. It wasn't every day all day at first. It was really sporadic for a while, and then I positioned myself so that I could do it every day. It took a few months.

So that's what I did for a year. Then I got caught, and I got in a lot of trouble. I never thought it was such a big deal. I wondered, *Why do people care? Why do the police care?* You can't do illegal shit and expect the police to not care about it. You can't live like that. I was on TV: "Jockey caught in a meth ring." I saw it in jail. It was surreal. It felt like a dream or a movie at first, then it did feel real. I was really scared and I was in a bad place. Because when you do that to yourself, you get out of touch with reality. It's a horrible drug. It fucks with your brain. I see why it rips people apart, and why they never get better. I'm lucky that I was able to get through it.

I got arrested a couple of times but didn't really stop because the first time I got bailed out of jail really quickly. I kept using because why not? Then I got in trouble again, and that's when I ended up in jail for 10 days.

I was just really sad that I got caught. I was really sad that it was over. I have always been a really low-energy person. My blood pressure is like 90/40—I'm just barely alive. I like to sleep. When I first did meth, I thought, *Oh my God, I finally feel like a normal person. I feel like I have energy.* A side effect is euphoria. So

I was sad that I couldn't do that anymore. And of course it was super embarrassing and so shameful. It was mortifying.

I thought, *My parents will never find out. They will never know.* Then I was arrested and my parents found out because it was on the TV news. My mom came for a little bit, then my dad came for a little bit, and my sister came, but I was still in the mindset, so nothing really changed. When I got locked up again, I called them and they just said, "Well, it sounds like you're where you need to be." They were glad I was in jail because they knew where I was and knew that I wasn't using. I was just incoherently bawling on the phone. My mom told me later, "I couldn't understand anything you were saying at all when you called me." Coming off the drug is so depressing. Besides the situation that you're in, you're chemically blown out. It was over a year before I felt normal. I knew I had brain damage. I could tell. You don't feel good. Normal stuff that would have made you feel good doesn't make you feel good. You've depleted all those things. That's why people use. There's no way to feel good. It takes such a long time to rebuild.

I have been approached a bunch of times about people who have problems or want to help someone else. I always ask them if they have been to jail. If they say, "Oh yeah, they've been to jail," I say, "Well, your best bet is to walk away." Because if someone's gone to jail and that's not enough motivation to stop them from doing it, then I don't know what is. For me, jail made me think, *I don't like this place. I don't want to come back here. I think I should stop doing this so I don't spend any more time in jail.*

In jail, you don't know what's going on outside because the windows are all cloudy. You can tell if it's light or dark, but you can't see the sky. As a person who works outside every day, to take that away was a big deal.

I really had a hard time with that. One day we had a day where they took all of us to the gym and let us walk around. They had normal windows, really high. You could see the sky. It was that grayish blue, but a little lighter. I came back and described it to one of the women. "Oh man, the sky! I saw the sky!" I told her the color, and how the cold air was coming into the gym and I could feel it on my skin.

I was on house arrest for over six months, and in drug court. That helped. I don't follow the twelve-step program now, but I appreciate how it works for people and the lady that was my sponsor is now my roommate. I haven't drank or used in 11 years. I don't even think about it. It isn't a struggle anymore and that's part of the reason why I don't do meetings anymore. I never really thought that I was an addict and this was a disease, but that's what they tell you. If people believe that, then that is good, if that works for them. But for me, I just thought that I messed with some addictive stuff and now I choose not to.

I had work release. So I was going out on a farm to gallop, because Churchill Downs wouldn't let me on the track. They said I made Churchill look bad, and I had to go to the Kentucky Horse Racing Commission with a lawyer to argue to have them give my license back. It was a big deal, and I tried, but they said no. It had never occurred to me that they wouldn't give my license back.

All through my incarceration and parole, I had to go to five meetings a week. I had to go pee three to four times a week. I'd call this number, and if my number came up, I had to go pee. I missed a drop once. Maybe I didn't call. I don't know. It got me at a busy day. I had a certain amount of time to go in and I missed it. I was clean. I wasn't doing anything—I just missed it. And if you miss a drop, you have to do five days in jail. They let me do it in C.C.C., which is a work-release jail, but part of the thing with work-release jail is that you're strip-searched before you come in. They'll let you out and then before you come back—every time—you get strip-searched.

It was just so humiliating. I was at work one day, galloping horses, and I was so in my head about it. *I can't do this again. This is the worst thing ever.* I was really panicking in my head about going through that experience again. You know how you get into a panic and it's just circle, circle, circle. You're just going to mess up your whole morning worrying about something that is going to take about five minutes. So I thought, *Wait. You get three hours outside of that place. You need to just enjoy it. Quit worrying about the strip-search. Stop thinking about it.* I kind of had this zen moment of enlightenment. It was like time slowed down. I was on a horse. I felt the breeze blowing my eyelashes and the sun felt like it was like glittering down. I was in the moment like I had never been before, able to experience every sensation. It was super magical. I felt enlightened for that 30 seconds. It's amazing what I got from being terrified of getting strip-searched. I don't regret it. On some level, it worked for me, and I came out.

I did end up getting my license and riding again. I did pretty good at first, but racing had changed. Races were cut back and there were not as many horses in races. I was still riding races, but it was getting really hard to make ends meet. Ron Moquett said, "Why don't you just get on a few horses for me before the 9 a.m. break? You can make that money every week, and then still work horses after the break for trainers." That was our arrangement for a year, and then I just quit riding altogether and started galloping for him. His wife Laura started teaching me the assistant trainer job—checking legs and taking care of stuff. I've been working seriously as an assistant to Ron for about two years.

I think they just saw the potential in me, that I could do it. I don't think everybody can be an assistant, especially jockeys. Some jockeys will go on to be agents or different stuff. I don't see a lot of jockeys being an assistant, but I was just willing. I like learning about the proper care for a horse, and what the best way is for me to do that. Laura's really good at natural horsemanship, as far as getting a horse to respond in a correct way, asking a horse to do something. That's been a huge piece, learning how to do that. I've learned so much from her. She's amazing.

It's been a learning curve working as an assistant. How do you manage people? I was kind of in a bad place about being an assistant for a while. "Do I get off the track? Do I need to quit doing this?" But I've since been in a better place, and I found out that you just fire the people you don't like and your job gets better. I've gotten really good at firing people and running people off. I'm just a real bitch. I need to work on being a little more kind and more motivating. I need to compliment people every now and again, because I have run off people that maybe I shouldn't have.

I don't understand how people on the track, like trainers or grooms, are so dedicated and they don't even get to ride the horses. Because riding is the best part. I think, for anyone, it depends on if you're an animal lover. Some people aren't. Some people just don't care if they have a dog or whatever, but that doesn't make sense to me. I want to be around animals, and a horse is just another animal to have a relationship with. They're really amazing, because they're so big.

I've heard that elephants look at us like we look at cats. The same thing that lights up when we look at a kitten, the same part of their brain lights up when they look at a human: like a little kitty. For horses it must be the same kind of thing. There must be something in their brain that says, "Aw. Okay, human! Let's go somewhere. Let's start something. Let's do it."

I also think part of it is, if you fall in love with just one of them, then you want to meet all of them. That's how it starts. You don't realize how different their personalities are, how engaging they are, and how much you want to be around them. It's like a dog you can ride. They're not smart like a dog, but they have individual personalities. They're really intuitive. That's why they started using horses in therapy: because they mirror whatever feelings you have. If you're incongruent—if you say you're okay but really you're mad—they pick up on what's really going on. You can't fake it around them.

If I'm mad at somebody in the barn and I get on a horse, I might be just a little tense with my movements, and they'll start acting badly or just not responding to what I'm doing. I can say, "Why are you acting like this? You don't normally act like this." And then I'll say, "It's probably me. I need to relax, take a breath, and this will be okay." It helps you be mindful of your actions and your thoughts.

Our big horse, Whitmore, is one of the smartest horses I've ever been around. He's a complete asshole, but riding him is like therapy. Because if there's something that I'm not comfortable with, he'll do it over and over again until I say, "Okay, it doesn't matter anymore." He'll lunge forward, lunge forward, lunge forward, until I say, "Fine, lunge forward." Then he'll stop. If there is some kind of fear or some other weakness in people, he exposes it. He thinks it's fun when a person is afraid of him. He likes that. He likes to intimidate other horses, too. He likes to bump them. It's just what he likes to do. He does it in races, and it's hard to find a good jockey for him because he's such a dick. I saw his first few days on the track. He was so bad. I said, "This thing is unrideable."

Yobani—this really great rider who works for us—got on Whitmore and the horse took off. Then he came sliding to a halt and threw his head up like a reining horse or something. Whitmore took off towards the inside rail, and I don't know what Yobani did, but his helmet slid down to his eyes. He was trying to see where he was going, and then the horse bolted off in the opposite direction. Laura got on him a couple of days after that, working with him in the chute, and just trying to get him to go forward. He wanted his own way. He did not want to be told what to do. Laura said, "You have to cut him. We can't ride him!" He got a little better after he was gelded, but it took a long time before we could work him. Maybe two weeks.

Then he ran the first race that he won at Churchill, and we said, "Whoa, he's amazing." And then he went down to Delta Downs and ran in that million dollar race there, and he was fourth. Once he started running, we realized, "Oh, wow. He's *nice*." Then he was three years old and campaigning on the Derby trail. He went to the Derby. He's super talented. He's really, really fast.

He came in second in the 2018 Breeder's Cup Sprint. I'm probably more emotional than others, but we all felt fucked up afterwards. He had been doing so well physically. It had all been coming together. Everything was perfect. Mentally, he was just really right, and he was at Churchill Downs, a track that he loved. He didn't have to ship anywhere to go run. We felt great going into the race. To do everything in your power to get the horse to be where he's supposed to be and to have him come so close—to have a horse of that caliber almost win the Breeder's Cup, a $2 million race. It was emotional. It was just hard to see him lose.

He's amazing. To be around a horse like that, it just doesn't happen often. /

Sophie Goff

SEAMSTRESS

I was born in Albuquerque, New Mexico. My mom was Isleta Indian. They have their own language which she spoke a little, but mostly she spoke Spanish. I was about six when we moved here from New Mexico in 1956. Mom met my stepdad when he was stationed in Albuquerque. Then he had to come back to Fort Knox and he sent for us. When we came here, Dad didn't like her speaking Spanish because he thought we were talking about him. Probably the first 10 years of my life we spoke Spanish, but it slowly got to be more and more English. Then finally we didn't speak any. I can catch one or two words and kind of know what the conversation is about. But to carry on a conversation? I can't do that anymore.

My mom sewed at home—made skirts and blouses for us girls—but she didn't do it as a job. She mostly worked in restaurants. She was a pretty good cook. She'd make us tortillas and a big pot of brown beans, fried potatoes, and sopapillas and we'd be in heaven. In restaurants here, when you order sopapillas they are like a cinnamon treat, but Mom didn't make them like that. They were more like bread instead of a dessert.

She worked at the lunch counter at Wagner's for many years when it was at 4th and Central. I was going to school at Manual, and I'd go over there and have lunch with her after school. I got to talking to Mr. Wagner once and I found out that they had a sewing shop upstairs. I sewed at home—I'd make a lot of my own stuff, a skirt or tank top—and I figured that sewing racing silks for Mr. Wagner couldn't be that hard. So I told him I'd like to try it out. When I graduated, he hired me, and I worked there for 17 years.

My mom had taught me to sew in elementary school. We had an old electric Sears-type sewing machine. She made me some skirts and I'd watch her and just soak it all in. Finally I started cutting out little squares, making quilts and stuff like that. So I could sew, but sewing racing silks was different than what I was sewing at home. It did take me a while to catch on to the way my boss wanted me to do it. She didn't want me to use straight pins. So I had to learn how to make it without straight pins and keep the material from sliding around. It took me a while, but I caught on.

When I first went up there, I mostly worked on the jockey caps. There were six pieces of fabric that are shaped like irons. You'd put them all together and put them on the helmet. If it was too big, you had to take it up, put it back on the helmet. If it was too tight, you let it out and put it back on the helmet. It was a lot of work, but after you get used to doing it, it doesn't take that long anymore. Making them with lycra now

out, and put it on the side of the machine. So I started working on it.

I sewed the colors for Seattle Slew in 1977. I didn't know it until I saw it on TV, because I didn't know the name of the horse. I just made the colors, and then I saw them on TV and he was winning. Black and yellow.

The shirts are all one size because they have to just stretch so much that if we make it to fit the jockey, they'll tear the sleeves out. It's got to be long enough that it goes in the pants, and still won't come out when he's stretching. These days, a lot of them like the lighter spandex-tight material which I don't like working with. It's just too stretchy, and the needles and the thread keep skipping. But that's what they want. I like the old fashioned material—the nylon or satin. Lycra is more expensive than satin, but I think satin is the prettiest because it's shiny.

Whoever owns the horse tells the trainer what he wants the silks to look like, then the design has to be approved and registered, to make sure nobody else has the same thing, and then the trainer will get in touch with us. And we'll go on and make it. If they're pretty plain, I can average a couple silks a day. If they have a bunch of stuff on them—lettering or diamonds or stars or something—I can do about one a day.

The trainers can be really picky about the colors. "That stripe's not two inches; that's two and a half inches," or, "That's supposed to be another shade of red." Well, we got one shade of red. You got to take it or leave it. If they want a light red, or a real deep red, they have to special order it. But a lot of times they don't want to wait a month, so we'll go on.

We start at $150, and then the more you have on it, the more it costs. An expensive set is about $350 or $400. It sounds expensive to me. I mean, if I went somewhere and ordered a dress, I wouldn't pay $350 for it.

is much easier, because it'll stretch. Jockeys would come up there and order their caps. The bills used to be bigger. The jockeys like the small ones now. I don't know why.

I did those for what seemed like forever until my boss finally let me work on the colors. I was probably working on the caps for about a year. Then one day she called me into the other room with her and had me get on the other machine. She handed me the pieces of a jacket and I started putting it together. It was kind of scary, but I'd watched her and I knew what to do. That's where it started. She'd already cut everything

And then they just don't take care of the things. They might use it two or three times, and then the trainer has to order another one. They're out there on the track and they get them all dirty and, even if you wash it, there's some stains that aren't going to come out. If you get the dirt off right away and put in the wash, it will be okay. Oil spots won't come out.

We've always lived somewhere in the South End. I've lived in two different places on Central. It's always been the South End. It's a nice neighborhood. It's gotten a little rough, but almost every neighborhood has.

Me and my husband have been married almost 50 years. He's retired from GE. He worked there for 35 years. He worked in air conditioning, and then when that went out, he worked in refrigeration. We raised two kids. My son, they call him Big Al. He's about 6'1", 225 pounds or so. My daughter Sonya passed away in 2009. She had two kids, Vanessa and Jonathan, and we took over after she passed away. They're pretty good kids. All of my kids and their friends turned out really good, and a lot of my kids' friends still come to visit us. They'll stop by and see us if they're in town. /

Ryan "Tiny" Rosely
STARTING GATE CREW, HORSE TATTOOER

I grew up near Marion, Indiana, in a farming community of 600 or 700 people. Growing up in a town like that, you didn't have to worry about anything. Everybody knew each other. You rode your bike. You knew every kid in town. You went home at dark—there was no checking in with your parents. Ain't got a crime rate. I lived there 18 years, never locked the front door. It's not like that as much anymore.

My dad worked in the RCA factory making TVs for 20 years. They ran three shifts, seven days a week. It was pretty good. My mom worked in fire restoration from water damage, stuff like that. She was one of the managers. I got a little brother, too, seven years younger than me.

I didn't really grow up around animals. When I got to high school is when I started getting around horses. I was 16 before I ever touched a horse. One of my good friends worked as a trainer at a local farm. They had their own track and everything, so I started going to the track and working for him. I started cleaning stalls, grooming.

I worked for him for two years, and then I got a job on the starting gates at Hoosier Park. I knew some of the guys that did it, and they needed somebody, so I started doing it. They don't race there no more.

I started from the ground up. They only let you shut back doors for a while, and then you start getting the hang of the way everything works. It's a trial by fire. You learn gradually. I still learn something new every day. You never know two horses that ever act the same. I still do the same job today as I did the first day at work.

I worked on gate crews in Indiana, Iowa, and Florida. While I was working in Florida, a guy that used to work at the starting gate at Churchill was going to become the starter, so there was an empty spot there. They needed somebody, and my boss called to see if I wanted the job. Churchill is three hours from home. Florida is 23 hours from home. So I came here and replaced him. My boss called and recommended me, and they knew each other well enough to take each other's word. Now I've worked every Derby since 2013.

In all reality, our job is just like a babysitter. Keep the horse calm, and if anything happens, you do your best to keep the horse and the jockey safe. You got to make sure the horse is standing good and relaxed. Last one comes, everything is quiet. We make a fair and equal start for everybody.

Horses pick up on nerves pretty easily. They're scared of people that are scared of them. You got to have a mutual respect with them. You got to be relaxed so it channels through. You can't be scared of them, but you got to know they're a big animal. Just remember: they can kill you, but they can't eat you.

Anywhere from five to fourteen horses is a normal race. We have 12 or 13 guys working the gate all the time.

If there's a 12-horse build, we load two at a time. You load the 1 and the 7, then the 2 and the 8, the 3 and the 9, the 4 and the 10, the 5 and the 11, the 6 and the 12.

The pony people bring the horses to us, then we take them from the pony people. You got one person leading them in, and two people that shut the doors. Once all the horses are in there, our boss starts the race. He's the one that hits the button.

It's a good day for the gate crew when everything just goes smooth. Nothing too exciting. No wrecks, no nothing. Everything's smooth, everything's quiet, and they're gone. Just a good, smooth day. Some races you're off, some races you're the one shutting the back doors, and some races you're in there. When you've loaded the horses, you're there with them until the race starts. It's fun.

Horses being unruly is a rotten day. Getting banged up, getting bruised, getting pulled at or kicked. It happens sometimes. I've been pawed in the head. I've been kicked in the legs. It just comes with the territory of being around horses in general.

When you're in the starting gate, you're very close to them. With a horse, the closer you are, the safer you are when it comes to them kicking, because they can't get the full extension of that leg. So it's a little safer being close to them.

If they get to thrashing around or something, you catch shots from their whole body. So you get bruised up. I got bruised up on my legs, busted knuckles, stuff like that.

The start of the Derby is especially cool. The crowd gets gradually louder the more the horses get in. Then as the last one comes, everything's quiet, and it almost pauses for a second. And then they're gone. It's a pretty cool experience.

There's about 30 thoroughbred racetracks in America, and about 15 people on average working the gate crew at each one. But here in Kentucky, we have Keeneland, Churchill Downs, Kentucky Downs, Ellis Park, and Turfway Park. We have five racetracks, and the same guys work four of them. Turfway has a whole different set of people.

Most of us only travel around Kentucky. We start at Keeneland in the spring, and then come here, and then Ellis Park and Kentucky Downs.

There's nine to thirteen of us that do the traveling. A couple of the guys gallop, so they stay here with that job. During the summer, most of the guys work here in the mornings still, and then they drive to Ellis Park Friday, Saturday, and Sunday for the races.

To be good at the job, you got to get along with everybody. You got to be for the team. Even though you're in the stall by yourself, you're still working beside the guy next to you. If something goes wrong, you're there to help the person next to you.

The guys here at Churchill are a lot more experienced than most places. This usually isn't a place where you get your first job. They're all a bunch of good guys. Some have worked here for 17, 18 years. And they worked elsewhere for years prior to that. So they have 30 years on the job.

———

I've been tattooing horses just two years. John James retired, and I took over for him. He did it for 12 years before his hands got to hurting too much. He had carpal tunnel. It got to where he couldn't do it no more. It was one of those things that I never really sought after. The opportunity just arose. John talked to me about it. He said, "Hey, would you be interested in doing it?

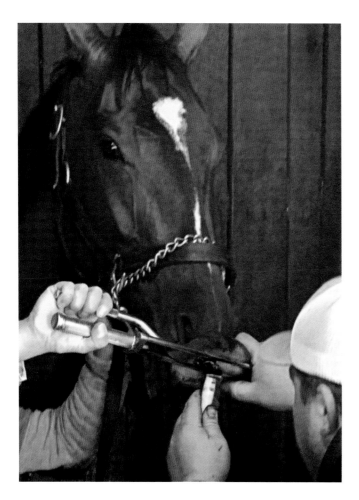

that you can't run the wrong horse under another horse's name. I don't know the exact year they started tattooing horses, but it was in the '40s or '50s. They've been doing it for a long time. Before that, they branded them. In 2019 they're going to start microchipping horses instead of tattooing them. So I might be one of the last horse tattooers in America.

The owners write descriptions of the horses when they are babies and submit them to the Jockey Club with photos. Then the Jockey Club puts on there whatever the owner submits. All the areas of the horse are identified for the certificate. Whorls or cow-licks. If they have a dark spot on them, they'll put that there. Say the horse has an indentation on his shoulder or anywhere, they'll put that on there. Patch of white hairs to right atop of eye-level, they'll put that on there.

If a horse needs a tattoo, somebody from the stable calls me and says, "Look, we have 10 two-year-olds that are gonna be running and need to be tattooed. Put me on your list." So I just keep a list of people that I go to.

I wanna retire in like a year and a half." He trained me to do it. I followed him around for about six weeks to help him do it and get the hang of the process. I thought it would be all right, so I started. And that's how it came about.

Before an owner can race a horse, they have to verify its identity and get them tattooed. They tattoo them so an owner can't run the wrong horse in a race—you can't run Secretariat with his stablemate who's about 99-1. There's so much money involved in everything, and you can't run a ringer. It's a federal law

They call me directly, or they call the identifier, which is Melinda. She's over in the racing office. They call her, and I have a list in there that people add themselves to. Melinda works for Churchill, and I work for the Thoroughbred Racing Protective Bureau doing the tattooing. The TRPB contracts and pays me. When I collect all the money, it's written to them. It's all a big collaborative deal.

Melinda's job is to read the tattoos and identify the horse at racetime and make sure that it's the proper horse. She makes sure the wrong horse doesn't come to the paddock. Nobody really tries to run the wrong horse anymore, but it happens unintentionally. People will send the wrong horse to the pad. It's happened.

There's not that many colors in American thoroughbred racing. There's gray, dark bay or brown, black, white, and chestnut. Most horses are dark bay. A registered black horse doesn't happen very often at all. There might be four of them running, right now, across the country. White horses are more prevalent. But both the black and the white horses are a rarity.

I've had people try to register horses as black, and when I get the papers, I know they're going to have to be changed. I go and look at the horse, and if they're wrong about the color, they have to be sent back. They're not allowed to be tattooed until it's properly marked.

The hardest part is that there's no uniform language for the way things are worded in those papers. So when owners might not be as experienced as a big farm, the way that they explain things isn't as good. So I can't think too literally about what I'm reading. You got to get in people's mindset to see where they're coming from when they're explaining it. Because when you read them every day, you know what it should say, versus what they actually make it say. It's trying to decipher it a little bit.

People are not happy about having to redo paperwork. If you do have to correct them, it can take up to two or three weeks. That causes the horses to miss races sometimes. And that's not the only thing they're dealing with. It costs them another $150. That's why people want to have it done early. Some people wait until the last minute, and some people want it done three months early. If you need to have them rushed, you can pay extra money, which goes from $100 to $500. You can get them back in two or three days instead of two to three weeks.

Those calluses they have above their knees, those are called chestnuts or night-eyes. It's like a fingerprint. Every one of them that have them, they're on the inside of all four legs. No two are the same on any horse. Those aren't actually on the papers, and they're not required to have pictures of it or anything. But if you're lucky they do take pictures of them.

If the horse's papers are wrong, but pictures of the night-eyes are right, I can usually let the horse go. They still have to do the process, but they get to run. And then after the race, they'll change the papers.

Once I identify the markings and make sure it's the proper horse, I then go about administering the tattoo. There's a stamp. There's a premade number of needles. You dip the needle in ink, stick it in their lip, and it's there. India ink. Waterproof drawing ink.

You got to put a little pressure into it to get a good tat. To get good, clean numbers.

If you don't push hard, they'll come out light. It's not that I'm pushing overly hard—you just got to apply hard enough.

The tool you use to curl the lip is called a twitch. There's multiple kinds of twitches, and they're for stretching. There's a different twitch for the ear and nose. It applies pressure to numb the nerves to where they don't feel it. It's more for the horse than anything. It doesn't bother them. It's all pretty humane.

Then I'll have to fill out all the paperwork that shows who tattooed the horse, who told me who the horse was, who witnessed the horse being done and everything. I send that with a picture of the tattoo to the TRPB, and that is kept in a permanent file in case there's ever a discrepancy.

I do, on average, 1,400 or 1,500 tattoos a year right now. It's a good side hustle. /

Neil Huffman

FARM MANAGER, TRAINER

    PHOTO BY BEN FREEDMAN

THE HORSE SPY

I was just starting high school when I got my first horse. A buddy of mine who lived two blocks down the street rode the horse into my backyard and said, "I gotta find somethin' to do with Rusty. I'm goin' away to Lexington." My uncle Ben Masden was there and bought him for $100. Saddle and everything.

I put him right there in the yard. I'd get home from school every day and saddle up, ride out Southern Parkway and around the park. My mom was ready to run me off. "You can't have a horse around here." I don't know why. I didn't see no rules. But before long I moved him over to 3rd and Kenton. There was two barns there. One of them had five stalls, the other one had six stalls, and there was a little arena in the middle of it. I'd stop in there on the way to school every morning and feed him.

My uncle Ben was a clocker here at Churchill. They called him the Horse Spy. You'd have loved to listen to him. He was a real character. Looked like Jackie Gleason, and funny. He was like me and had started climbing the fence onto the backside when he was a kid. He knew horses. He was good right off the bat.

Uncle Ben worked for the *Daily Racing Form*. Back then the clockers worked for the *Racing Form* instead of the track. Bill Cunningham was the clocker, and he was the one who taught my uncle Ben to clock. Ben would come back here with his own stopwatch, and Cunningham taught him how to split and how to catch two horses at once breaking from different poles. This went on for a couple of years. And one day Cunningham's boss, the head of all clockers for the *Racing Form*, flew in and told Cunningham, "After the meet is over you're going to a new racetrack." Cunningham said, "Whoa, whoa. Wait a minute. Where?" They'd just built Aksarben in Omaha and Cunningham says, "I ain't going out there. I'm too old. That's Indian country out there. They race quarter horses with cowboys. I ain't going." My uncle was there and Cunningham introduced him. He said, "This is Ben Masden. He can clock better than I can." The guy looked at Ben and said, "You want a job?" He never had a job before. All he'd ever done for work up to then was place 50-cent bets at the Steiden's Grocery next to where we lived. There was a bookmaker in the back, and Ben had been beating the bookie to death. He made a hell of a living. So my uncle tells the guy, "Yeah I want a job!"

He come running home to my grandmother's house that day, got his wicker suitcase, and my grandmother said, "What are you doing?" He said, "I'm taking a job. I'm gonna be clocking horses.

I'm taking a train to Nebraska." Ben got on a train to Omaha. From there, they sent him to Oaklawn, and then he worked just about all the racetracks. He ended up at the Fairgrounds, at Oaklawn, Keeneland, Churchill. And then they built Cahokia Downs in East St. Louis and they sent him there. Ben said he made more money there than he did at any other place.

He had three jobs. He worked for the *Racing Form* as a clocker, but for the track he was the I.D. and the paddock judge. The horse identifier is the one who turns their lip up to see the tattoo number in the paddock. Every horse gets a lip tattoo. And when every horse comes in the paddock, the I.D. is standing there. He has a stack of papers with I.D. numbers for all the horses that are in that race, and he turns their lip up to verify their number. The I.D. has to take down the markings too. Ben had page after page of horses with their markings.

When a horse shipped in or when they got tattooed, he'd go physically identify them by the white marks, the blazes, the birthmarks on their necks, how many white stockings they had, and how high up they went or how low they were.

Now it's all computerized, but back then keeping track of all those horses was difficult. They didn't have saddle towels identifying who the trainer was. The towels were either white or all red. There weren't initials and there wasn't no gap attendants like Bob DeSensi to tell you this horse is working five-eighths. If Ben didn't know who they were, he'd follow them back and find out which barn they went to. He'd go from stall to stall and had a book with the horse's name, the trainer, a description like: *dark brown three-year-old gelding, blaze left front over, and right front under, back*. He had a whole book of the stuff.

Ben's last job was at Cahokia Downs. He got sick, went to the doctor, and had rectal cancer. They just sent him home. There wasn't much treatment for cancer back then. They didn't have nothing they could do for you. There was no chemo, no radiation. You got it, and that was it. He was 46, and he would've been the youngest state steward in the country. He was only married about a year before he died. They brought him home and my mother took care of him. He went from 240 down to like 60 pounds when he died. It was hard on my mother. She lost an older brother and a younger brother, and another brother went out to Waverly Hills. He had tuberculosis. My mom lived to 92.

Ben's dad, my grandfather, was a railroader. Patton Masden was an engineer on *The Hummingbird*. That was the top job at the L&N Railroad. Passenger engineer. *The Hummingbird* ran from New Orleans to Cincinnati. Mom used to take us down to the railroad track on Kenton because he'd tell us exactly what time he'd come through there and he'd blow the train as he'd go by. On his day off, he'd put that suit and that watch fob on and go to Latimer's Barber Shop.

That barber shop was at the back of the parking lot at the fish fry on 3rd and Southern. That was Harry and Doc Latimer's place, and that's where everybody was at, reading the *Racing Form*. I went home from there one time with a haircut, and Dad looked at me and said, "Well, you have to go back." I said, "Why?" He said, "Harry didn't cut but half your head." He forgot one side. He was too busy running to the back room and taking him a shot and making a bet.

Next to the barber shop was the N&S sandwich shop. That's where my dad met Victor Mature. Victor Mature's dad was a knife sharpener. Right on the corner there by the fish fry was a Steiden's Grocery. That was before Kroger and all of them. He would be in there sharpening knives, and Victor would come over to the pool room right next to the barber shop. Victor had that hair. He'd comb that hair and he'd tell my dad and everybody in there he was going to be a movie star. He was going to Hollywood. Sure enough, one day he didn't show up. His dad was next door sharpening knives, and they asked him, "Where's Victor?" He said, "Got on the train and headed to Hollywood." And then he became a big movie star. Ever heard of John Wayne, Humphrey Bogart, or James Cagney? Well, Victor Mature is right in that group. Played Samson in *Samson and Delilah*, pulled the pillars down. That's Victor Mature.

I was born during the flood of 1937. My dad had 11 brothers and sisters, and they were born in Colesburg down around Lebanon Junction. As they grew up, they got away from the farm and he headed to Louisville. Before he got a job at the L&N he had an ice route. There was a little ice house over here on Central Avenue, right across from where the Derby Museum is. He had a wood-bedded pickup truck and he got a job there delivering ice. That was before refrigeration. That's where the term "ice boxes" comes from. They had them hooks on their shoulder, and he delivered ice all around South Louisville for a long time. All he ever did was work. He loved to go to the races on Saturday. He loved to sit there and handicap.

He also worked at the first Ford plant in Louisville on 3rd Street and Eastern Parkway before he got on at the L&N. He started out as a fireman, before the trains had diesels. The fireman had the hardest job. You shoveled coal up and down the roads for eight, ten, or twelve hours. Finally got promoted to engineer, the job he always wanted. The engineer just sits there. They had a pedal, they called it a dead man's pedal, and you had to have it down with your foot before the thing would run. That was to keep awake. Well, they figured that out real quick: They had a broomstick they would use instead of their foot and they could do whatever they wanted.

Derby winning jockey Roscoe Goose (left) and trainer Tennessee Wright

My grandmother took in boarders during the meet when all the jocks were in town. She lived right there where the fish fry is now. There was a bunch of them that stayed there during the meet or during Derby week. She had all the great riders stay there at one time or another: Charlie Curtsinger, Willy Nash, the Iceman George Woolf. The Iceman rode Seabiscuit in the match race with War Admiral at Pimlico in 1938. That was one of the greatest match races of all time. That was a great day in racing. The stands only held 36,000. In the parking lot, there was 100,000 with the doors open on their cars and the radio on, listening to the call of that race. Millions listened worldwide.

It was like the nation just kind of froze for an instant. Seabiscuit beat him. The greatest race ever. Look it up. It'll make the hair stand up on the back of your neck.

When I was 12 years old I started hopping the fence to come on the backside. That's how I started working for Tennessee Wright. He was in the barn right next to the track kitchen. I just showed up back there one day.

I was going to Holy Name, and I climbed the fence. I wandered in Barn B over there by the kitchen. That's the way it was. You had to climb the fence and make it through the high weeds. I just walked in the barn and Tennessee Wright handed me a horse. They hand you the shank and tell you to start turning left. That's about it. That doesn't take a hell of a lot of know-how. I got a job walking hots down there.

Tennessee Wright was the leading trainer in America for four or five years. He was an amazing horseman. He reminded you of Humphrey Bogart: had that long gabardine top coat that went down about mid-shin, that hat, and a cigarette always in his mouth. When he walked around the shed, if he'd stop and linger in front of a horse's stall very long and get that condition book out, he was getting ready to enter it.

Tennessee didn't like to work horses. Working a horse is letting it go as good as he can go, just a little less than race time. Tennessee liked to two-minute lick horses. He'd let them gallop open and bring them back. I remember he was spitting and cussing one morning during Derby week. Roman Line was one of the favorites in the Derby, and he trained good. Grissom, the owner, was coming down, and he wanted to see the horse work. That's why Tennessee was mad, kicking and spitting. "What's wrong?" I said. "Grissom's coming down in the morning and wants to see the horse work," Tennessee said. He had to work him, just because the boss was coming down from Lexington.

This was Derby week. The horse come back all right but then finished second by a neck in the Derby. Tennessee always swore if he hadn't have worked him, he'd have won.

THE HORSEMEN OF SOUTH LOUISVILLE

There were a ton of people who rode around here. There were a ton of houses on Southern Parkway that had a barn in the backyard. We had two riding academies on Southern Parkway. Carla Grego's parents owned one there on Ashland Avenue off Southern Parkway.

We'd get stupid sometimes and race on Southern Parkway—go right across the streets. Luckily, there wasn't a car pulling out.

When we were all stabled on Southern Parkway, the big ride was the Friday night moonlight ride. Just out the parkway and around the park and back home. There was over 100 of us. It was all over and done with by 12:00 or 1:00. We'd all come in from South Louisville and meet where the AutoZone is now, across from Iroquois Park. It used to be Parkside, one of them drive-ins where you pull in and the waitress came out and took your order and then brought it back to the car. Right across New Cut Road in the park, they built a big hitching post. It was 50 feet long; you could hook up 30 or 40 horses. So we'd all ride up there, tie our horses up, and walk over to Parkside and get a beer and whatever.

Right on down to the corner there was two beer joints. The one on the corner was a motorcycle joint. The one next to it was the saddle club, where the horse people went. Did that every Friday night for I don't know how many years. A long time. After midnight those two crowds didn't get along. Motorcycle riders would climb the fence drunk and try to get on somebody's horse, then the word would come in and some stuff would start.

Later, we moved up to Holsclaw Hill in Fairdale where we could do some real trail riding. The riding was so much better out there. A thousand acres up there between Holsclaw Hill and Mitchell Hill that you could just ride through for ever and ever. On Saturday, we'd ride from Holsclaw Hill to Lake Elmo at Mitchell Hill. They'd always have a country band in there. We'd go over there and put our horses in the barn, drink beer and listen to music, and then ride back. It was good. They had a fishing lake, and they had Saturday night dances out there. They'd have traveling rodeos come through there. They had horse shows. We'd all go there for all of that stuff. And then you went on Mitchell Hill and went over the top and kept going to where Knob Creek is running. Ain't no bridge, but you cross the creek and come up and around on top of Holsclaw Hill to make the whole circle. We'd leave before dark. We'd all get off of work and saddle up and head out. We'd get back putting them horses away at 4:00 or 5:00 in the morning. It was a long way. That's a lot of riding. We spent a lot of hours out there.

Believe me, it couldn't have been any better. But there was some dedication to doing it. I mean, none of us had trucks. I had a station wagon and when you'd go up Holsclaw Hill, which was pretty straight up, ain't nobody maintained the road. So when it snowed, we'd have to park at the bottom and walk up, which was about two miles. And a lot of times we'd have a bag of feed on our shoulder, or a bale of straw or hay, because we couldn't get nothing delivered out there in volume. We'd have to haul it out in the trunk of our car, three or four days a week, two and three bales at a time.

We had a big mud-bottom pond in that field, and all our horses spent half their life in it rolling and playing and fighting flies and what have you. That's where I broke all of the babies I raised out there. I'd just go out in the pond with them, roll up on their back, keep them turning, and they couldn't buck. It's the best way in the world to break a horse. And after a few days, you just let them walk out of there with you, and they're broke.

BEGINNINGS IN RACING

I was in and out of school and walking hots in the summer. Then I ended up buying the first thoroughbred I ever had. I was working for a guy named Old Man Rogers. We used to have a stockyards here in Louisville, down in the West End. A lot of them guys would sell cold-blooded horses every Thursday at a horse sale in Rushville, Indiana. I was working for Mr. Rogers helping him. He'd take a load of horses that he bought here in Louisville up there to sell them at the sale. Then he'd buy more up there and bring them back. I'd go up there and help loading and unloading. One day I was up there with him working, and it was the biggest cold-blooded sale in the country. They'd sell like 600 head at Rushville. That's a lot of horses.

The first 400 they'd sell were what you'd call "killers." These were old, sick, crippled—horses going to be dog food. That's not legal anymore. The last 200 horses were riding-type horses. I was up there with Mr. Rogers one day and this poor mare came through, skin and bones, both ankles were what you call "fused"— they didn't bend no more. Pitiful-looking. The horses would stop right in front of two auctioneers, Hob Lee and I can't remember the other's name. They'd open up the horse's mouth or lips, and they could tell you how old they were. Horses have cups in their teeth, and if the cups were still there, you're looking at a four-year-old or a six-year-old. Once all those cups

are gone, they're what's called "smooth mouth." They brought that mare in there and they said, "Got the papers. Got a thoroughbred here." She was bred by Brown Hotel Stable. She was by Seven Hearts who'd won the Arkansas Derby. I knew the breeding right off the bat. They got up to $200 and I bought her. I had $200 in my pocket. That was the first thoroughbred I owned. I brought her back and took her right up there on Holsclaw Hill. I got her as fat and pretty as a horse could be. I just spoiled her rotten and ended up breeding her to a horse called Valiance, the last son of Blenheim from Claiborne. Blenheim horses all had a history of being bad. Seven Hearts were the same way. But I got two in a row out of her and they were the best foals ever. The first one's name was Valicat. I foaled her, I raised her, I broke her, and did everything you could do.

The game plan was to run her up at Latonia. I said, "She's good. I'm gonna take her up there, I'm gonna give her one." That was a scene too. It was so cold. The track was half froze and they didn't call off the races. The race was for first-time starters, and they named a bug boy on her and I didn't even know him. He came in there from California with Mitch Tenney's brother. We got to the paddock in the freezing cold, and that little kid come out there. He looked like he was about 12, and he said he wanted his instructions. I said, "Look, let her break and just sit still. Don't move." I didn't want her to win; I wanted her to get beat as far as from here to Wagner's. But that kid held his hand up and said, "I'm a Mormon. I don't cheat." I said, "I don't want you to cheat! Just sit! Don't move!" I was hoping she'd get beat by a city block.

She got beat in a four-horse photo finish: nose, nose, nose, nose. She was 90-1. If I'd told him to ride hard, she'd probably have won. I didn't bet anything on her. But Freddy, Bobby Smith, and Pat Bowles all went

down town the next day and bought new cars. I put her on a van the next day and sent her to New Orleans, where she won and only paid seven dollars.

I got two foals out of Valicat, and then I had her back for the third time and lost her foal. It was what you call a breech birth. The foal was backwards and you don't save them kind. Me and Doc Watson worked all night trying to get it out of her and couldn't and we lost it.

I had worked for Doc Watson out at Douglas Park walking hots when I was a kid. Doc was the premier veterinarian at the time. As a matter of fact, he mentored Doc Harthill. Doc Watson was a famous veterinarian who did all the work for Calumet Farms back in the day of Citation, Cold Town, Bewitched, Sunshine Nell, and all the great horses up there. They raised nine Derby winners. They knew what they were doing.

Doc Watson was an unbelievable vet. That was back in the day before they had all the medication they have now. I saw him do things they don't do anymore. He had me hold a horse for him one day up at the farm.

"What are you gonna do?" I said.

"This horse has got a sinus infection."

I'm holding the horse right underneath his eyes, right in his face; there was the sinus cavities on each side. These days we have scopes we can look in and see it, and antibiotics to clean it up. It's not a big deal. But back then, he bored holes right through the face and into those sinus cavities, and then he took two shoe strings and soaked them in iodine, and he just stuffed them back in there. Every day we'd pull out a little and cut it off, and by the time you got all that shoe string pulled out of there, you had cleared up the sinus infection.

I saw him do a lot of things that I never heard of people doing today. Like firing, which was a rather new technique to deal with leg problems like buck shins, acolytes, things like that. Thank God we don't do it much anymore. It's when you burn a pattern on them with a red hot iron. It's like getting a third-degree burn, and then getting over it: It's going to get to its worst and then it's going to start getting better. The leukocytes in the white blood cells speed up the healing. That was the idea behind it.

Doc Watson pioneered equine x-rays. Calumet Farm came in with General Duke in 1957. That was the best year of horses for the Derby there ever was: Bold Ruler, Round Table, and Calumet had General Duke. They got to Keeneland and General Duke had a problem. Ben Jones called Harthill over. He x-rayed it and said, "Well, I'm gonna send the x-rays to Doc Watson in Louisville and then we'll go from there."

The guy who drove them down was a trainer, Johnny Cuznar. I was tending bar at the time at the Say When Club. It was a busy Saturday night and Johnny came in, top coat on. I was at the back bar, and he give me the head nod—he always liked to be a little cagey for some reason or another. I said, "I'm busy! I'm busy!" It's three deep at the bar, and he said he had something inside his coat he wanted to show me. He wanted me to come out and go to the band room. So I finally got unbusied enough to go out. We went in there and he said, "You ain't gonna believe what I got."

"Well show me, I gotta get back to work!" I said. He pulled the X-rays out. I looked at them and said, "Looks like an ankle."

"Yeah, yeah, yeah," he said, "But *whose?*"

"I don't know, John, whose is it?"

"It's General Duke," he said. General Duke had won the Florida Derby and was coming into Kentucky as the Derby favorite. "The news ain't got out yet."

"Where you going with them?"

"I'm going to Doc Watson's to look at them," he said.

Watson said, "Scratch him." So Calumet ran their backup, Iron Liege, and Iron Liege won the Derby. Bill Hartack rode him against all them horses. That was an unbelievable field of horses, and he beat them. Willy Carstens rode Bold Ruler, and he was the one that taught Bill Hartack all he knew about riding. Rumor had it that when they turned for home—Federal Hill was in the front, and Iron Liege was getting ready to go by him—Carstens told Hartack, "I'm through. Go get the money." And Hartack did, but he was lucky that Gallant Man's jockey, Shoemaker, stood up prematurely at the sixteenth pole. Shoemaker thought the sixteenth pole was the finish line, but he had another pole to go. He sat back down and started riding again, but it was too late. He misjudged the finish line. That's one of the most famous of all Derby stories. When he stood up, that cost him the race.

EARLY YEARS AS FARM MANAGER

In hindsight, the biggest pleasures I ever got out of fooling with horses was on those farms. When you win a race, you get a picture in the Winner's Circle. Thinking back, I wish to God I would've had somebody take a picture of all those mares and foals, as soon as those babies got up, shaking in the cold and wet, trying to nurse and all that. You take it for granted after a while. I foaled 1,830 mares.

I didn't have what you call a real good job in 1967. I was tending the bar and dealing cards and stuff like that. Messing with horses was a part-time thing. I'd usually have a horse and be working for somebody, but it was an on-and-off thing. Skippy Dunn owned the Say When Club, and I had tended bar for him.

He knew nothing about horses. Zero. In '67, he came and got me and said, "Come on. Take a ride with me." I got in the car and said, "Where are we going?" He said, "I bought something." It was the farm right on the other side of Hermitage in Oldham County. So we rolled out there and we pulled in. He said, "I bought it." That was 1967, and I was there until '79 when I went to Calumet.

It was Tindor Farm back then. Later it would be called Skylight. Skip named it for his two daughters, Tina and Doris: Tin-dor. The farm wasn't complete. There was a barn that was half done, the paving on the farm was half done, the fencing on the farm was half done, and there were horses everywhere. But we moved out there. I was married with two children. I hadn't been there very long when the barn burned down. It was all over the newspapers. I lost 13 mares in it, and saved one. I think it was an electrical fire in a wooden barn with a loft full of hay and straw.

I had just left the barn when it happened. I got through watering all the horses and checking the mares. I walked across the yard to my house, which wasn't very far. I was taking my coat off in the kitchen and looked right out the window across at the barn, and fire was coming out of it. We had one of those glowing, plug-in heaters to keep the pipes from freezing, and I think that's where it all started. I headed right back out. I went in and got one horse out. I couldn't get back in because the smoke was billowing down. The barn was gone that quick. It was a terrible, terrible ordeal. You don't forget that.

I've been in three fires. One was down at Miles Park. That was a bad one. And the first one was at Old Douglas Park in South Louisville. It's no longer there. When I was a kid, I heard on the news that they had a barn at Old Douglas Park that was the longest barn under roof in America. In the winter time they'd train

inside. You could gallop in there it was so long. And it was wooden, of course. A lot of the winos would lay up in them lofts and sleep up there. Smoke and drink and what have you. That's what they said did it.

They turned horses loose to get them out of there, and them horses made it all the way to Iroquois Park. Horses running everywhere. And people trying to catch horses and bring them back. They were catching horses in South Louisville for a week. It was terrible. Horses are so scared. The stall is their home as they know it, and that's why they don't want to leave. Once you get them out, sometimes they'll turn around and want to go back in.

Skip Dunn wasted no time after the fire at Tindor. He was cleaning, he had the architects out, and they started building that barn right away. Immediately. Thirty-two-stall barn, and I haven't been in a barn anywhere in the horse business any better than that barn. Calumet's was all wood and very traditional. This barn was concrete block and ultra-modern. Most beautiful barn in Kentucky. There was an office in the front, and the apartment upstairs for the night watchmen, an enormous loft in there, I could put I don't know how many thousand bales of hay and straw up there. The foaling stalls were the best. It was a tremendous barn. I miss that barn.

Then Skip went to jail in 1971. My friends always tease me. They always say, "Don't fool with Huffman. You'll go to prison." Everybody I ran a farm for went to prison. Every one of them. Skip Dunn, Dan Lasater, and J.T. Lundy. People say, "Huffman, how did they not get you in any of those nets?" I say, "I didn't do nothing."

Skip owned Prudential Savings and Loan and was politically assassinated. Wendell Ford had asked Skip for the use of his plane when he was campaigning, and Skip turned him down. Said he was backing the other man. Ford told him, "If I'm elected, you're out of business," and then he got elected. Six weeks later he appointed a new banking commissioner who showed up at Prudential and demanded to see the books. Skip was innocent as the day is long. But he pleaded *nolo* because the trial would have been longer than O.J.'s if he had decided to go to court. They would have brought people in you can't believe, from celebrities right on up to the White House. But he didn't. He pleaded *nolo* and did his time. He did 18 months at La Grange and 18 months at Lexington at the federal jail. It killed me when they got him, really made me mad.

Dan Lasater bought the farm in 1972 and I stayed there to work for him. Claiborne Farms was dispensing their racing stock. They were having a paddock sale. Lasater and David Vance went up there, and he called after the sale and said, "Well, I got us a Round Table colt."

I think they give $100,000 for Royal Glint, and a physical specimen he was not. When he came in he was thin, slab-sided. I put him up in his stall and he was a cribber—which is a bad thing for a horse to be. He also had bad feet; you could've took your thumbs and almost pushed them through the soles of his feet. And he had a bad attitude. Round Tables all have screws loose. They'd hurt you. You had to be careful around them. He only had one testicle down, which made a cryptorchid and the other testicle up in the sleeve was banging around like the gong in a bell and made him miserable.

But he could run. He was a solid top-five horse in the country for two or three years. He was the nineteenth millionaire.

He ran the Massachusetts Handicap and won it. After the wire, he pulled up and collapsed. There he is, laying in the track. The trainer, Gordon Potter, ran out there, and the vet and the car— everybody got up there. Then they brought out the ambulance. He's laying there gasping and every time he'd breathe, blood was coming out his nose, his mouth, his ears, everything. They thought he was just going to die laying there on the track. I don't know what he was doing with it, but that vet had a whole load of estro in his truck; that's a female hormone, and it's a blood thickener. He started pumping that estro in that horse while he was laying there bleeding, and finally his pulse slowed down. He quit bleeding, rolled up on his haunches, looked around, got up, walked on the ambulance, and went back to the barn. He went back to Monmouth the next day and was running again.

Royal Glint didn't break down until he was in Chicago. He broke both sesamoids—they're the walnut-shaped bones that sit right at the back of the ankle and keep the ankle from going all the way down. And the attachments stem halfway up the back of the leg.

They put an air cast on him and shipped him back to the farm. They probably should have put him down, but they sent him back to me at the farm instead. He was awful-looking.

Doc Lavin went looking for a guy named Red Meeks, a harness maker who could make anything. He was famous around Lexington. He'd work hard through the season and make a ton of everything: bridles, breast plates, halters, reins. He'd get so much made and go sell it, and then he would drink for the rest of the winter. He wouldn't work—he'd just stay drunk. But he was the best. He could make absolutely anything.

So we looked at that leg, and Lavin said, "We need to find Red Meeks. Where's he at?" Nobody knew, so we called Sallee van line and got Bobby Maxwell on the phone.

"Where's Red Meeks?"

"I don't know, drunk somewhere."

They found him over in the back of a shop in Nicholasville, Kentucky, and they sent a driver to pick him up. Brought him all the way down there to Oldham County to the barn. He came in and Doc Lavin was describing what kind of a prosthesis we needed made to keep this horse together. It had to be a real thick foam, covered outside with leather that would go underneath a bar. We had a bar and shoe made that raised him up, and a leather strap hooked into the bar shoe and went up behind, where the sesamoids should be to replace them. Then it went all the way up above the knee to the elbow for an elbow-to-the-ground prosthesis that would be able to bend so he could walk in it. It was an enormously complicated prosthesis.

Red Meeks looked at it and said, "When do you need it?"

Doc said, "Immediately."

Royal Glint 1970-1976. Racing's nineteenth millionaire

Red went home and made that thing that night, and brought it back the next day. We had the blacksmith there. We put the high-heel shoe on him, and that big buckle went up the back and fit like a glove.

What usually happens to horses when they quit using one front leg and start favoring the other, the one they're trying to protect isn't the one that malfunctions. It's usually the good one they use too much. At six weeks, he was doing really good. And then his off leg started getting pulse, and pulse is a bad sign in the heels. He started pressure foundering in that good foot. There was a big insurance policy on him, so we knew he had to be put down. You had to have three vets look at the horse and agree before they could okay it.

Doctors Coplin, Lavin, and Harthill came down and everybody agreed he had to be put down.

It was a tradition at a lot of the farms in Lexington to bury their great horses. Most of the farms, like at Claiborne, just cut their heads off and buried the heads. Calumet buried the whole bodies. The graveyard at Calumet is unbelievable. All those champions are buried up there. I loved that graveyard. Every day I visited just to see all those headstones with all their accomplishments on them. They really did it right up at Calumet.

So I dug the grave and Eddy Leat—he was the carpenter and the heavy equipment man at Oldham County—built a casket right in the barn out of plywood. It was well-built, and half as big as a tack room, and deep too. We put it right in the aisle and then put Royal Glint down in the stall, and then we moved him into the casket and covered him up. We had it on runners, so we hooked a tracker to it and drug it out of the barn all the way around the farm to where the grave was on the other side. Then after we got him buried over there, I had a big monument built with his name and everything on it. All total, I spent about $30,000 getting him buried, but he made $1 million.

Dan Lasater won 1,200 races in four years as a novice owner just getting in the business. It was unreal. He didn't get in the business until about 1972 and then, all of a sudden from 1974 to 1978, he was the leading owner in the country. We were really hitting on all the cylinders. It was one super operation. And Lasater was lucky enough to have hired a whole bunch of guys who not only knew what they were doing but liked doing it. They were all hard-working guys that just loved to get up in the morning and go to work.

We had accumulated a broodmare band that was unbelievably good. Lasater wanted to be the leading breeder, and if he'd have stayed around, he would have been. He would've been right there with all of them, because he really had some good mares.

We had a system. We were claiming fillies for broodmares, and we had the only library in the country. It was handmade by Ed Cooper. It had little index cards made from sales catalogs that would come out. He'd get his nephews to go through each sales catalog, page by page, and anything that had black type, they'd make an index card with the breeding and the reference. Large black type in the catalog tells you that the mother won a stakes race. We could all read pedigree. You take into consideration who the sire was, what they stood for, what the mare did in her offspring, but the black type is the key thing.

So we had all those index cards alphabetized in the office. Then I'd get seven *Racing Forms* every night at the main post office. I'd take them home, and me and the kids would go through and circle the fillies. Just the fillies. In the *Racing Form* it shows you the mom and dad. Say the mom was Warriors Girl. You'd go through them index cards, and if Warriors Girl is in there, it means this horse has some pedigree. Then we'd find the catalog, pull it down, and look to see what we think it's worth. Then we see what it's running for. We only circled the fillies that were running for a claiming price. Then we looked at the catalog. This horse is in for $5,000 and we know that this horse is worth every bit of that and maybe more. There was no bloodstock research then, and the Jockey Club didn't have it where you could pick up the phone and call somebody and they could mail you a pedigree three or four days later. This was instant.

We had somebody at the track the horse was running on if we wanted to claim it. We just picked the phone up: "J.R., there's a filly in the third race today. She looks all right. Go ahead and take her." Sometimes we'd think it's going to be pigeon-toed, or splay-footed, or back at the knee—something horrible—because they'd be running way too cheap. But every one of them couldn't have been better. Couldn't find nothing wrong with them. I kept thinking, *God Almighty. Nobody else knows.*

That's the way we got most of the mares. We'd bring them in there and breed them. We didn't buy most at the sale.

Lasater was on his way to being not only the leading owner in the country, but also on his way to being the leading breeder. We were putting together a broodmare band second to none. I didn't have a bad-looking mare in that barn, to be honest. Had good looking babies in there running, playing, kicking, sucking, and nursing. We had a barn full of good mares.

One of my favorites was Ephonia, a dame of Cutlass. She was foaled to Secretariat at the time Lasater told me to get the van and go buy her; he gave me a check for $300,000. So I took the van up there, and she was a gorgeous broodmare. Just gorgeous. She was big—didn't even look like a racehorse—an enormous mare with tremendous pedigree. But she was pigeon-toed, and they wanted $300,000 for her. I had the check in my hand and I said, *Lord-a-mercy, I'm gonna give $300,000 for a pigeon-toed horse?* I mean, her feet were facing each other, and she had only run three times. She couldn't run much. She broke her maiden, but she was so pigeon-toed. I called Lasater and I said, "Do you know this mare's pigeon-toed?"

"Well, what's that mean?"

"Well," I said, "it could mean anything. Usually what's hereditary is knees. If she has a bunch of pigeon-toed babies, this might not be a good idea."

"Well, go ahead and buy her." He wanted the mare because she was the dame of Cutlass and in foal to Secretariat. I wrote the check for $300,000, loaded her up, and brought her back. Then I had to make the worst phone call: She slipped that foal two weeks later, and I don't think we had any insurance at the time. This was an expensive piece of merchandise. I've had to make a lot of bad phone calls, but that was a bad one. It was awful. I bred her back to Secretariat and the foal she had by him was straight and perfect. A big foal. A Secretariat foal. It was a little dishraggy, and we really had to work on her for a while to get it going, but it finally did. It won some minor stakes, but it wasn't a world beater.

Other than being pigeon-toed, though, Ephonia was one of the most beautiful mares I ever saw. Even my kids remember her. The kids fell in love with her. Every one of them. They all had to run and see Ephonia when they'd go to the barn at night with me to water off. She would look at you and it was like just looking at your mother or something. Her eyes looked right through you. She knew what she was doing there, what she wanted. She knew what you were thinking. She was just intelligent, and her babies were all really smart. Never had another one like her. One of my favorite horses. She's way up there.

Then Lasater went to jail while I was working for him. That's why he sold the farm and decided he was going to get out of the business, because he knew he had to go. He had a big dispersal with all the horses and sold the farm to Dr. Lavin.

That's when I moved to Lexington to manage Calumet. Calumet was bigger than I was born to do, really. So many great traditions up there around Lexington: Dixiana, Claiborne, Green Tree, the Idle Hour farm, Elmendorf. That was Max Gluck's farm, and Jim Brady ran it. He was a good horseman. From the '70s,

Elmendorf was the leading breeder in the country for 10 years. Everybody wanted to take credit for what the hell they was doing there that them horses were running so good. There was a nutritional professor at Ohio State who made a pellet for horses called Tiz Whiz. They were feeding Tiz Whiz at Elmendorf, so he took all the credit in the world for why they were running so good. And them horses were running.

Elmendorf had that creek that run through there, the Elkhorn. They showed a picture in *BloodHorse* one day of Brady sitting on his pony out in the middle of the creek. It's crystal clear, runs fast and has a limestone base. He'd sit out there on his pony when they'd come back from the track in the middle of the creek, holding the shanks of three horses with their legs in that cold water for hours. When I saw that I thought to myself, "He knows what he's doing. It ain't Tiz Whiz pellets."

That limestone water's got a lot to do with it. I've always thought them old-timers migrated here on account of that. That and the bluegrass. And for many, many, many years, there wasn't nothing fancy going on like it is now. Nowadays, you could walk in at Luckett's Tack Shop and look up on that wall, and I don't know how many different jugs of vitamins is up there. All of them are bragging about this, that, or the other. And supplements for everything. Back in the day, what they had was that grass and that water and good hay. That was it, nothing else.

But Calumet was the one with the most. The most famous farm on the planet, not just in Kentucky. There's never been one since to surpass it. As famous as Claiborne is, they never produced the Derby winners Calumet did. Calumet just kept winning: Whirlaway in '41, Citation in '48, Ponder in '49, Hill Gail in '52, Tim Tam in '58. It just goes on and on, and that's not even to mention the fillies. That's a famous place. They did it right.

The barn Neil built at Skylight Training Facility

When Lasater sold the farm I knew I was going to leave. It wasn't like Lundy got me out of the phone book; I'd known him for a long time before that. It was J.T. Lundy's wife's grandmother, Mrs. Markey, who owned Calumet. When she died, they didn't owe one bill and there was like $176 million in the bank. They owned all the stock at Calumet Baking Powder, and they owned a gas field in Texas that pumped a million barrells a day. It was in great shape. J.T. Lundy called me when Mrs. Markey died. He said, "She died. Pack your bags." He was fascinated by all the races that we were winning when I was with Lasater. He couldn't figure it out. He wanted to know what in the hell we were doing. Lundy was good on a farm. He knew horses.

Calumet was way beyond enjoyable. I'd been working every day. I was getting my hands dirty. I was worn out when I got home at night, but at Calumet, I wasn't *allowed* to do anything. There was a little over 900 acres and 51 men, and it wasn't but 85 head of horses. I was used to anywhere from 150 to 300 head of horses. All I was supposed to do is just ride around with a beeper on my belt in a car, make sure anybody got any questions, tell somebody what they're doing. It was the best crew ever. Most of them been there all their life. They all knew what to do. Didn't have to tell anybody nothing. I didn't have too many decisions to make. It was pretty much boring. I wasn't used to that.

Those guys had the best farm jobs anywhere. Most of them guys were taking care of three groomed mares.

They'd come in in the morning and walk them out to the gate, open the gate, turn them loose. Come back in. Throw the stalls back. They had a "warming room" that had refrigerators and a stove and a couch, a TV. It was like home. As soon as they turned their horses out and cleaned their stalls, they'd come in there. They was there until lunch. At 2:30, they'd go throw the stalls back down, put the feed in, and then walk out to the gate, lead the mares and foals back in. Then at 4:00, the farm bus would come to all the barns and pick all the men up to take them to their cars. The best jobs in the world. They all loved Mrs. Markey, and she loved them. When she died, she left every one of them $50,000, including the last man hired, who had been there about six months.

ALYDAR

Alydar got beat by Affirmed three times in the Triple Crown. He just could not get by Affirmed. But when they retired and went to stud, Alydar became an unbelievably successful sire and Affirmed did not—he was kind of a wash out.

Alydar was the real deal, but if you walked in the stud barn and I told you to pick out the one that wasn't a stud horse, you'd pick him. He was not a big, massive, aggressive type of horse. He was very nice and docile. You wouldn't ever have thought of him as a stud horse. He was the easiest horse in the world to take care of and to breed. Simple as ABC. He sired 77 stakes winners, and he really didn't live that long.

Alydar

For a short stud career, that's amazing. He sired Derby winner Alysheba with Van Berg. Then Easy Goer was a champion. Turkoman, Althea, Criminal Type, Strike the Gold. It goes on and on, the great horses he sired. He won 14 out of 26 races and right at one million. Pots weren't as big as they are now. Today he'd have won way over two or three million.

He was a foal of 1975, and I wasn't around when he ran in the Derby against Affirmed in 1978. But there was an incident that happened while I was there—four or five years before Alydar died—that was kind of scary, when Alydar got sick. It was a hot, hot day. I was on the backside of the farm. We had radios back then, and they called me from the stud barn around 2:30 when they bring them in and give them a bath. They called me and told me to come to the stud barn immediately.

I got in my car and I drove over. They had Alydar in the shade of the breezeway between the breeding shed and the stud barn with a hose on him. It was really hot that day, and when he came out of the paddock, he was walking drunk. They figured the same thing I did, that it was a heat stroke. So they had the water on him, and I got the phone right away with Dr. Priest, who was doing the farm work there. He was in Versailles worming horses and said Dr. Harthill was somewhere between Louisville and Lexington, where he had a surgery to perform. I got hold of him and told him to forget the surgery, to come straight to the barn, and he did.

Alydar wasn't any better by the time Dr. Harthill got there. Doc went all over him and couldn't put his finger on anything. Then Dr. Priest got there. The first thing they did was they took blood and ran it to the lab. Doc got a case of fluids out and started hanging jugs in him.

We ended up staying with him all day and all night, and the horse never improved at all. The lab tests came back good. That's where we really got to scratching our heads. They started calling in experts. They did every test you could ever imagine. A girl from Ohio State—the premier for neurological disorders in horses—came in. We'd get him out and let them all look and walk and try to make him do all this stuff. Everybody was coming up blank. They couldn't figure out what in the hell could be wrong.

The key to this whole thing was his insurance was supposed to run out at the end of the month. He was insured for like $36 million, but he wasn't going to pass an insurance exam before that had to be renewed. My god, Lundy was pulling his hair out. Dr. Harthill and me sat up there many a night in that warming room up there in that barn worried about him. He'd stagger around in the stall, eating slow; it was like he was drunk. Well, we found out it was very simple.

One of them University of Kentucky technicians came over, and he got to taking samples in the paddock and on the boards around his paddock, on the window sills in his stall. He took them all back to UK, and couple of hours later the phone rang. He said, "I know what's wrong with that horse. He got lead poisoning." And then it all made sense. That's just the way they act when they get lead poisoning. Lundy was having the old roof replaced, which was the old tar paper, which is lead, and it was up there cascading down. It had been going on for weeks. And then the wind was carrying the debris into the stalls with the windows open.

All you do then is give them calcium edetate, which rounds it all up, pushes it through the kidneys, and out it goes. We'd taken blood right off the bat, within hours, but they missed it in the lab. It wasn't like we'd failed to dot all the i's. The lab screwed it up. We found out what was wrong and gave him the calcium, and he was fine just as soon as we did it.

It was day 29. One more day and that insurance would have run out.

BLACKIE

I was at Calumet for three years. I came back to Louisville in 1982 and went back into business with my brother out of Skylight Training Center. That was a big business we had there from 1982 until 1987. We had two barns out there. I had a barn, and my brother Blackie had a barn. We'd usually break about 60 horses every fall and winter there. We had a whole lot of people send us horses to break, and we had horses out there that just trained, that we raced out of there. And sometimes there's a problem with a horse, or the horse just needed some time. Say a horse has gone to get blistered, it's gone there to get turned out, get some time, and now it's ready to go back in training. They don't want it back at the track; it can't start. So it would go to a training center like mine or Blackie's and get it started. And then we get it going, and when we get it close to racing you want to holler at your man, see if he's got a stall, and get it in there to the track.

Blackie did awfully good. But he didn't want to get in the winner pictures. When the horses would win the race, he wouldn't even get over. He won the Stephen Foster at Churchill Downs, and I don't think he got in the Winner's Circle. He's just one of those guys. He didn't want no publicity. He didn't want

Blackie Huffman

anybody to know who he was. He just had that edge to him. Everybody misses him.

Blackie could tell a story. He was just one of them kind. He could convince you of anything. He was that good.

He never played a sport. Not one. But he could go out to that gap and convince anybody that he'd hit a baseball 500 feet from either side of the plate. First one in the neighborhood to dunk a basketball. Had all the records from all the football games. He'd convince you, but he'd never played one sport. He was the best.

Blackie would go to Wagner's three or four mornings a week. He never paid for a meal in there. Ever. When he'd get through, he'd go wandering around. He knew everybody in there, of course. He started talking and, next thing you knew, he'd be drifting towards the door. Next thing you knew, he was out of there. Somebody'd say, "I'll take care of it." He was good at that. Never carried any money. Never. He'd come to me, and he'd have some change in his hand. He'd say, "You got 30 cents?" And I'd say, "Yeah, why?" And I'd reach in and I'd give him 30 cents. "I gotta get a pack of cigarettes." He always smoked. Smoked up until the day he died. Terrible.

We had a coffee truck here on the backside. The kitchen truck. It would pull up out there every morning. If we had some owners in the barn that morning who'd come see their horses, Blackie would always go out there when that truck pulled up and he'd holler at all them guys, "You want any coffee or anything? Sausage biscuit?" They'd all say yes. I knew he didn't have a nickel in his pocket. So he'd stand there and they'd start lining up, "Five sausage biscuits, five coffees." Now, it's just about time to pay up and just as he's going in his pants pocket like he's going to get the money out and pay for all that, he'd look back toward this tack room like somebody was hollering at him.

"All right! I got a goddamn phone call," he'd say. And he'd take off like he had a phone call. "I'll be back. I'll get this. Don't worry about it." Of course, they were going to step up and go ahead and pay for it. That was one of his smoothest moves ever. I've seen him do it so many times. He was the best at it. He was famous for them kinds of stories.

There was a guy in Lexington that used to work for Keeneland. Nice guy. Always showed up here Derby week. Always comes down to see me. He couldn't wait to get here on Derby week to talk to Blackie, because he knew he was going to hear some great stories. He'd heard them all before, but he wanted to hear them over and over, like everybody around here.

When Blackie passed away, this guy from Lexington made a point to come back here and see me and tell me how bad he felt. He said he thought of him as one of his best friends. I said, "Yeah, we all miss him pretty good." And he said, "The way that you two have made it, I just got so much respect for you." I said, "What do you mean?" I didn't know what he was talking about. He said, "Well, the way y'all were adopted and were orphans on the street." Blackie told him this story he could've made a movie about.

I just said, "Well, the only thing is, it's not true. We weren't orphans." He started, "Why would Blackie go to his grave without straightening it out?" That was Blackie. He didn't want to straighten it out. Any of the stories that he told down there at the gap, they'd all come to me. I'd hear it two or three days later, and I'd just shake my head. Where does he get it? He was good at that stuff. It never came back on him. He done it all his life. They had hats going around back here that said *Lying Blackie*. Everybody had a *Lying Blackie* hat. He left a bit of a legacy.

Oh, Blackie. I miss him. We had a good time.

BEER JOINTS, BRAWLERS AND BOOKIES

Louisville during the '50s was good. There was industry here, and every one of them was running three shifts. This was the greatest town in the world if you wanted to work. There was a job for everybody. It was prosperous. GE was starting up, the Ford plant was rolling, Harvester was rolling. They were building the cigarette plants downtown. And then we had all the paint companies—must have been half a dozen. American Synthetic. Oh my God.

Everything was so simple back then: It was baseball, horse racing, and prize fighting. The best of what I remember was before television, like when you got down with your ear next to the radio and listened to a ball game. When they started tearing stuff down in Louisville, that's when it started downhill. They tore down Parkway Field, then the Parkmoor. When they blacktopped Southern Parkway, no more riding academy. Everything started going the wrong way. They just let Colonial Gardens collapse. That was a super place. Big dance floor, big bar, lots of people. A good joint. Simple as that. Sunday night was the best night out there. Every dance floor in town was packed. You knew what nights to go where. You knew where the bands were.

The first bartending job I got was at the Say When Club. It's where the Foxy Lady is now on Berry Boulevard. That was the spot. It was almost like there was a sign out front that said "no ugly girls" because it was just 10 after 10 after 10. Me, Weenie Faurest, and WeeWee Robertson was the three bartenders back then. We were limited to 75 people in there and the ceiling wasn't much taller than your head when you stand up. Of course everybody back then smoked, so you couldn't hardly see in there. The place was a log cabin.

Neil Huffman, Bill Denzick Sr., and Weenie Faurest

It had been there a while. Sixty-five cents for good whiskey, 60 cents for bad bourbon, 35 cents for a beer.

Back then you didn't have to know much to be a bartender. You could make six drinks because nine out of ten of them's going to be Jack and Coke, VO and ginger, or Tom Collins. It's going to be relatively simple. Wasn't no piña coladas or any of that stuff. Keep cold beer, and just some ordinary types of whiskey, and you can get by. Sold a lot VO and Canadian Club; that's blended. Little bit of the good stuff, Calvert Reserve and Crown Royal. That's the best. Once you start drinking Crown Royal, you'll never even think about bourbon again. The smoothest bourbon that compared to the good stuff was Yellowstone 90. During closing time we would look over the bar, and if the good whiskey was way down and we didn't have any more in the back, we'd just top it off with Yellow 90. Nobody could tell the difference, that's how good it was.

We had all kinds of heavy hitters in the Say When. We were getting a five-dollar cover charge back then, and we'd put 300 people in there. The fire warden limited us to 75. Bo Diddley was at the

Say When Club one night. Rumor was he couldn't read or write, so his sister traveled with him to do all the money. She's the one we paid off when they was about to leave. We had to get him to turn down so the place didn't fall apart. Bo Diddley got on stage, and when he cranked up that guitar and hit that first chord, I was standing there with all the bourbon on a shelf behind me, and I started hearing this tinkling. I looked behind me, and the mortar between the cabin logs was coming loose and it was trickling down on all the whiskey bottles. It was so loud I was afraid the place was going to crumble. So I hollered at Ronnie or Luther, one of the bouncers. I said, "You're gonna have to turn it down some—this place is coming down! He's bringing it down!" And so they had him crank it down a notch or two. They were good.

The place was packed every night. On Sundays, you had laws back then that you couldn't sell beer until 1:00. But my man knew how to keep a crowd. Instead of being open on Sundays, he'd have two or three of them dancers come in and give lessons. So we always had good dancers in there. And there was a dance contest at all the joints in Louisville, and they'd have it at a different place every night: Tuesday it was at the Say When, Wednesday it was at the Fabulon, Thursday it was at the Red Bull, Friday it was Colonial Gardens, and the next night was Chamberlains. Everybody had a night for the dance, and it was $50 to the winner. Those good dancers never had to work; they made a living winning dance contests. I was never a good dancer, but I put many a mile out there. Good or bad, who cares. The only two dances you seen was the slow dance and the jitterbug. That was it.

Louis Jackson and the House Rockers were at the Fabulon. The singer was a girl named Ruby, and they were the best. That place was packed. Ruby could sing—good God she could sing. That place was full every night. She was black and she was from Indiana. She could flat sing. They'd play "Ruby Bring Your Love to Town" every 10 minutes. She was a knockout. Back then you couldn't sell whiskey on Sundays, so everybody would smuggle it in. Bring it in our coats. Most of those guys would bring wine. Big jugs. And about midnight, when they finally finished them, they'd set them empties down on the floor, and they'd get to kicking them around. Next thing they was banking off them walls and busting them.

———————————

7th Street Road was divided in the middle with Shively on the west side and Louisville on the east side. On the Shively side there was the Arch Club, the Fabulon, the Domino, and the one on the corner of 7th and Algonquin where I dealt cards for a while. The only thing we played back then was five card draw and stud. Wasn't no seven cards and all that other shit.

On the Louisville side it was Stuart's restaurant, and then the Riss Terminal, where I ran a truck line. Then going on down, there wasn't but one joint on that side going all the way to Algonquin: the Green Mouse. Catty-corner on Berry was the Merry Go Round that Dick Asher owned. The Merry Go Round was a strip joint, and it was classic. There wasn't no poles on the stage back then. They had them big fans, and they could move them fans around and you'd never see nothing. You'd bend your neck trying to see; they were good. They had Gypsy Rose Lee, and Lili St. Cyr. These were famous strippers. These were really high class strip joints.

I bartended over at the Shady Lawn on Dixie Highway at the corner of Ralph Avenue. That was in 1967. That was a money maker with all them distilleries right there. Come 5:00 when everybody got off, here they came. It's a boilermaker and a half a pint to go.

Fridays we was cashing checks, and then Sundays we was bootlegging maybe 200 half pints. We'd close up on Saturday night and fill up half-pints of Heaven Hill, Early Times, Yellowstone, because you couldn't sell whiskey on Sunday back then. That's what you call bootlegging. So we would sell 10 cases or so on Sunday, when it was not legal. And every one of those guys that was there on Saturday night could've bought a half pint for $1.60, but they'd rather come back on Sunday when it was illegal because they thought they was getting by with something. It's the nature of a man: He's doing something and the law don't know it.

Jerry Moreman owned the Shady Lawn. He was an All-American basketball player at U of L in the '40s. Nicest guy that ever lived. Died way too young of cancer. His wife was the whiskey taster at Yellowstone or Brown-Forman. Jerry came in late one night. It was midnight or so, and nobody was in there except the one-armed bartender from the Thelma Lanes bowling alley who was down there shooting craps in a box with Wayne.

Jerry says, "What's going?" He had just woke up. I said, "Nothing. They're just down there playing. I don't know if I'm gonna stay open to 1:30 or not." He wandered down there. Wayne had done busted the one-armed guy. He said, "I'm going home. He done got me." So Jerry decided, "I'll play a little bit with you." The next thing you know, Jerry came back to the bar and said, "Give me the cigar box." I kept the cigar box in the back and it had all the cash in it. I'd unload the cash register and put it back there. That's the way we did it. So he says, "Get me the cigar box." And he wasn't sleepy no more; he had a look in his eye. Wayne had done took everything he had in his pocket.

Jerry didn't know what he was doing; this is all luck. Wayne don't know. He was throwing them at seven, throwing them at eleven, made bad points.

Next thing you know, I got the money out here, give it to him, he went down there, and he wasn't gone five minutes until he came back. Wayne done got all of that too. He got it all. And Wayne didn't want to win; he was trying every way in the world to lose. Next thing you know, Jerry said, "I ain't got nothing left except this bar." Next thing, he started looking at me funny, because I'm the only guy there that knows Wayne. He thinks that Wayne's something special, and then he finds out that Wayne just got out of the joint.

Anway, I talked Jerry out of it. Wayne could have very easily owned the Shady Lawn. Wayne just wanted to get out of there. He kept thinking that he wasn't going to make it to his car, that somebody was going to make him. He probably walked away with several thousand.

———————

Peg Leg was a bouncer at the Club Fabulon on 7th Street Road. It was gravel out there, and Peg Leg was a motorcycle rider. One night he was in the gravel doing donuts showing off, and the bike got him down and just chewed up that leg; so they had to take it off. He worked for Jones Dabney, the paint company, moving 55 gallon barrels on the dock. When he came back to work at the paint company, he had a peg leg but he was still a powerful man. He was huge and strong as a bull. Paint comes in 55 gallon drums and weighs 550 pounds a barrel. I know because I hauled them when I ran the trucking line. On Friday, when those guys would get paid, he'd bet them that he could lay three of those barrels down and upright, all three of them at the same time. Them guys would say, "Naw. You can't do that," and get their wallets out. Peg Leg could hook his fingertips on the outside rim of the two outer barrels, he'd hook his collar bone on the barrel in the middle, and then he jammed that peg against the dock. And up he'd come, and he could upright all three of them at the same time.

Peg Leg was bouncing at the Fabulon at night, and that was a bad place. The first of the month was when the soldiers got paid—Fort Knox and Fort Campbell—and they'd all come to Louisville. The characters at Fort Campbell wasn't much bigger than jockeys, and none of them could drink, though they all tried to. You needed a couple of bouncers when they came, and when they'd get started them bouncers could stack them up, 10 deep. Peg Leg loved to fight.

Willard Norman owned the Fabulon. Willard was some kind of guy. Always drank VO and ginger. He had a palsy—his hand would shake—and when he come up behind you, you could hear them ice cubes shaking in his drink.

Nub Milton was the chief of police in Shively. And when Nub would pull up out front, you had to rush out with his vodka and it was time to make a payment to him. Everybody had an envelope with some cash in it so they could serve underage drinkers in there. That's what everybody paid Nub for.

Possum was one of the bartenders in the front there at the Fabulon and Louisville Louie was the other one. Possum was a little guy. He had a sawed off shotgun there at the bar and he wouldn't bat an eye. He'd shoot you. Just as simple as that. He shot McCorkle one time in the ass. He ran him out across 7th Street across the parking lot of the tobacco warehouse. There was a fence back there, and McCorkle was going over the fence and Possum shot him in the ass.

Willard would see Nub out there, and he'd holler at Possum, "Nub's out there!" Willard was nervous, and you could always tell when he got behind you: You could hear them ice cubes in his VO and ginger. Possum would say, "Don't get nervous. Don't get nervous. I see

him!" He'd reach in the till and get whatever he got out of there: $20, $50, $100. They'd run out there and give it to Nub and take him a drink in a cup. That's the way life was over there.

Nub was 300 pounds and about five-foot high. And when he locked you up, he loved to take the gun off, go in the cell with you, and give you a major ass-whooping. You didn't want to get locked up in Shively. He was going to beat you half to death once he got you in there. Nub was bad. Nobody screwed with Nub.

He'd roll up and down 7th Street all night long locking people up. There's one famous one who got locked up one night, and he was bad. Big time bad. He's still alive right now. That's why I can't mention his name. When he got him in there, Nub whipped him pretty good. When he got out of the hospital, he knew he was going to get even with Nub some way. He wasn't going to take that kind of beating. So I'm at the Fabulon one night, and everybody came in. They said, "Why's so-and-so sitting in his car down there at Arlan's?" That was a department store on 7th Street Road—it ain't there no more. Then somebody else would come in saying, "What's he doing sitting in his car down there?" This kept happening all night. I'd say, "I don't know what he's doing down there. He's sitting there. He does what he wants to do." Well, he was setting up. He knew Nub was going to come down 7th Street Road, rolling two or three times a night. Later, we figured out what happened. He pulled right out in front of Nub and took one in the ass end of the car. I think he got $100,000 out of it from Shively—that was one way to get even. He was hoping he killed him.

But there was a dozen guys like that. You seen *The Magnificent Seven* and *The Dirty Dozen* and all that? All these guys in the Navy SEALs? Believe me, they're altar boys compared to some of these South Louisville guys. You can't believe how bad they were. If you had to rank all them guys that loved to fight, it would be hard to say who was number one.

They were booking in the daytime over at the Fabulon. There was a peephole in the door where the bookmaker is. You got a doorman back there, and he can look out through that little peephole and see if he knows you or not. We had it set up perfect.

Buddy Bauer had his book in the coat room there. One of the best books in town. They did all the dancing/night club part, and he had stretch calls coming in there in the coat room. You'd walk in there and they had sheets and forms all on the tables, then you walk right up to Buddy and bet with him just like you would a teller over here at Churchill, and he'd give you a ticket. We could hear the race being called—the stretch, not from start to finish, just the stretch.

I bet pretty good with Buddy. We'd settle up every Saturday night at the Downs Cafe on 4th and Central. That was settle-up time. All the bookmakers would show up and you're either collecting or you're paying off, one of the two. I went to get my money one night and Buddy was sitting there with his head down; he had took a beating. He reached in his pocket and got my envelope out, and he said, "Neil, if you take this envelope, my kid won't be going to Notre Dame." I reached out, took the envelope, and said, "I guess he ain't going to Notre Dame." I never will forget that.

Earl Garr is as famous a name in Louisville as you could ever find. He was a powerful man. He had everybody on his payroll. It's why he could get by with the booking and running the card games, and doing whatever he wanted to do. Because he took care of City Hall people. He was a no-nonsense, no-bullshit

guy. He was big, he was heavy, and everybody liked him. If he didn't like you, you were in big trouble. It wouldn't do to start any kind of trouble, or not pay, because you couldn't do anything in there with him around, and nobody did. They didn't want to fool with him.

Back then, Earl Garr ruled 4th and Central. *Life* magazine or *Look* magazine or one of the others rated it as the third toughest corner in the country. Farnsley was the mayor, and Carl Heustis was the chief of police, and Earl Garr was running 4th and Central, and Doc Harthill was running Churchill Downs, and Nub Milton was running Shively, and Johnny Bose was running Portland. There was somebody all around, and it worked. It all worked. It was a great, great, great town. You knew where you could go, where you shouldn't go, you knew who ran what, and it just worked. This was a great town when it was that way.

Earl Garr was so powerful, he ran the City Hall. On Friday and Saturday nights, there'd be a paddy wagon that circled 4th Street. They'd roll down Central to the alley, up the alley to Heywood, Heywood to 4th, down 4th to Central, and all around all night long. They just kept going around there to lock up whoever needed to get locked up, or whoever Earl Garr said to lock up.

One night, a couple guys no one had ever seen, pretty big boys, came in—the place was always packed. Out front was the bar and the drinking, and in the back they had the food counter and a club where they had music. Earl and me were back there where the food was, and somebody came by and said, "Earl, there's a couple guys out front looking for you. Looks bad." Both of these guys was bigger than him, but Earl just waltzed his ass out there and knocked one of them down. He was after the other one, but the guy ran out the back door to the alley behind the joint. They found him hiding behind the house of Roscoe Goose—he rode the Derby winner Donerail, the longest odds to ever win the Derby: 90-1. So this guy was hiding underneath Roscoe's Cadillac in the backyard when the police found him, and they put him in the paddy wagon.

Then they stopped out front and they came in. They said, "Earl, we got them. What do you want to do with them?" Earl said, "Pull around back," and they pulled that paddy wagon around back. We was all standing out there smoking cigarettes, and Earl came out back and said, "Open the door," and he climbed up in there. I thought the shocks and springs was going to break on that thing. Finally there wasn't no more noise. Garr knocked on the back door, and they opened it up. Earl stepped out and them two guys was both beat half to death. Earl left them both in the paddy wagon. We found out later that they'd come from Portland. They'd heard about Earl Garr and they thought could make a name if they could whip him. When the cops asked Earl, "What you want to do with them?" He said, "Take them back to Portland and turn them loose. They won't be back."

Garr had a dog that everybody knew. Brownie. On Friday, everybody who worked at American Air Filter would cash their checks at the Downs Cafe. So Earl would go over there to First National Bank and he'd get the cash. He'd stuff $50,000 in his pocket, and he'd put $50,000 in Brownie's mouth, and they'd go across the intersection to the Downs Cafe.

He had a plane, but they grounded him because he put Mickey Gant in the plane one day with a whole big thing of toilet paper and he buzzed around and threw toilet paper everywhere on the track. Earl really liked Mick. They'd cuss each other all the time, but it was one of those kinds of things—he thought the world of him.

Downs Cafe

Mickey Gant was a bookmaker. Short and fat. He was a no-neck. He had character written all over him since the day he was born. He'd go to Churchill Downs and book at the track. They'd catch him, and so out he'd go. Threw him out. But he had a whole bunch of stuff in the trunk of his car that he could use to disguise himself. One day he pulled up in the Longfield parking lot, opened the trunk up, and dressed up like a nun. He went in as a nun. They use to have different windows. If you wanted to bet two dollars, there was a two dollar line. If you wanted five that's another line, and then lines for $10, $50, and $100. And it was the same way to cash it—you'd have to go to that line to get it cashed. When Mickey dressed up like a nun, he went up there in the better part of the racetrack and stood at the back of the $50 or $100 line. When those guys would come out, he'd say, "A little something for the church?" And them guys couldn't say no. They'd throw him something. But he waited too long and they spotted him, and hauled him out again.

Earl's uncle, Sam Garr, was always around the Downs Cafe running things. At the time, I was running a truck line over on 7th Street Road. I had one of those white collar and tie jobs—terminal manager. I'd go over to the Downs Cafe for lunch because that's where the bookmakers were, and I'd bet at lunch time. Back then, we'd get a scratch sheet and doubles of five or six tracks and straight bets, parlays, turn-arounds. I'd go over there and Sam would always come up and whisper in a tip in my ear: "Take Breedlove in the third. Breedlove in the third." He was one of them guys. There just ain't them kind around anymore.

I played both sides of the game: the bettor and the booker. Bernard Roby was the bookmaker over there in the round house at the L&N yard. We knew all the guys there. Just about everybody that lived in the neighborhood worked there, and he did all the booking. His son Jerry was working over on Taylor Boulevard for Dial Finance. That's where everybody would go when they were busted to get a quick loan. I was running a big truck line. I was hauling one million pounds a night out of Detroit to the Ford plant. Well, Ford was on strike, so I'd laid off just about everybody. I had six phones on my desk that had five lines on each one of them, and many a time they were all going at once. It was busy. I had 30 city drivers, 150 road drivers, 300 trailers, and 150 tractors—this was big. Jerry Robby called me up one day and said, "What are you doing?" I said, "I've got my feet on the desk. I laid everybody off. Ford's on strike, I ain't doing nothing." He said, "You wanna book at L&N for a couple of weeks?" I asked why and he said his dad was going on vacation. So me and Jerry Robby started booking.

Them railroaders were the best handicappers in the world. After about the first week, I said, "Listen. Your dad's gotta come back and work with us soon. They're beating us to death. We're gonna have to take

out a loan." Jerry was one of them hyper types, and he says, "I know it, god dammit! They can pick everything but their nose!" Finally Bernard did come back, but we ended up having to take a loan out to pay everybody off. They beat us to death, them railroaders did.

But bookies were the best guys in the world. There was no bad bookmaker. I didn't know a bad bookmaker, and I knew just about every one of them. Buddy Bauer ran that one over on 7th Street Road. Rufus Allen ran the one down at the Domino. There was a bookmaker everywhere. They're the best guys in the world; they don't bother nobody. Couldn't have been a better way to spend the day.

Bobby Kennedy shut it down. He was going to cut the race wire service off. Back then, we was getting wire service stretch calls from racetracks. All the bookies was getting service and you'd know who won the race as soon as it was over. It facilitated bookmaking and gambling. Kennedy said he was going to cut the call services off. He said when he would do it. We were all waiting to see if he would, and he did. That was the end of the race wire service.

Then the Open City thing happened. One of them undercover reporting jobs. Fly Raymond had a book in the back of the Arcade. It had a doorman. A good, good spot. A lot of people in there all day long, reading the *Form* and betting. A reporter managed to get in there with a camera. Then it was 6:00 breaking news. "Exposed: Louisville gambling ring." Are you kidding? The nicest old guys in the world come there to bet their two dollars. They ain't doing nothing to nobody.

They used to have the trainers' dinner at the Brown Hotel the week of the Derby. I only went once. That journalist that snapped the pictures and did the chirping on Open City showed up, and I heard they took him by his ankles and they held him outside the

second floor window of the hotel, scared him to death. He left town shortly after that, and a lot of guys shut down their book for a while.

Making the rounds back here, after talking to lots and lots of veterans with lots and lots of know-how, having all that information does not work that often; once they ring that bell it's all up for grabs. There's not that many of us around. We've been here forever, and we've seen everything, but we still can't walk over there and pick eight winners a day—or maybe not even one. As much as we know, it's still not an absolute dye-in-the-wool thing.

I've played some good licks, and then after it's over and you walk up and you cash that big ticket, you know that it probably ain't going to happen again for two or three months. It don't happen that much.

You don't ever think about taking a pencil and getting a piece of paper when you're in the horse business saying, *I lost this much* or *I made this much*. Forget it. You're in it. You do it. And it don't make no difference. Just doing it in the horse business is the reward, really. /

Linda Doane

RETIRED ASSISTANT TRAINER, DRUG AND ALCOHOL COUNSELOR

Our family has a hearing disability. We have what is called Waardenburg Syndrome. It's a genetic disorder that can cause deafness, different coloration of pigments in our eyes, and patches of white pigment in our hair. My brother Randy has a great big white patch of hair and he's profoundly deaf. I have cousins and grandparents who are deaf, and most of us who aren't completely deaf have hearing loss in one ear. I don't have hearing in my left ear, and I've got what they call key holes, which is a blue patch in my eyes. One of my cousins has one blue eye and one hazel one. My whole family is affected, so it was normal for me. We were normal.

My brother and I did a good job raising our parents. Mom was a home ec teacher and worked in dietetics in the hospital later on in life. She was a strong, strong woman. Big backbone. My dad was the Boy Scout master; my mom was the Girl Scout leader. We had cookies on this side of the garage and a paper drive on that side. They were terrific parents. My dad was a teacher, too. They were just of that structured teaching world, which was really a great thing. In education there were all sorts of different philosophies on how to accommodate our disability, whether signing or not signing or oral.

When we were young, my brother and I would make up our own signs. We converted to American Sign Language in adulthood, but when we were kids communicating with each other, our parents couldn't understand us. My dad was into language as an educator, and he really thought we needed to prepare everybody with a disability to fit into mainstream life and to hone in on verbal skills for the hearing impaired. He said, "We're going to help Randy. We're going to help this family by helping him in an oral world." Lip reading and using voice is very difficult for a hearing-impaired person to mimic when you don't hear it. I can understand my brother, but it's too embarrassing to go in public and have such an odd-sounding voice. We would be in restaurants and I would voice for him what he would want and make phone calls for him. You don't really understand the issues of it until you start to see their pain about fitting in. He's very well adjusted into his own circle of friends, but it hurts me still. You just don't like to see anybody hurt.

We lived in a little town called Ellington where Dad could commute to the University of Connecticut at Storrs and Mom could drive Randy to the state school, the American School for the Deaf.

They didn't want him living at the state school. They wanted him to remain a part of the family so my mom made that commitment and drove him back and forth. That's a hard thing for families to work with.

Junior high is when frustrations really set in with him feeling isolated, trying to fit into the hearing world, especially at school. A lot of trauma, a lot of anger, a lot that didn't work well. And then, just adolescence. Whether you're hearing impaired or you're just a normal kid, you're rebellious, you're trying to sort yourself out, you're trying to fit in to a peer group, you're trying to establish yourself as an adolescent or as a young adult. The boys wanted long hair and my dad said, "No." It was a rebellious time in our world. The Vietnam War was on at that point. Compound that with trying to fit in with a disability, trying to excel academically when you're not up to par because of language issues and education styles. In my eyes, Randy is a superman. He was tough.

My upbringing was obviously a key factor in the career choices I've made. My experiences growing up with my brother definitely brought an awareness of misunderstood adolescents. I always got along with the bad kids in school and the misfits and the outcasts. There was one gal the kids constantly picked on. She was a big, tall girl. Her family had a big commercial kennel of Siberian Huskies and Schnauzers in their basement, and the whole house smelled like a kennel. It just had that aroma, like a horse has an aroma. She cleaned the kennels before coming to school, so she'd always smell like a kennel. She was a good friend of our family, but kids would pick on her and she said later on in life, "You always stuck up for me." I don't know what I did but she said I always stuck up for her. As an adult, she continued to show dogs and became a professional dog handler, and she was one of the few women to run the Iditarod.

Linda and Randy

In Minnesota, I had a babysitter, Lulu, who lived across the street from me and loved horses. She was taking riding lessons and me and my mom would go watch. That's all it took. I was stuck on Lulu like glue. It was pretty funny. She was an only child, and I was the little sister that would never leave her alone.

I fell in love with those horses and started formal riding lessons in Michigan when I was five. I did my first horse show and started jumping when I was six. It was a quarter horse. It wasn't a pony, it was a big horse. I remember hanging on to those reins. I always wanted to touch them, comb and brush and smooch on them

and all that stuff. I'd go in the tack room where all the saddles were and I'd just put my hands on the reins so my hands could smell like horse.

As we moved around, my parents kept me involved with horses. I took riding lessons all the time—twice a week, or whatever could fit into my school schedule. Lulu rode hunter/jumper, so obviously I was going to be like Lulu. The prestigious jumps, the huge jumps, I never went that far. Four feet was probably my highest jump. They can go eight feet, ten feet, twelve feet. It's unbelievable, some of these massive jumps. Like at the Rolex in Lexington: The first day is dressage,

the second day is cross-country, and the third day is stadium jumping. One horse has to compete in those different disciplines. I'm in awe at that caliber of athleticism for an animal.

Look at a racehorse: six furlongs is all he does, and he goes left at the turn. Then look at three-day-event horses who have to do a multitude of things. But they are also eight, nine, ten years old and racehorses are two, three, four years old usually. Don't get me wrong: I have tons of respect for the racing industry. There are just different disciplines of horse. Each breed has a specific purpose or is known for certain ways of movement that would be better for certain disciplines.

Your quarter horses are a more muscular breed that can make some quick turns. They're not the big, tall, lanky ones like a thoroughbred. The Arabians are much more fine-boned. They can do endurance as well

as being a good riding horse, but they definitely look different. When I talk to friends and family members that are not familiar with horses, they all look the same to them, but every breed has their own look. People that know trucks can obviously tell the difference between a Chevy and a Ford.

I won a blue ribbon at my first show. I was five. The next couple of shows I got second and third, and then I got another blue. When you're a little girl in love with horses, that's all there is in the whole world. Nothing else compares. Every book I read was about horses, everything that I wanted to do had to revolve around horses. It was pretty sick. Every Christmas present and birthday present had something to do with horse riding: boots, saddles, jodhpurs, feed tubs, or brushes. The Sunday clothes with the little pointy shoes and the dresses with the little puffy things that pinch the underneath of my arms: that was just not me. Barn boots and pitchforks were my thing.

As I got older I wanted to work, I wanted a car, and there was less time for horses. I was not interested in going out to the big circuit of shows anymore. I just kind of outgrew it, and I didn't compete at all in high school. At that time I was ready to give up the horses. My mom said, "Thank God," and her prayers paid off. She was always concerned that I was going to get hurt.

I went to University of Wisconsin-Stout, got my undergrad in vocational rehabilitation, and worked in a crisis center. I loved it. It was a rewarding job. If you like kids, you like kids. I was probably only three or four years older than some of the kids in there. I was 20, and you've got juveniles in the facility that are 15. I think when you grow up with someone who has a disability, you just end up taking some leadership roles and getting a lot more strong-willed and focused.

Kids in crisis centers have a lot of issues. One attempted suicide young, and 10 years after I left, news got back to me that he finally did commit suicide. But I understood it. He was badly abused, tormented, living in a dog crate, beaten, and molested. Incest is a lot more common than what people would ever think. Incest really does a number on how men think about themselves. Changes their DNA, so to speak. He shut down and was made fun of in school, and it was an awful life for him on this earth. He just wanted the pain to end.

People get really angry when it comes to suicide. They lose compassion for the pain being felt. They don't really want to die, they just want the pain to go away. The family members and people around those who are suicidal think of it as being selfish: "How dare they." I have a different view on suicide. So when he finally committed suicide on the third attempt, I understood it even though it was upsetting.

I completed my master's degree and got a school counseling certificate with a concentration in education and schools. I was working as a counselor and teacher at the crisis center, but after two years, I wanted to be with horses again and a friend said I should meet this family out in rural Wisconsin who were racing thoroughbreds. I said, "There's no thoroughbreds in Wisconsin. What are you talking about?" But sure enough, they had thoroughbreds, and they raced at a little racetrack in Chicago. They said, "Well, do you want to come down for the summer and work with us?" I showed up, and after a week I thought, "Oh, I'm home." I was 32.

I'd never hung out on racetracks before. It was a different discipline. But a horse is a horse: you love them, they smell great, it's connecting with the animals that you really like. I knew there was the Triple Crown.

I followed Secretariat, obviously, and whatever was covered on NBC Sports, but I didn't understand the whole realm of thoroughbred racing. I was like a sponge, and I knew at the end of the week that this was going to be great. So at the end of the summer it was time to go back to school and I said, "I'm gonna take a year off, folks." Then I traveled with racehorses for 20 years. I was a groom and then an assistant trainer for 15 years.

I started at smaller tracks. When I decided that I wanted to go to the bigger tracks, the people I worked for kind of laughed at me. They thought I wouldn't survive. I think they wanted me to stay with them at these smaller tracks, and I didn't want to. I wanted to see bigger racetracks, better horses, more money, a different atmosphere. They thought I was silly, dreaming big, that I should probably just stay small. I was an adventurer, though. I was footloose and fancy free and having a great time. It was a great time.

I had a dually truck and a six-horse trailer that I used for moving my own horses and hauling for others. So I went to the track kitchen and put up a sign where people would put up little notes like, "Need a groom. Need a hot walker." Mine said, "I'm going to Churchill Downs. Six-horse trailer. Empty. Looking for a load." Dale Romans's dad, Jerry Romans, had six horses up at Beulah Park in Ohio, and he said, "Yeah, I need to get these horses down to Churchill." So I left Ohio and I drove down here. I'd never been to Churchill before. I drove around the city with a trailer load of horses not really knowing where I was, and this was before GPS and cell phones. But I finally found the place. To drive in and see those spires—man, I got goosebumps. Sometimes I forget about that until people come here on the backside tour and they're enamored with the sport, and I'm like, *Oh yeah, I remember that feeling.*

I dropped off the horses, parked my trailer, went and got something to eat, and went to find an apartment where that Mexican restaurant is on 4th and Central, El Molcajete. That used to be a flower shop, and my apartment was on the third floor—hotter than hell, no air conditioning. I'd go to Sears and sit in the TV department with a bag of popcorn. I found that apartment, then I came to the stable gate and looked for hot walking, grooming, exercising, whatever they needed, but I had a hard time finding a job and I didn't get one. I hauled more horses to Ellis Park, another trailer load just so I could get some more money. I didn't want to haul horses, I wanted to work with horses. Then I got a job with Bernie Flint, who's a trainer here.

I lasted for a couple of weeks before they told me I was fired. "What? What'd I do wrong?" I had never been fired from anything. I didn't know I was supposed to rake the shedrow until the rake fell apart. We didn't rake that much at Beulah Park. I'd just rake a little area and thought I was done, so I left. It broke my heart. Tracks like Beulah are pretty rough. They're very impoverished-looking. Everybody has the leftovers of everybody else's gear: if you have a stable you might have a red feed tub, a blue water bucket, and green cross-webbing. There's just not a lot of money in the game for those kind of places, and making the whole place look pretty was not part of the growing up I did at those tracks. You'd rake to clean it up, but not to make it look like what Bernie Flint wanted. So I got fired. Then I had to look for another job. I called a friend who was a jockey agent up in Ohio and said, "If you know anybody down here that might be interested in finding a groom or an assistant, then it would be helpful if you'd give me the name."

There was a trainer named Del Carroll—a big name in the business—and I gave him a call. He said, "Yeah, but we need to send you to Lexington for a

couple of weeks and see how you work out, and then maybe go to New York." I packed up an overnight bag and stayed in the tack room in Lexington for a couple of weeks. They said that I fit the bill, so I went on to New York to stay with Weekend Surprise, a nice filly on a stakes trail who later became the dame of A.P. Indy and American Squall, a couple of really good Derby contenders.

I stayed at the Del Carroll stable in New York for the winter. That's a hard way to do it: December, January, and February, the most brutal time of the year. The horses grow winter coats, you're working in overalls and hats and mittens, and you're not able to bathe a horse. You have to just wash off their legs. It's hard. The following year I hauled horses to Florida. Didn't have a job, just packed up my truck and went to Florida and got a job there.

When I returned to Kentucky, I went to Keeneland and worked for Phil Hauswald, who I ended up with for a long long time. When I went into the barn on the backside with three horses, Phil didn't think that I could be a groom. I was somebody different: a tall woman in a man's job.

I came into racing just as women started in racing. There weren't a lot of gals back then. There were some tracks that wouldn't even allow women on the backside. Did we get harassed? Yeah. The whole Me Too thing is not any different here. Men flirt, men say inappropriate things. Here, you're just cut a little tougher. I suppose there's a handful of ladies that might get picked on more, might be a little more vulnerable. But the women riders that I've known are strong gals. I guess I'm supposed to say, "Oh, it was so awful. They treated me badly." But if they did, I didn't notice.

They must have said it in the ear I can't hear out of.

I grew up in my 30s and 40s doing exactly what everybody does here: worked with the horses seven days a week, traveled with them. I moved into the stable. I just rolled up my sleeves, worked my butt off, and was happy doing it. I went on with it.

Usually, when you first start working for a stable, you don't get the good horses. You're at the other side of the barn with the horses that are hardly able to do anything or the young horses or whatever. I got into that barn and within a short time I was given some of the better horses. This didn't sit well with a lot of people that had been there for a long time. There was some gossip, trying to exclude me, not being nice all the time, some resentment, jealousy, envy, anger. "Why does she get those horses and I don't get those horses?"

I was busting my butt. I was organized. I out-shined them. I out-worked them. I just had that in me. I loved doing what I was doing and one groom said, "She deserves it. She out-works all of us. She's good."

Then I became the assistant of that same shedrow within a year's time even though I really didn't want it. I was rubbing one or two of the better horses and helping run the shed. I was quick, I was able to take care of my duties and help other people who were not as fast as me or couldn't organize their time as well as me. I'm a workhorse. I know what needs to get done. I organize. But I didn't want to be the assistant. You're at the barn all the time. There's no days off. You're on call all the time. You got one headache after another: help not showing up or not being on time, the wrong silks in the wrong place, the vet has to treat this horse at 4:00 in the morning and someone's got to be there, the night watchman doesn't show up. The assistant gets to take care of all that. Why would anybody in their right mind want to do that? The good part is the extra pay. They treat you well, you get more of your travel expenses paid, your apartment is taken care of, your percentage of the wins or stake money is higher, but there was a huge trade-off: all the work you had to do.

I got the job by default. Phil said, "Linda, you're going to be the assistant. I need more help." I really struggled with that. I didn't want that headache, so I told him I'd just do it for the winter in Miami. And then I stayed at Hauswald Racing Stables for 15 years.

When I came on the racetrack, women weren't embraced all that much. This was in the '80s. The workforce back then was black and white and mostly men. Then it seemed like it changed to a mostly Hispanic population overnight. We needed the help, they showed up great, and then all of a sudden a bunch of them showed up. When one got fired or let go, there'd be somebody else right behind them.

Some people think the Hispanic workforce doesn't have the same passion for horses. I don't know if it's because of the language barrier, but I know the Hispanic guys that I work with talk about their horses all the time. They're very proud of their horses, they want me to photograph their horses galloping out there. There *is* that sentiment, there *is* that connection.

When a groom rubs a horse, they're supposed to rub their shoulders, their hips—rub and massage those muscles like any good athlete. You sit under their legs and rub a leg with liniments and you're supposed to massage those ankles for several minutes and then put the bandages on. But these days grooms sometimes just "slap and wrap"—slap that liniment on and wrap it up.

The economics of it is that when stables would have good horses, your grooms would only rub one or two horses and really give those athletes the best attention: walking him an extra half yard, doing the extra leg work, doing the extra body work if the horse needed to have therapy, putting them in ice water. That was the rule. Those grooms would take care of those horses, and also might do a little extra work in the shedrow. Now, due to the economics, they rub three and four and five horses because they get paid more if they do that. And when you rub four or five horses, you don't have the time to give the extra care for that athletic horse. You pretty much *have* to slap and wrap.

When I finally decided to make the job change to a counselor at Churchill Downs, everybody said, "Linda, why are you doing this? You're so well-respected, you make great money." That made me feel good. I knew that, I felt it. But it was just time for a change.

I couldn't imagine myself doing anything else. I still wanted to be with the horses, still wanted to be part of that scene, wasn't ready to give it up. Not at all. I know the culture, I know the game, I also know counseling, and I know issues. That was kind of my experience before I got into racing, and even when I was still working with the horses, the man that had this job before me would say, "I've got a gal who's struggling a little. Would you be interested in talking with her?" And I'd say, "Yeah, no problem." Or when I was down in Florida the minister there said, "Would you mind talking to a couple of the women on some things?"

I made myself available for them. I knew the issues and I knew a couple of the girls that were getting into trouble, so I would be the first one to say, "This is me. I'm a racetracker too. There's some activity you might wanna be watchful for."

I worked in addiction, alcohol, and drugs all through college. I never wanted to do it because it's hard. It's just a crazy world. The insanity, the thinking is bizarre. So I never wanted to do that. When I was offered this job, I thought I would just take it for a year. Now, I've been here for 16 years. This job enables me to stay in one place. When I first quit racing and stayed here a full year, it was the first time I ever finished a jar of mayonnaise.

I'm the Director of the Healing Place Lifestyle Program at Churchill Downs. It's an employee assistance program and my office is in the stable area on the backside. Any kind of big corporation will have an employee assistance program implemented in the work atmosphere. There's always issues in the workplace that will be problematic for the employer and the employee, so there's got to be something in place to have policies and procedures when trouble comes up. As in other industries, one of the biggest problems is drug and alcohol related issues within the workplace. I'm kind of like the guidance counselor in the workplace.

Anybody that gets in trouble out on the backside where security is involved will be referred to me. I'm kind of like a triage. They come here and I filter out where they need to go, who needs to be accountable, what the frontside needs to know in terms of health and safety and security for that person, as well as for our industry. I help folks utilize community resources so that a client can stay in racing. Or if he needs to take a little break, I help him find a residential treatment facility. We know our industry is always hurting for help, so we're trying to do as much as we can for people to stay within the work atmosphere and plugged into their jobs. Their employers depend on them, and they've got a good working relationship with some of the trainers they've been with for a while.

So if we can treat some of the issues, primarily alcoholism, where they can still remain on the track and employed, we'll do that. But if they keep on relapsing and relapsing and relapsing, then we have to take a look at something more residential or intensive outpatient.

The door's always open. I get a lot from trainers or assistant trainers who say, "Gosh Linda, I've had this groom, exerciser, hot walker, whatever. He's been really great but he's messing up so much. What can I do?" We talk about options. This an entertainment and sports industry, and we have to be accountable and vigilant for the safety and best behavior back here.

I do this job because I love people and I love the industry. It's really important for our industry to come to grips with what the people bring to the sport, the people that do all the hard work.

The perception of backside workers is that we're all riff-raff. That anybody that moves around a lot is not a stable person, that we have to have everything provided for us, that we're needy. I don't like that. We're hard-working people back here just like everybody else.

We have families. We have houses. We have car payments. We're not riff-raff that can't hardly make a living. You have exercise riders making $600, $700, $800 a week, and you have a groom making $450 or $500 a week. That's a lot more than what McDonald's pays. There's a trade-off: We work very hard for that. But if you're willing to do it, it's an honest living.

I see a lot of success. You do see failures, but a failure doesn't always mean it's not successful. Success for some might be staying sober for two days. Success for some is eight years. It depends on each person. I've got one fella that's been sober now for two years, and I didn't think I'd ever see him sober that long. There's an assistant trainer who's not on the track anymore, but when he first started here he always relapsed. He was always in and out of trouble, in and out of jail, in a problem situation. I don't know what happened—a moment of clarity, something stuck for him, maybe he'd just had enough, sick and tired of being sick and tired—but he's been sober now for many, many years. When I introduce him to other fellas who are young and trying to get sober and clean, the young guys go, "Man, I can't even imagine you out in the madness!" I'm thinking in the background, *I couldn't even imagine him being sober.*

There's always people that change. I have a bigger appreciation for hope because it's pretty bleak when they're at the bottom. I've just seen too many people there that have made some really big changes, so there's always hope. They don't have to be that person.

There is an expression, *Alcoholism is a slippery disease.* Racing can be considered a slippery lifestyle. In and out of cities, very long work days, a disconnect from families and friends, and a limited time to get away from it all. It is the perfect breeding ground for problems to grow.

It takes a complete village to put on the greatest two minutes in sports, the Kentucky Derby, along with many other races. Like other communities, the race-track community consists of hundreds of people from all walks of life, and with all the issues and problems that come with being a human being. It makes sense to reach out to help backside employees, to strengthen the working backbone of our racing industry. To maintain and support a strong and vital work force and healthy work environment adds to the integrity of our sport.

I continue to love the horses, the sport of racing, and the people that dedicate their time and energy to care for the horses that put on the greatest show! /

Mark Simms

TRAINER

I was in the Army for five years right out of college as a military intelligence officer. I had been thinking about being a special agent in the FBI for a long time, and they said if I wanted to be an agent, I needed to be an intelligence officer. I was stationed at Fort Worden, Washington, and when I drove to Arizona for my intelligence officer training, I stopped at every racetrack on the way. I knew that a guy from my Indian reservation who had brought horses down to Turf Paradise. So I would leave training on Fridays at 5:00 p.m., drive three hours to Phoenix, get there at 10:00 or 11:00 at night, wake up at four in the morning, work with the horses all weekend, and Sunday after races drive back to Fort Huachuca, Arizona, to do the Army thing. Horse racing was always in the back of my mind. It just gets in your blood and you cannot shake it. I've had every opportunity to shake it, but I always find a way to be tied up with horses. Everywhere I've been, I find the horses.

I lived in Korea for a year and worked with a Korean soldier, Dak-Ho Wong. He was called a KATUSA, which stands for Korean Augment to the U.S. Army. He kind of facilitated for the U.S. Army. He'd take me to the racetrack, and I would take him back to a different military base and we'd go eat at Chili's or something. He got a little American, and I got a little Korean. On the weekends we'd go to the races.

The program would be in Hangul, the Korean alphabet, so I'd look at the horses and Wong translated the program and figured out how to bet them.

Racing was a bit different over there. One thing that stood out was that they weighed the horses after a race to see how much weight they lost during the race. It was weird. And there's a lot more turf racing over there. The turf here is on the inside, but over there the turf is one the outside and the dirt track is inside. The jockeys ride a little differently over there too. Their posture, the way they sit on the horse. They just ride a little funny, they set their stirrups a little bit lower.

I was in Korea for a year, then went to Kentucky, then to Afghanistan. I got promoted to lieutenant and realized that I've been moving my whole life. I wanted some stability. I knew I was born to train horses, and the horses decided that I loved Louisville. I was assigned to an infantry brigade at Fort Knox, which was closer to my wife, who was in nursing school at the time. I don't know if I would be here right now if it wasn't for my wife's support. She knew I was passionate about horses and training racehorses. She researched a bunch of horse farms for me to check out, so I started emailing all the trainers in the area. A lady named Tay Henderson took an interest in me and hooked me up with the Romans team. They have a farm out in Goshen, Oldham County. Liberty Lane Training Center.

I would drive out there in the mornings just to be around them, just to learn. I'd get in the stalls and help out to get practice, then drive back to Fort Knox.

Dale Romans has opened so many doors. I went to the Keeneland sale with him, buying yearlings, and he was introducing me to top guys in racing. "This is Mark. Here's his background. He's getting in the business." Initially I was planning on going straight to the racetrack, but I had my daughter and my wife. Dale told me, "Don't transition fully. Do something else. Do horses on the side." I took a job at GE, and that was an opportunity to make a really good salary and still pursue my passion. I just figured I'd do horse racing on the side, but then my grandpa died, and I thought, "Man, this is not right. It's in my blood. I gotta do this. At least take a shot at it."

My grandpa trained horses. His name was Mike Nelson. He'd tell you, "I learned how to walk walking to a horse barn." His dad was a jockey, and my grandpa was an awesome horseman. He worked with quarter horses on the reservation. My mom's whole family is on the Turtle Mountain Indian Reservation in Buckhorn, North Dakota. We're Chippewa Indians. I've always considered it home. The reason they call it Turtle Mountain is that it's got these small hills all over and when you fly over it, it looks like the backs of turtles. They call it God's country. The sunsets are really pretty, it stays bright really, really late, until 11:00 at night. Biggest mosquitoes you'll ever see.

My mom and uncles don't care for horses that much because when they were little, the horses were a priority. If it it was freezing outside, they had to go up there and bust ice buckets and make sure the horses were fed and watered before they went to school. My grandfather was a tough guy to get along with. He and I had the relationship we had because of the horses. I loved the horses just like he loved the horses, so we always had that connection. Family shouldn't have favorites, but he loved me and another cousin who was into the horses. We really enjoyed spending the summers together. I'd jump in with him and be with him all day just trying to learn more about horses.

He was a vet tech for a long time and traveled all over the country. He had a cool life, just doing whatever he wanted, bouncing around, trying to learn the game. He had been to racetracks all over, from Florida to Washington. He would float around from racetrack to racetrack running horses, then he owned and trained horses. He'd get horses from guys like Van Berg, horses that just couldn't make it on a circuit like Churchill. They would have injuries and he'd work on them, do all these little cheap tricks to try and nurse horses along, and he had a lot of success doing that kind of stuff. He was carefree. The only thing he worried about was his horses, and he instilled that in me. Just a passion for it.

They didn't have pari-mutuel racing in North Dakota, so he raced horses in South Dakota and neighboring states. He got tired of traveling all over to run horses, so he said, "Hey, why can't we just do it here?" He talked about how sad it was that they had to travel to South Dakota or Canada if they wanted to run horses because they couldn't figure it out in North Dakota. He fought for pari-mutuel wagering and helped build that out, and now they have two racetracks in North Dakota. He was one of the founding guys, and he was the first guy to manage the racetrack up there at Chippewa Downs.

When he was young he was mean. A lot of folks on the reservation were scared of him. He was mixed race, and being on the Indian reservation, the first thing people want to say when they're mad or drinking is the n-word. Some of the folks on the reservation don't want to see folks from different cultures coming in.

Him and his brother would have to fight all the time. He was known for knocking people out.

As he got older, he got a lot softer. I never knew the mean side of him, except when he got a little irritated once in a while if I showed up late to the barn or didn't do what he wanted me to do. Just a good old man. When I go to the reservation, if I say I'm Mike Nelson's grandson, people always say, "Oh, I loved your grandpa." They really appreciated what he did and the impact he made on that reservation. A lot of folks came out to his funeral. It was a lot more hands-on than some of the funerals you will see around here. It was intense. Me, my cousins, my dad, and our uncle took care of him, shaved his face and stuff, made sure he was sent off properly. It was cool to be able to be there with him.

His funeral was a combination of a Catholic funeral and some Native stuff as well. They played the Indian drums when we came out the of the church and we hooked him up to the wagon. I am a small guy compared to my cousin, so we had to squeeze in the back of the wagon. We put him in the wagon and carried him to the cemetery in a horse drawn carriage, and when they put him in the ground they dropped tobacco leaves over the top of his casket before we put the dirt on him. My uncles have told me thousands of times, but I just cannot remember what the significance is. It has something to do with the spirit on the other side. I had just talked to him a couple of days before.

He'd gotten such a kick out of being able to watch me on TV once I came to Kentucky to see the horses running, and he'd go brag to his buddies, "That's my grandson." He was extremely proud of what I was able to do here, just really ecstatic to see me on TV. When he'd call me on the phone he'd be cussing, "You little motherfucker, you over there livin' my dream, you little asshole." Raising hell, but all in good fun.

Mike Nelson

The Romans team had this horse who couldn't cut it here. He won twice, but just wasn't up to par. I told my grandpa about it and we bought him together, put him in a trailer, and shipped him to North Dakota. When my grandpa died, I went back to the reservation and told my uncle, "Let's go make him win, but we gotta train him my way." So I got that horse cleaned up. I trained him a little bit. I would travel up, check him out while my uncle was doing day-to-day stuff. I had my trainer's license up there. I won my first race as

a trainer in 2017 back in North Dakota. Once when my grandpa was watching me work, he told somebody, "That kid's a horseman." That was definitely one of the biggest compliments I've ever gotten.

I have a ton of patience with horses. My wife will say I don't got a lot of patience with people. But I just really get in tune with horses. I love getting in the stall with them, trying to understand them. I really get a kick out of it. It's a big sense of accomplishment for me to take a horse they say is crazy, to understand him and get him to go do what I want him to do, and be willing to do it. I was around cheaper horses when I was younger in North Dakota. They're not bred as well as these horses here in Kentucky, but I learned how to train them. I went from $500 horses to $500,000 dollar horses. But if you spend a million dollars on a mare, that doesn't mean that horse is going to make the racetrack.

This guy from Canterbury Downs named Mack Robinson came here last year for the yearling sale and bought a filly for $20,000. She ran the highest Beyer Speed Figure this year. She broke her maiden—won her first race—by like sixteen lengths. Her name is Amy's Challenge. She can really run. They spent $20,000 on her, and she'll be running against fillies people paid $200,000 or $300,000 for. That shows that the guy with all the money in the world still can't win the Kentucky Derby. That's what really appeals to me—there's always hope as a trainer. You always have a two-year-old that makes you think, *Maybe this is my rock star. Maybe they'll get me there.* That's the kind of dream trainers have.

I'm a little bit nervous about going out on my own as a trainer, but I'm passionate about it. My biggest fear of making the transition is that there's a lot of racetracks shutting down. There are not a lot of race-tracks opening up. Twenty years ago, there were a lot

in this area, and right now I'm hoping that we're going upwards. A lot of horse tracks are doing pretty good trying to promote it for a younger crowd who are more excited about racing again. Churchill Downs is doing a pretty good job. Having later post times, night racing, doing stuff like allowing beers is attracting a younger crowd to the game. I think it's working. I think we're getting more people into the game, even though it's an expensive game.

I think the business has changed. A lot of times these guys talk about "back in my day," but horse racing was basic. It was extremely primitive, and now we got so much other stuff going on. We're a lot more connected now. Trainers have Facebook, we have websites, you can reach out to people digitally, owners can own horses in New York and run them in California and still watch them. I can send them pictures or videos from my iPhone when their horse is working and send it to them. A lot of older trainers still don't do that kind of stuff. I think the younger businessmen are getting out there. Those guys really want to see that kind of stuff. I think you have to connect the dots and show them your horses. I mean, they're spending a lot of money. They're going to want to see that animal. So we're a lot more connected now, and nowadays you have to be connected. You have to be able to reach out, to do a better job of promoting ourselves. Horse racing is old school. A lot of the newer guys, like myself, if we're going to make it we have to evolve with the business.

I tell people my spiel, shake hands: They got to know who you are. When somebody says, "Hey, I'd like to swing by your barn," you have to be ready to roll. If you're going to be a successful trainer, you've got to get some horses. When you get horses, next thing you need is stalls. You've got to have somewhere to put them. It is a lot easier to get owners to invest in you when you already have stalls and a couple of horses and they can come out and see what is going on. If you only have one horse, you probably don't want to hire a groom, because a groom's going to cost you about $500 a week, depending on how many horses you're grooming. I got my first couple of horses in March of 2017. I had them out at Skylight, and I applied for my stall at Churchill Downs. I got stalls over at the Spectrum. I have been running horses since then. I have been learning a ton and really enjoying it. I got a couple guys over there that work for me. I am really trying to build this thing out. Initially I didn't have anything, so it was really selling the dream to folks. Luckily, I had some folks who knew my dedication and how many hours I put in and how much I loved it. They were willing to put some money up and really support me and help me get it going. They have been there every step of the way. Horse racing is tough.

What keeps folk around is hope, because they hear a lot of cool stories all the time where somebody came in with $5,000 and made $100,000. Those stories are few and far between, so I definitely try to be realistic with my expectations. It is a tough game. What I don't want to do is tell a bunch of folks about all the roses and how good the game is, because then folk come in with an expectation that they are going to make all this money or they get sour with it really quickly. If you are doing it strictly to make money, it is going to be tough. On the other hand, my kids still have to eat.

It's tough to get folks into the horse racing business because it's so expensive. It's not easy getting young folks into the game and telling them, "I'm going to charge you $85 or $100 per day to train this horse." So my parents, a couple guys I was in the Army with, and I pooled a bunch of money to go find horses. That's how we got it going. I told them, "We will split this money up and put it in a pot and we will use this pot to train these horses without taking any money."

Just trying to see if we can get things going. It worked out well. We got really, really tight at the end, but we were able to win a race and replenish the pot and keep going a little bit longer. I haven't had to go back and get into more money; we've just been working through that pot for now. If we are able to win another race or two races, everyone will at least get their money back. I think those guys are excited for us to get money back so we can reinvest it and try to get a better horse. So it's been good, it's been a lot of fun. For the two horses we bought, we had 20 starts. The horses have been healthy and been able to run. A lot of times you pay for a horse that may never see the races.

Most trainers charge a day rate. But that day rate is going to fluctuate. Every trainer does it a little differently, but it's going to include room service to care for the horse: straw, bedding, food, hay and oats, getting that horse running. Anytime the horse jogs, when he works, you've got to pay somebody to get on him, and that's 15 bucks a day. Bills can rack up pretty quickly. There have been many folk in this business go broke because the owner hasn't paid the bills because it is a hobby for them. But there are a lot of folk on the backside—trainers, grooms, exercise riders, ferriers, vets—and this is their living. When folks don't pay the bill, people get put into really, really tight spots. I have heard plenty of stories of guys having to put liens on horses and things like that just to get paid. I think communication is key. Be up front with owners; people don't like surprises. I keep a spreadsheet and I say, "This is where we are, this is what we are spending our money on." That way they are completely aware when that bill comes around. Or if these horses win and we won $20,000 but the owner still didn't get any money, the owner understands it's because we spent the money on these different spots. Just being wide open and clear with folks is how you reason with them.

You're not going to make that much as a trainer. If you've got one horse, you've got to do it yourself. Once you get upwards of 10 horses, you can hire an exercise rider that you can keep fully employed and you're getting day rates from 10 different owners, so you got that cash flow. It takes a little while to get that going. You have to make sure you get feed, straw, wire, and you've got to have tack. That's a big thing, and tack is expensive. I've been acquiring tack for three or four years. I got my saddles, all that stuff. Depending on what kind—there's different metals or different quality—they charge about $200 for a bridle, $500 for

a saddle, and each trainer's got their own saddle towels. I got all my saddle towels, and I got silks.

When I was in Afghanistan I wanted to do something cool with my uniform when I came back, so I had my uniform turned into blinkers. I knew early on I needed some silks, so the seamstress took my colors, and then used Army camo for both the sleeves with black, white, and my symbol on it. The body part, the chest part is black, and then that red and white S and J is on the chest and on the back. I used my grandpa's colors, red and white, and Dale's color is black, so that's where the black comes from. /

Darial Navas

ASSISTANT TRAINER

Everybody has big names in Guatemala. My father and my mother wanted to use two names for me, so they call me Sergio Darial Navas Orantes. It's too many names.

I'm an assistant trainer for Phil Bauer. I like to work here. When I came to the United States, I started to work for this guy as a hot walker. I learned a lot. Later he told me, "You're young and you can be a shedrow foreman." And I started to take care of the whole barn, like 20 horses. He saw that I was still working hard, so he told me, "You're gonna be good for assistant trainer." And my boss started to teach me. Now, sometimes he leaves for Saratoga and I take care of the 18 horses here. Only me and two riders.

I didn't play music when I moved to the U.S. But once I was here, I wanted to get a keyboard and start playing music. So about four years ago I started learning to play keyboard, and I watched YouTube to learn a little bit. One day, my friend had a party. He told me, "I have a bunch of meat—we could have a good barbecue." I went there and we started to play keyboard and sing. They liked it and started to dance. The next week, they had another party and I found another guy who's much better than me to play keyboard and I sang. A month later we went to West Palm Beach to race, and we found another guy, and he played the guitar. The band was getting big now, and they started to pay us a little bit. Everybody said, "Hey, you did a good job. Keep doing it. Keep doing it."

When I came back here to Churchill I found three more guys. They're good. I said, "Hey I have two keyboards. Do you want to practice here?" And we started playing together here on the backside in the big room, the loft above the barn. Sometimes security comes by because the music makes too much noise, so I turn the speakers down a little.

The name of the band is Complices de la Sierra. I picked the name. We play norteño music, like border music. We play *duranguenses*, and *quebraditas*— romantic music, something you can dance to with your girl. I like the music. I'm sort of the boss for the band. I have six guys in the band. I like the guys who work for me. They're really smart. I want to tell them I appreciate everything they do. They work hard. I put a little pressure on them to come to practice music, to learn a couple different songs. Every time we practice music, we try to do better and better and better.

When I started four years ago, I didn't have a good voice. After a lot of practice I'm starting to get better. Practice makes you professional. Last year, we were doing good. We've played probably 30 concerts. And this year is much better. I've had four already this month.

We'll be busy Friday, Saturday, and Sunday: three days per week. People are coming from Mexico and different countries and they never forget the music they heard at home. They want to keep the music they like. That's why bands in the United States are doing this music—because sometimes they miss the family and they want to sing a couple songs for the family. Like me, I want to make good songs for my family or for my girlfriend, because she's in Guatemala. I want to write her a song and sing it in my band.

We played in the infield last year. It was so good. There were probably 300 people there. Paige from the rec hall said, "Your band should come play this concert." So we went there, me and my six guys, guitar and keyboard and drums and everything. We made a big party and everybody was dancing. Everybody had a good time. When you see people starting to dance you think, "Well, everybody likes the music. We're doing a good job." I know the people from Mexico and Guatemala—when they don't like the music, they don't dance. They sit down.

A lot of racetrackers are from Guatemala and Mexico. They have almost the same music. That's the music we heard back home. When I go to bed I put the phone next to my ear and listen to music. There's couple songs I like about mother and father. I hear a lot of songs where guys have moved away and lost their fathers and they write a song about their dads. There's one called "Sólo Dejé Yo A Mi Padre"—"I've Left My Father All Alone." I know another song that talks about coming to the United States, "Cuando Me Vivir al Norte"—"When I Came North." The guy who wrote the song came here and somebody called him from Guatemala and told him, "Your mother has died. She passed away." He made a good song about it. He tried to go back there but he didn't find his mother. Everybody liked that song. He says, "When you have your mother, or your family, you need to take care of them. If you leave, when you come back, you might not find your mother, or your kids, or your brother."

When I go on at a concert, I need to do a good job. I need to sing very well, from my heart, to talk to everybody. Everything comes from my heart. When I'm at the concert, I think about how I need to work harder to see my kids happy, to see my mother happy, to see my father and my brother happy. My whole family, I want to see them happy. I send them videos so they can see me and see that I'm doing a good job.

When I call my mother, she tells me, "Congratulations. You're doing a good job. You're my favorite kid." She's really happy. In the band, I don't make much money right now because we try not to charge too much for the music. When I make $200 for playing, I send $100 for my mother. $100 for me, $100 for my mother. And I tell her, "Mother, last night I sang and I made $200. This is gonna be for you, and you can use it for your medicine. You can use the money." She tells me, "You're the best. Thank you." I like to hear that from my mother.

I want to write a song for my girlfriend. I want to tell her how much I love her, and how much I miss her. I want to tell her it's very hard to be here and for her to be there. It's something nice I want to do. I want to tell her she's sweet. I miss her really bad. There's a lot of stuff I want to tell her. I want her to be in love. I want her to tell me, "Wow, you're my hero." Enrique Iglesias has a song called "Hero." I want to make one like him because he speaks good English.

I want to write one song in English. Sometimes I confuse some words and I say something wrong, but I've been speaking English for about five years. I use English in my second job at the feed company, and when the vet comes in to work on horses, I have to hear everything.

Sometimes I went to the Backside Learning Center. It's why I talk a little bit of English now.

Being in a band and working with the horses is hard. It's too much pressure sometimes, like if people need the music to start at 5:00 p.m. I lose concerts because we finish work in the barn at 4:30 here. Other times we play so late. One time we had a concert and we finished at 3:00 in the morning, and came back to the barn and started working. Because here with the horses, we start about 4:00 in the morning. So we only had one hour to come back and start work again. That's not good for me. It's really hard.

I try to be smart. I tell everyone, "Hey, I've got to do this, I've got to do this." And my boss is real nice. He told me, "When you have a concert, let me know two days before and I'll let you go and I'll come back to feed the horses for you." He's a good boss. If I'm

really busy, I'll pay a little money for somebody else to come fill in for me at my job so I can go sing.

I want to be famous one day, but not for money. Everybody makes money in music. I want to let everybody know about doing something good in your life. Don't waste your time. Don't be into drugs. Because some people use drugs, and they forget where they come from. I don't forget where I come from.

I come from Guatemala, and I remember when I came here I didn't have money to buy my shoes. I didn't have money for eating. And my father and mother didn't have money. They loved to take care of their four kids. I never missed a meal. My father fed us. He worked hard. He worked hard every single day. Every single day. I appreciate my father because he taught me you need to work hard to do everything you want. /

Andy Spalding
RETIRED RIDER

PHOTO BY LINDA DOANE

I grew up in a small town called Springfield, Kentucky, in Washington County. I got hooked on the horse business at a real early age just by going around horses and working with them and just loved it out of the gates. Springfield at one time had three good-sized horse farms: Kalarama, High Pointe, and Barbara, which used to be right there in front of Saint Catherine College, not too very far from where we was born and raised in a little place called Rosary Heights. We used to sneak down there all the time before we was even old enough to get jobs—hanging around stables, helping them with anything. They'd give you small stuff to do like mucking stalls, throwing hay, leading horses or holding horses while they bathe them, or taking yearlings out and holding on to them while they graze. We were young kids, so we liked it. Every now and then we'd get lucky enough and make 50, 75 cents—that was a hell of an incentive then. That was a candy bar or two.

When you come up in it in that way, the next thing you know, within a year somebody says, "You wanna get on this horse?" They'll see if you want to be a rider. Back then the older guys used to put the younger guys on there and get them bucked off. You learn how to ride real quick. It's trial and error in that game.

You get jacked around pretty good. You learn quickly. They said we had to use common sense or finesse or whatever you want to call it, and you ain't going to win by force. When you hit that ground two or three times and still had the nerve to get on back up there, then you made it.

I started getting on a lot of horses at about 12, and I was a pretty accomplished rider at 15 years old. I was riding the hell out of horses and breaking babies. We'd come in so handy they'd pick us up and slip me four or five dollars a week. We got to where we were valuable.

There was about 100 of them old country guys you never heard of that showed me the ropes. They were out there on the farm breaking babies. Good family men. That portion of the horse business is really good horsemen you never even heard of. This old guy come up there once. He was going to ship a couple horses, and he knew I had a pretty good hand on a horse. He said, "If you work a couple weeks now and get these horses right, I'm going to give you $100." My ears stood straight up. We worked and we worked, and—I never will forget it—he gave me $100. That was the first time I ever had a whole one in my life. I said, "Oh man, this is where I want to go." That was a lot of money. Cash money flashing around.

Other places of society, there wasn't that much cash money floating around. Back then, money had some value.

I come out of a huge Catholic family: eleven sisters and six of us boys. Seventeen of us. Dad lived until he was 80 and Mom lived until she was 86. Dad was a cement contractor. He always had six or seven men working for him all the time. I worked a little bit for my old man, but never could get into that work—talk about manual labor! They had just started building subdivisions, and one of the first big jobs that he had was turning one of those big horse farms into a development of thousands of brick homes. Old man had all the concrete. The driveway, the basements, the sidewalks. They'd leave Springfield every morning and have a caravan of vehicles.

He was pretty successful. We were lucky he made a decent living more than others. He sent all of us to Catholic school. Old man was a freak on education and civics, like voting. You brought your report card home, and Old Man and Mom would be sitting in a chair and judge it right there: look at the report card and look at you. We went to Holy Rosary. Our house was right beside the church. Back then, when you were a kid in elementary school you had mass every morning at seven. Every morning. Mass was in Latin and we took Latin every day: *In nomine patris et filii et spiritus sancti.*

I was an altar boy and I told this boy one time, "You come start serving mass with me and I'll get you some wine." He showed up about a week later. The priest was out there doing something, so I poured him some wine. He drank it and he liked it. I liked it too. One morning when I wasn't there, he went over and stood there and the priest asked him what he wanted. He said, "Andy told me I could get my wine." He told Mom and Dad, I knew they was going to kill me then,

but they didn't say nothing. I said, "Oh my God," but nothing happened really. The priest just started watching us when we poured it up, then he'd close the closet and lock it.

Our parish was always integrated. The white people would come to the church. We was integrated back before restaurants was integrated. White kids, black kids, we all played on the same basketball court and on the same baseball field. It wasn't no big deal one way or another. The church was integrated but the schools were still segregated. Back then everybody wished they was Catholic, because we had asphalt basketball courts outside and all the amenities where the public schools didn't have them. My oldest two sisters had to go to Lebanon for high school because Springfield didn't have a black high school. Then they had this all black boarding high school in Shelby County called Lincoln Institute. My two older sisters and my brother graduated from there.

Our house was right on the road. It used to be just an old two-lane highway. We had a huge garden. I thought it was hard labor watering that. We raised hogs and had cattle. Hog killing around Thanksgiving weekend. There'd be six to seven families get together and they killed 20 to 25 head of hogs. We killed beef every year too. Ten to twelve years old I'm rabbit hunting with shotguns and squirrel hunting with .22 rifles; that was just part of the upbringing out there. I had it made pretty good coming up. But everybody wasn't quite as lucky as I was, I guess.

I was the only one in my family that messed with horses. When I got up into high school, I'd come down here to Louisville and gallop horses at Churchill on the weekends and in the summers. Gallop boys were in demand. Back then there were a whole bunch of black gallop boys, but that's gone by the wayside. Most of the time we got on six to eight horses in a morning for two dollars a head. Sixteen dollars was a pretty damn big chunk of change in the mid-1960s. I'd come down here and stay in the tack rooms for a couple months or sometimes I stayed with my aunt Dorothy Lee. I got in with all these hot walkers and grooms, so I was grooming and walking too. We'd get up every morning and muck stalls and exercise them. We did it all. We did whatever. We was "whatever boys." We stayed around the racetrack. It was good to get away from home and fool around the barn. We had fun. We lived good. I think we were making $35 or $40 a week. Those were good times.

Then the meet was over 30 days after the Derby and people would take the shoes off their horses, ship them back home and turn them out. Same in the fall after Churchill's fall meet—everybody went home. In late August to first of September everybody would bring their babies to the farms to break them. Leading them, tying them to the wall, and picking up their feet is all a part of breaking. They'd have mud on them, feet hadn't been trimmed; it's pretty rough work if you don't know what you were doing.

You start breaking them when they are two-year-olds, and when you start giving them exercises they start muscling up quick. When you bring a baby in out of the fields, before long they don't even look like the same horse. People don't realize that is when they start developing their bodies—when you start putting that structure and routine under them every day.

Nothing better than seeing a young horse come up. I guess it's the feeling a school teacher has about a kid. For horses, it only takes two or three years and you see the whole process—you see a young horse just grow up right in front of your eyes.

A guy named Paul Hampton had a farm. He was in construction, eventually went into coal mining—a wealthy man. He had thoroughbreds with a man

named Dr. Gaulbert, a veterinarian in Bardstown. They raised babies. Got them broke and going good, and then they'd send them out to their trainers. LeRoy Jolley was a big time trainer, a hot name back in that day. We'd get them broke and send them to Jolley at whatever racetrack he was at, and they would go ahead and finish them out, get them ready to run. That's how I really got on them, watching the young babies come along and develop. In about 90 days we'd have them broke and galloping a little bit. Couldn't do much because their knees weren't closed. Young horses got what we call bucked shins, which is when the blood vessel that runs down the front of a horse's leg gets sore from pounding the ground. When that happens, they turn them out so the shins can heal and the baby's knees can develop.

When they're born their knees are open, leaving room for growth, and they don't close until the body is basically through growing up. The bigger the baby, the slower the knees close. If you go putting a lot of stress on the joints in the knees, you start chipping bones and creating a lot of problems—too much activity for an immature body. They race them before their knees are closed and that's why so many horses break down. Usually the knees close when they are two or two and a half years old. That's the problem with horses. They're big and strong and they're much more powerful than their body is developed. Of course that's what those $30,000 purses make you do. With that kind of money, people are going to do whatever they can do regardless. That's just the game now and the game has changed.

The second year is when people start putting them on the track. Horses' birthdays all fall on January 1, but a lot of them babies aren't born until April and May. So you look at the babies that are really born in January—you give a baby a three or four month jump

BETTER LUCKY THAN GOOD

on another baby, he is huge in the early part of his life. They have what they call Oklahoma yearlings: that means that he was probably born December 1. But when they go to register him they put January 1. When you take 30 days on the baby in his first two years, it's huge to be that much more physically and mentally matured. When they finally go out to race, he'll be quite a bit ahead. In the early years, they won't catch up really until they're three and a half to four years old. That happens all the time but nobody ever says anything. How can you prove it?

I was around good horses, but they hadn't developed yet. The advantage I had was training and buying in on a lot of cheap horses with folks who'd say, "I'm gonna get this horse and if you train him, I'll split half of the bills and we'll split half the purse." I did a lot of that and some deals worked out real good, and some didn't. I'll never forget the first $10,000 I made was with this guy named Quayland. He was from Colorado; his dad was one of the original developers of Steamboat Springs. His daddy had a lot of money and he bought a horse called Rainbow Benny. Quayland said, "I tell you what, you do the work, and we'll split it right down the middle." Then we trained him out in Bardstown, Nelson County, out on his farm and he was coming around real good. This horse was big and strong. Damn near black was how dark he was. I said, "This damn horse acts like he wants to be a racehorse. We better see if we can get a stall out at Churchill. We gotta see how he's going to turn out."

So we got him a stall and drove to Churchill every day and trained him. He was just blossoming. One day a guy walked over and said, "What you boys want for this horse?" Quayland said, "Oh no. We're not even thinking about selling him." I thought, *What you got to say about selling my part?* So I asked the guy how much he was thinking about paying and the guy got up to 20 grand, and I said to Quayland, "I've got to sell my part. I've got to sell it." So he got on the phone with his daddy and his daddy sent me a check for 10 grand to stay on board and keep training. So then I said, "I'm with you baby, I ain't gonna give up!"

We got his gate card, and he was ready to run. We'd been watching this allowance race at Keeneland for $23,000. That was big money back then. We went back to the farm with him, planning on running him later that month. He was in his stall, and somehow an old broodmare got down there by his stall. She must have been in season, and Lord, you know what a young colt will do when he's horny. He got to kicking and pawing and everything. He got his foot over top of the gate and messed up that tendon, and that was the end. He never did get to run. I made $10,000. Quayland lost $10,000.

He put him out to stud then ended up selling him for a pretty good price to some guy in Oklahoma, who was doing what they call an appendix breeding. They would take a thoroughbred stallion and breed it to a quarter horse mare and run them like that.

Me and Quayland ran together for 10 or 12 years. One time we had about seven horses we were training. None of them worth a quarter. We had this idea to take them up to Waterford Park in West Virginia. We had this four-horse trailer, bumper hitch at that—wasn't a gooseneck. Loaded up four of them. Waterford Park was rough. Purse was $1,500; I think we got like $800 for the first-place money. To make a bad story good, we was there for about two weeks. All four of them won and got claimed, and we headed back with a pocket full of money. That's how bad the horses were at Waterford back then. I think we got like $2,000 for each of them, headed back with pockets full of money. I'd never do it again, though.

I worked horses at Churchill, but I wasn't really a traveling guy. I didn't go to New York or Hot Springs or Fairgrounds like most guys. I wasn't much into the traveling. I pretty much stayed right here. Then I started out at the farms in Oldham County. When you train at the training centers, most of the time you've got Sundays off because they train six days a week. At the racetrack you don't get off. Somebody is training seven days a week. I was living on Rose Island Road for eight or nine years working at the training centers. Skylight Training Center had about 60 to 70 horses.

Van Berg had a half mile track and a two mile synthetic track. Right beside that synthetic track was this old slave cemetery. It wasn't a big one, but there were some headstones back there. Van Berg kept it cut and cleaned up real nice. Well, this old black cat set up on that fence and watched us work out in the mornings. I never did take the time to walk out there and check it out, but we'd get back to the barn and tell each other, "That black cat is setting out there again this morning." I remember an old hawk who sat up in this old dead tree too.

One time I went out and galloped this old horse, and when I pulled up I saw all these people running across these fields and carrying on. I figured there was a loose horse or something until I looked out in the parking lot, and I saw this school bus. I thought, *What the hell is going on?* I rode on down and came back to the barn, and it was real quiet. When I walked the horse into the stall, he spooked, and I looked down and there was a Mexican up against the wall stooping down. He looked at me and put his finger to his lips like "shhhh."

This big black dude came down the shedrow toward me with a big old gun on his side. He was with Immigration, and he asked me about some Mexicans. He says, "Where's the guy that works in these stalls?" I look around and say, "I don't know." Well, there he

is in the corner of the stall. Now this guy told me he was a Puerto Rican, but if he was he wouldn't have had to run. I'd been working with him every day for almost a year. Jose. Real good groom. Hard working man. Good guy. He liked to sit around and have a good conversation. I'm pretty sure he had a wife and a kid living with him in the dormitory. He got away. A bunch of them got away. A bunch of them stayed back in that field until dark. They got 20 of them. But they missed a good 20 too. When they got through rounding them up, they had a bunch of them and fined Van Berg $5,000.

About a year later, the newspaper and TV said there was a turkey giveaway for Thanksgiving. They had it set up, promoting it seven days out. They made sure the word got out, had flyers hanging up. They wanted to welcome the Mexican people to the country and all that, so come get a free turkey the week before Thanksgiving. They said to show up at the courthouse. They showed up and hell, it was a sting. They was arresting them. Locking them up right there in Oldham County.

Spanish speakers are probably 90 percent of the workforce on the backside of Churchill Downs. You go back there now you and don't see too many black guys anymore. Not that many white guys either that ain't galloping horses or training. There's still a few, but it used to be predominantly black. A lot of English speaking folks blame the Mexican folks for the degrading of the horse business. They want to complain about, "This sumbitch is takin' all the jobs." Well, there's nobody else back there to get them. Americans ain't going to work seven days a week. Ain't no sense being hard on the Mexicans because they want to make a living and will work seven days a week. Quit cryin'. Leave them alone. Let them work.

I used to make a lot more money. In the '80s I was making $800 a week. They're not even making that much now. If a horse won a race, a groom could count on having $100 to $150 in his pocket the next morning. The owner would always give you $50 to $100. The trainer would kick you out $50 and the jockey would have his agent come over and bring you $50. That's on top of your paycheck. But that started to dry up 25 or 30 years ago. When they found out Mexicans would work seven days a week, with very little accommodations, four-deep wanting a job, and didn't expect to get a cut from the jockeys and owners, the stakes dried up.

You kind of feel sorry for them. All they want to do is make a living. I've never seen guys work harder than they work. I used to put them in my car and bring them in to work, fill out their Western Union forms. One time I said, "Why don't you just send the money to a mailbox in a money order?" and they said, "No, no, no, you can't do that." I said, "Why?" They said, "They steal it." I said, "Who steals it?" They said, "The people who work in the post office steal it. They know when money comes from America like that." Those Western Union prices were eating them alive. They worked seven days a week to send that money home, and live on just a little bit. They could put together a meal pretty cheap, though. A good meal. Lord knows I ate with them thousands of times. I don't remember eating anything they fixed that I didn't like.

———————

I was working on a horse one time at Skylight, going the wrong way, backing up, jogging the horse. I come out of the turn and look up at the racetrack, and I see this dude who was just learning how to ride. His horse was drifting like it had a DUI on the horse's back. I said damn, this boy look awful raggedy on that horse.

The normal protocol for that is you holler, "Inside! Inside!" Everybody hears you, get their ass out of the way, and leaves the inside wide open for you. But this dude didn't move and then I'm right on top of him, then I was going to zig or zag one or the other so I zigged it looked like he was going to zag. I went down to the rail and here he comes, right back in and hit my horse right on the tail end. I could feel it.

I had to get real forceful and just jerk him to the inside just to miss him. Me going that fast on a horse and collide with another horse, it ain't good for riders, the horses, nobody. I heard the bone pop. I said, "Oh Lord."

It seemed like it took a million years but finally I got him pulled up, jumped off, and sure enough, he'd busted that sesamoid. That's the ankle of the horse. I walked him back to the barn. Doc came out and looked at it and said, "Yeah, that's a busted sesamoid." So we took him on out there, and Doc went and he got the shot. It's a cocktail of three drugs. One is a tranquilizer, then they give them another one which lets you ease him down backwards and let them sit down on their ass, then you give another one and it stops his heart. Doc just eased him down, and he did all the right things and he got stiff. The wagon couldn't get there until the next morning so we all ran around and covered him up with a blue tarp just to show a little respect. We put bricks on each end so the wind wouldn't blow it off, and we got in our cars and we all went on home that night. You always feel bad when a horse breaks down like that. Something wrong with you if you don't.

This is the truth. I come to the barn the next morning and I notice all these cars in the parking lot. I said, "What in the world is going on here?" This girl named Amy said, "Andy!" I thought something was wrong the way she was hollering. I put on one of them

Usain Bolt sprints around there to see what's going on, and I had to take a double take: The horse we had put down was standing there grazing. I'd held his head as the horse went down. We covered him in a tarp. But he'd gotten up, and he was grazing and standing there in the round pen. That blows my mind. The drug evidently just did not work on him. Don't many of them get past that drug cocktail, but there he was grazing! He wasn't even sick.

That was a story for years around there. This horse really is standing. The manufacturer admitted that it was a bad batch of drugs. I just shook my head, and Amy said he was going to live out the rest of his life and she was going to breed a few mares to him. She took the horse home and turned him out, and two or three years later the horse was still kicking. After a while he never even limped anymore. I guess those old bones just healed on their own. She even put an old western saddle on him and rode him a little bit.

————————————

I had to give it all up because I was going blind. I got stopped at a roadblock one time coming in the back way from Bardstown. They stopped me there and checked my license; it had been expired for six or seven months. I said, "I'll be damned." I didn't know it. He said, "I have to give you a ticket, but if you go get your license then they will probably throw it out." So I went to go get my license, and they told me I had to take the vision test. They had these three-leaf clovers and one of the leaves had a dot in it, and you had to tell them which one has the dot in it. You had to get seven right to pass. I could not get no further than three. After the third clover, I couldn't find the white dot. So, that knocked my driving out starting right then.

I had glaucoma. I was going blind fast. The optic nerve from your eye to your brain starts to spring loose.

It's something I could have avoided if I'd had regular eye exams. They could have stopped it. When they found mine it was already out of control. I was probably in my middle to late 30s. It just went downhill from there and I had to give up training. I started galloping horses a lot more. I could get on and keep them straight. I kept galloping for a long time and I made a good living doing that. That used to blow people's minds. Can't see good enough to drive but I could gallop. You do it so long and it just becomes natural. It was no problem to ride with my glaucoma. I just couldn't drive. When you're a little man in a one man show, you got to do all the driving—getting hay and straw, moving the horses around—to keep labor costs down. I was still galloping when I was 55, but I had to quit soon after because I could not see. Horses would be jumping around and I wouldn't know where they were jumping.

I got my apartment at the Old School 16 years ago. It is the only place in the city where I can get to the doctor and live independently. It has a bank close by, transportation to my doctor's on Eastern Parkway and different places. At the time they opened it up, it was just going to be for racetrackers. They couldn't get it rented because a lot of racetrackers are only here for a short amount of time. They wouldn't pay their rent and all that. You know how racetrackers are. I have seen a lot of racetrackers come and go and die. Especially those old timers. I am the only person who has lived in my apartment since it opened up 16 years ago. There's about five racetrackers here now. Used to be a lot more. I was still going over to the racetrack then. Walking hots, tracking horses, cleaning stalls. Then one year when they closed at Churchill for the season and the horses went over to the Spectrum, I wasn't going to get rides, so I just quit. It was an adjustment, but you got to adjust. I stopped messing with horses entirely about seven years ago.

I still get up at four in the morning. I can't help it. Eyes pop open. I drink some coffee and walk outside. Come back and have a little bite to eat. Around 6:30 or 7:00 I watch the news. Then I go outside and just mingle around with guys heading over to work at the racetrack. If I could see I'd be over there walking hots too. I still love it.

There are always people passing through on their way to the racetrack, keeping you filled in with what went on that day over there. You'd be surprised by the amount of horsemen and racers that come through here and over to the Dairy Mart on 4th. There are a lot of horse players around the neighborhood here. Six or seven of them come through all the time. It's pretty easy to stay up on it right here. Lot of times you get a good tip and you make a bet. Sometimes you win and sometimes you lose. Different ones walk through here. Catfish comes through. He was a groom for years, and a good one. He was the type of guy that if he rubbed four horses he was always the last one to leave the shedrow. He took care of a horse. It's kind of crazy now that they're all old, retired, getting checks like me,

but they get up and go over there every morning and still love it.

A lot of people have *Racing Forms* around here. I got two or three friends around here who will read the *Form* to me. Read the line, start from the beginning: Where did he run last time? Read the fractions. Where'd he end up at? Read the comment line. Closing, fading, steady. Go to the next line if you're interested in that particular race. They just read like I was reading it myself when I had vision. Little stuff will pop up. When you listen, the numbers don't lie. What numbers sound good and what don't is all part of the game. Who he's running against, what caliber of horse, whether he's on the drop or on the up. I pay a lot of attention to jocks. Jocks do make a difference.

Horse racing has been good to me. Met some good people, been to a lot of places and met some people I never would have met otherwise. I'm not going to complain. The game has changed, but the game is good. I love the game. I'd probably do it all over again. /

Wayne Kestler

EMPLOYEE, WAGNER'S PHARMACY

PHOTO BY JOE MANNING

*I*was born over on Longfield Avenue. Been around here all my life. I wandered over to the backside in a diaper once through a hole in the fence. I was gone for hours. Walked over there and got familiar with the people from the racetrack and they brought me back. It's a wonder I didn't get killed back in them days.

I was probably 10 years old when I started walking horses. My mother didn't want me over there, but I went anyway. I used to hide my stuff out on the back porch and go to the racetrack every morning. I'd go there to walk horses, or ride a pony, or break a baby. You got to be very easy with them because they might try to kick you or bite you or hurt you. It's a big job, breaking yearlings. A big job. It ain't no part of your day. It's time consuming. I've been thrown off a few times but I never did get hurt.

It was very exciting back in them times. When we was young a lot of guys worked on the racetrack. Didn't make a lot of money, but you made a little bit. Everybody was poor anyway. There was kids that used to follow me over there and work too. One guy that used to follow me to the racetrack ended up becoming the senior vice president of Churchill Downs. Danny Parkerson. He started out potting flowers years ago and he progressed. We went to school together at Semple.

I used to jump on horses for J. Graham Brown. Seen Mr. Brown many a time on the backside. He had a black chauffeur with a black hat, black vest, white shirt, and a suit on. Old Man Brown never did get out of that Cadillac. He'd be at the three-quarter pole gap and from the car he'd watch us work them horses out of the gate. He'd just sit there by the fence. I can see Old Man now. They called him Bulldog. He didn't look like a bulldog, but they said he had a bulldog that lived down there on Broadway in that hotel with him. That's what I've been told.

He had good horses. He had a horse called Run for Nurse and a horse called He's a Pistol that got burned up at Churchill when that barn burned, if I'm not mistaken. I can't recall what year that was, but they had a fire over there, and that barn burned up.

To heat the tack rooms there used to be pot belly stoves in those barns and they didn't have no water heaters. They just had a 55-gallon drum of water with a fire underneath it for hot water. They didn't have hot water coming to those barns. You'd dip that hot water out to bathe the horses and to make the mash for the horses: oats, carrots, eggs, different things. Stir it up, put it in the feed tub, put a little salt in there.

They used to have mules and Clydesdales to rake the track or pull the float across it. I can see that man in that seat with a team of mules going by. And back then they had the old black kitchen. I used to hang out there. It was an old house with a rail going around it with a porch on the front of it. The blacks went in the black kitchen, and the whites went in the white kitchen back in them days.

I remember the old donut man too. He drove an old flatbed truck from the '40s with donuts and a couple pots of coffee. In the fall, when it was cool, you could smell that coffee, and you knew that donut man was coming.

The peanut man had his piece of plywood and his old nail apron on him for his money. He had one arm. He had peanuts, candy bars, tomatoes, apples, oranges—all kinds of fruit and stuff. Better not take them peanuts in that shedrow, though. That horse won't go to no race. That's a jinx on the racetrack. Ask anybody on that racetrack. They ain't going to throw no peanuts in the shedrow. That's the way it is. I don't know if they're bad for horses, but I know one thing: You better not take no peanuts to the shedrow. They'll run you out.

I've done everything you can imagine on the racetrack: galloped horses, worked horses out of the gate, mucked stalls, walked horses, broke yearlings. The only thing I didn't do is ride a race. I had the opportunity, but I passed.

I was getting ready to ride races and I left. I gave it up. I couldn't put up with them drunks. Back in them days there was a lot of winos on the track. I was young, and I couldn't put up with them drunks coming in there late at night in the tack room and raising hell. They'd come in the tack room at night and snatch your blanket off you and get all loud. They were too rowdy. I said, "To hell with this. This ain't for me. I've got to go."

I told the trainer to give me my money and put me on that Greyhound. When I got back to Louisville I was glad.

I've been clean for 31 years. I'm me. I'm nobody else. I don't try to please nobody. I made up my mind that I was tired of what I was doing. I wanted to live. And you can't live by fooling with chemicals. That ain't no life. You only fool yourself. You got to make a decision somewhere in your life. And if you get sick and tired of what you're doing, you'll give it up. And that's what I did. I used to go to AA. I learned that word "no." If I'd have kept living the way I used to live, I wouldn't be here today talking to you.

I'm 78 years old. I've worked here at Wagner's for 20 years. I did some painting and some stuff for Mr. Wagner when he was alive, and I just fell into this. We used to take care of all the silks in the jocks' room. We did that for several years. I'd go up there and get the silks, take them to the laundry, take them back to the jocks' room. They got their own dryer, washer, and stuff in the jocks' room now.

Everybody knows me. Most of the riders know me. Pat Day knows me. They all holler at me when they see me. The track is my home away from home. I was raised over there. I have a daughter got married over there in the Winner's Circle. I go over there all the time still. I never look back. What happened yesterday, I don't care. I'm looking forward to tomorrow. Living a clean life and positive thinking, that's what gives me joy. /

Clarke
Otte

RETIRED GROOM, PHOTOGRAPHER

I got into horses in the '40s when I first heard the Derby on the radio. My father and mother had gone to the Derby in 1941. They liked a horse called Our Boots and one called Mr. Long Tail. Whirlaway won the Derby that day. My grandfather and I listened to it on an old radio. I liked the horses back then and my mom started taking me to the track. She was a fan of the races too. My father wasn't particularly fond of horses, but he had a box at Churchill.

He was the Commonwealth's Attorney from 1930 to 1933. He was fairly prominent in law. One of the fellas he went to school with in England, Frank Murphy, became a Supreme Court Justice in 1942. My dad was pretty knowledgeable. He had a lot of famous cases. Hard cases. He had 43 capital convictions in three years, more than any prosecutor back then. I think that all affected him, because later he came out against the death penalty and switched sides—by the time I was born he was a defense attorney. He won a lot of cases doing that. He had 17 consecutive acquittals.

My father had a client who was a professional hotel thief. I met him once when he came to our house on Eastern Parkway. He was a very dignified fella. I don't know if he wore a pince-nez or a monocle, but he reminded me of a Frenchman. He and his wife worked as a team. She was a nurse of some kind. His voice was very distinctive, sharp, and forceful. He presented himself very professionally. He seemed like he was an influential fella, but he was a con man.

My mother said he traveled around and when he was here he'd retained my father for something. He had given my father a few things, including the camera that I used to shoot some of the pictures I took years later on the backside. It's a Zeiss Ikon. He got it probably back in the '30s. Nice lens. Good sharpness. That camera belonged to my mother, but she could never seem to take a picture with it. She said, "You should try it." I took a couple of pictures with it when I was in high school in the 1950s, but then I forgot about it.

Then later on I had come back from California where Silky Sullivan had been really prominent. He was a great stretch runner and he won the Santa Anita Derby in 1958. I read in the paper that he was coming to Churchill Downs to prepare for the Kentucky Derby and that he was going to land in Louisville. So I went out to the airport and met the plane and the trainer, Reggie Cornell, was there. I talked with him and said, "If I get a camera and follow you around, I'd like to take some pictures." And he said that would be fine.

Clarke and his grandfather reading the *Racing Form*.

I went home and found that little camera I'd tried out in high school. I bought some 127 film which made an inch by inch-and-a-half negative. I got to the track and found him in his barn. They were coming in from training and getting ready to graze the horse. I took a few pictures with my mother's camera. The shutter speed would only go to 1/75 of a second, and you had to guess the distance to focus. You didn't have all the sophisticated technology. It was a little challenging, but I was lucky and got some good pictures. When Silky Sullivan and Cornell got back to California, he wrote me and asked me to send him 25 copies. He said they had a Silky Sullivan fan club out there.

The first time I worked with horses was when I separated from my first wife in 1966. I had a drinking problem that ended that marriage. I made some bad choices. I went and got a job with Spendthrift Farms. Dick Fischer was the trainer, and Shelby Clark was the assistant. Coincidentally, Shelby was the jockey who'd ridden Whirlaway as a two-year old at Arlington Park in Chicago. I worked a couple years with them but I couldn't travel because I couldn't keep up with the expenses; I had two girls and had to keep up that responsibility. So I got a job at a distillery and later at the Ford truck plant.

I met my wife Marylene in 1968. We've been together 50 years now. We started over again and I started trying to recover from my problem. You are never cured of it: You arrest it, and you make a recovery, and then you maintain that through a spiritual program. We're spiritual beings in a human condition. I would have destroyed myself, except that some grace was holding on to me, guiding me where I didn't know. In my heart I wanted to be better. I wanted to help people. I wanted to do the right thing.

I had experience with horses. I loved them and I kept up with them. It was 12 years before I got back

to the track. In that time I really got into the camera work. I took photography courses at night out at the Louisville School of Art when I got off work at the truck plant. I learned about the camera and the chemicals and the developing—the technical part of it. I also took a painting course out there. I took photographs because I just like to remember the images. The ones that I really liked, I painted.

When the girls graduated high school, I told Marylene that I couldn't stand working at Ford any more. I didn't like it. I said, "I'm making a decision today. I'm gonna leave." I left one of the top factory jobs around to go back to the track to work with horses. It was a decision that I made in my heart. I said, "I'm gonna accept whatever comes up. I'm going to trust in the Lord." It was an intuitive decision. I didn't understand it. But I think the most important decisions you ever make are intuitive.

I came back and started working with Arnold Werner in 1979 and then I worked on the gyp circuit doing everything I could. I spent a winter in Sabinal,

Texas—down around San Antonio—hauling horses from Texas to New Orleans. Jobs would run out and I'd get another one. I was a holder for a blacksmith. I even had some assistant training. Finally I got a job with Neil J. Howard in 1986.

Working with horses was something that kind of worked on the nature of my mental state. I felt comfortable with the horses. My mind was better suited for that. Some of those years were tough. Sometimes I would pray that Serenity Prayer over and over when I was walking hots. You know, the last line of the Serenity Prayer is asking God for the wisdom to know the difference. I made the commitment and it strengthened me. I was grateful I got to go on another day. It was a part of my journey. I had a lot of help from Marylene and now I'm able to take care of her. I'm glad I'm able to do that.

Working with horses was just something I wanted to do and be a part of. I didn't achieve any great success. But I saw a lot of things that are very interesting. I was around interesting people and good horses. So it was worth it to me. /

Photographs by Clarke Otte

Papa Jim was from New Orleans. He worked for Louis Roussel there on Louisiana Downs racetrack. And he helped Harthill when he was down there in the '82 or '83 season. Harthill had a horse—Real Westport—that he was hoping to get to the Derby, but didn't make it. When Harthill came back, Jim came back with him to work a while. Next time I ran into him was about five or six years later down at Louisiana Downs. I was down there with Summer Squall, and I went over to the kitchen to get something to eat, and I ran into him there. His name was Jim. Papa Jim, they called him. He always had that cigar. —*Clarke Otte*

That's Percolator Bates. They called him that because he'd percolate that chicory coffee down in New Orleans in the morning. He always had a fifth of good bourbon too. Bates was with Doc all the time. He knew how to handle Harthill. Doc could be racist in his talk. He might cuss them out and call them racist names, and some guys couldn't handle it. But Bates and Eddie Bonefont knew how to handle Doc. They never paid any attention to him. They just knew how to handle him, and Harthill took care of them. —*Clarke Otte*

Tommy Long goes way back with Harthill. Way back. His name was James Crawford. He ran a lot of horses for Doc. Baylor Hickman was Doc's father-in-law, and he owned a distillery in Canada. Hickman gave Tommy that car. Left to right: Houston, Roy Dixon, Tommy Long, Beady, Red. —*Clarke Otte*

Slim had one leg longer than the other. He was a good dude. He and my stepdaddy used to be drinking partners. They liked Old Forrester and ET, Early Times. They were good horsemen. —*Catfish*

When I was working for Neil, Tommy Long had come over saying he wanted me to do something. "You want me to dress up, and you'll take my picture?" He kept asking me until I agreed and met him over at the rec hall. He put on some silks, and wanted his picture in them. I took this one of Tommy and the guy who ran the lifestyle center, Bill Chenault. —*Clarke Otte*

Scotland Yard liked me and he kind of took care of me. Here he's pulling a $10 win ticket out of his pocket to show me. He was on to some horse. He was connected with everything and he knew everything. That's why they called him Scotland Yard. He had a real sharp line and could talk slick. You might say, "That guy's lucky," and Yard would say, "He could fall out of a jet plane, shit through the eye of a needle, and land on a haystack without a scratch." I had a picture of the horse Mahmoud who won the '36 Epson Derby. It was a great black and white, a snow scene. He's where you get a lot of your grays in this country. First one to show his blood is Determined, and he was the first gray to win the Derby. Well, Yard liked that picture. He said, "Man, I'd like to have that picture sometime." Well, that photo had been given to me in 1954, but once, when Yard was in the hospital, I gave it to his son to give to him. It was in a nice white frame. He knew something about Mahmoud, and he liked that snow scene. I wrote an inscription on the back that said, "To Scotland Yard, good friend and co-worker." A couple years later, I got a hold of him and said, "You know, Yard," I said, "let me get that picture that I gave you. I'm gonna make a copy of it." And that's where I got my copy. He was going to his job at the Spectrum, where he was a guard. He knew everybody. He'd come around and see everybody. He had a heart attack. John Robertson came in the barn and told me. —*Clarke Otte*

That's PJ. He galloped horses for John Hill and also for Old Man Leroy. He come from across the water. Cuba or something. —*Catfish*

Doc had this horse, Real Westport. They wanted to make him a Derby horse. That's Neapy. He was a good hand, but he couldn't take Harthill. He went on to study plumbing or electricity. Anyway, he went into the trades. He got away from the track. —*Clarke Otte*

Jim Keefer won a lot of races at Miles Park and Churchill. That's a groom named Sam. We worked together a couple times. They were both good horsemen. —*Catfish*

Janie MacDonald and a horse called Ralph. —*Clarke Otte*

Mr. Potter (left) knew me through my parents. He was a photographer around town and has all of his pictures over at the University of Louisville Archives in the R.G. Potter Collection. —*Clarke Otte*

That's Royal Orbit. He ran fourth in the Derby then he won the Preakness. That's Reggie Cornell who trained Silky Sullivan. —*Clarke Otte*

Maurice Sanchez gave me this picture. That's Eddie Sweat bringing Secretariat over to the track on Derby Day. This was taken near the gap over by Lukas's barn. —*Clarke Otte*

In 1959 I was working for Sears giving roofing estimates. I was driving around down by the track one day and I saw Northern Dancer grazing over by Longfield Avenue. I'd seen him on TV and recognized those white stockings of his. He was a little horse, only about 15 hands, but well muscled. I went back there and took these pictures of Northern Dancer and his groom Willie Brevard. —*Clarke Otte*

That's Old Man Ferris on the left and Sam Dixon in the back. Uncle Willard is on the right and that might be his stepson Jay. The little one looks like another Dixon. —*Catfish*

That's my cousin James Earl Richard. He's Red's brother. Later on he worked on the maintenance crew. —*Clarke Otte*

See all them guys in flat hats? Every morning you'd see them out there in front of Wagner's. That's Lefty Erlanger on the corner. He ate breakfast at Wagner's every morning. He's the only bookmaker in town that would book baseball. He was the only one who knew how. —*Neil Huffman*

Mo and James Albert. They worked for Mike Law. —*Catfish*

This is Bob and Gene Rice. They were brothers. That's the Churchill Downs blacksmith shop. That's where the ferriers hung out. —*Clarke Otte*

Jack Reynolds was a famous horseshoe man. He was a specialist. The feet are so important, and there's quite a bit to it, shoeing a horse. Jack was kind of a hero. He learned horse-shoeing and ferrier work in the cavalry in World War I. Harthill really idolized Jack. He'd fly him in from Independence, Missouri to Louisville or California and pay for all his expenses. I think Doc always had the urge to be a blacksmith or something. Doc would get all excited when Jack was coming. He'd put on his chaps like he was going to shoe a horse himself. He shod a lot of great horses, like Spectacular Bid. That's Gayle Brumlee who always worked for Harthill. —*Clarke Otte*

At that time Willard Pinkston was one of the best exercise boys on the backside. I remember one time I was working for Suddie Whitaker; we called him Little Man. Uncle Willard and Little Man galloped this horse in the snow in the winter time at Churchill to get him ready once. When they got him fit here galloping in the snow, they took him somewhere and he won by 15 lengths. He was the best. He could handle a mean horse. He could really handle a rough horse. He was a good horseman. He raised me. I lived right next door to him. —*Catfish*

Willard Pinkston was the first guy to show me a few things when I came back to the track in about '79. I'd worked with horses earlier in the '60s for a while, but it had been a long time, like 15 years. Willard showed me some ins and outs, little things like how to put on a twitch, hook it back on the halter, and clip it to the wall so you can work with a horse in the stall. He retired and went blind. He lived over there on M Street, a couple streets down from Churchill, in The Hill. He sent a message once for me to come see him. He wanted a picture that I'd taken of him walking a horse. That's why he'd sent for me. I couldn't imagine why, but he wanted to give it to his grandchildren. He galloped Federal Hill, who ran fifth in the Derby in '57. That was the year Iron Liege won. Iron Liege, Gallant Man, Round Table, Bold Ruler, and Federal Hill was next. And Willard galloped him. —*Clarke Otte*

That's Bimp on the end. My wife did his taxes. I don't remember his real name. He worked for Calumet when he was younger. Then he went to work at International Harvester, and then he came over and worked at the track for Arnold Werner. Next to him is Tommy Long. That's Centerfield Slim. He got hit by a car and had one leg shorter than the other. He was a night watchmen and did odd jobs. That was his little dog there. Angel Montano had a dog called Wino and he'd come over because he liked Slim's little dog. That's a guy named Ferris there in the chair. He was a retired fireman. He's probably waiting for one of these fellas to get free and help him with his horses. —*Clarke Otte*

That's Tommy, Arnold Werner, L.C. Cook, and James Wilson. Mr. Wilson lived right on Central Ave. in that good looking house they just remodelled. That's where he lived.
—*Catfish*

Everybody respected Tommy Long. White, black, whatever—everybody respected him. Tommy was just a hell of a guy to be around. Just a pure horseman. Me and some friends started working with him when we were around 11 years old. He was more like a father to us than our fathers were. Tommy would come through the neighborhood and say, "What're y'all boys doing? Let's go. Get in the truck. We gonna go see some thoroughbreds." Mom would say, "Where y'all going?" And we would tell her we were with Uncle Tommy.
—*Plummie*

That's my man, there. Tommy Long. He was from Highland Park. His real name was James Theodore Crawford. He practically raised me. I was around him all the time and learned a lot from him. He was one of the blacks that always had a horse or two. He worked for Harthill. Harthill was a tough man, but Tommy was all right with him.
—*John Lee Robertson*

Larry Melancon was a good rider. Only jock who won more stakes races at Churchill is Pat Day.
—*Neil Huffman*

Chelsea Bailey

EXERCISE RIDER, MMA FIGHTER

I grew up on a farm in Enumclaw, Washington, east of Seattle. It's the last city before you get up to Mt. Rainier. We had cows, chickens, goats, sheep, and pretty much any animals I would collect and bring home. When I was young I always wanted a horse, but I started out with a pony. Our place was actually inside city limits but had been grandfathered in, so we were technically allowed to have horses. Our neighbors on each side had parcels of land—there were about six houses, each one sitting on about three acres. On the back of our property there was a Safeway parking lot.

A lady my mother worked with had an old barn for saddlebreds with a bunch of leftover things—a whole entire tack room—that she ended up selling. Mom told her that I had gotten a pony. The lady said, "I have a pony cart," and Mom got it. It was meant for miniature horses. It was pretty rusted and the harnesses that were left in the barn were too badly molded and broken. My mother found someone with a harness for sale and wrapped it up at Christmas time so that I had no idea what it was. My pony had never had anything on her, and I went out and threw everything on her right then and there, just jimmy-rigging and tying things together. Then I went on YouTube and looked up "how to do a pony harness," and that got me about 80 percent there, but she did just fine.

She was old. Her name was Molly. She had previously been a lesson pony, so she was pretty well-mannered and bomb-proof. At first she was a little confused, like, "What's behind me? What's going on?" I took her and I led her around to see how she was steering, making her turn. Then I hopped in, took her around, and she would make little figure eights. Later we'd get in that little pony cart and go to the McDonald's drive-thru, or I'd take my brother to the skatepark. No cops, no police, nobody ever said anything. Everybody knew where we lived and who we were, so it was kind of a no harm no foul.

That lady I had gotten the harness from had some Arabians that were in racing. She said, "I have horses if you want to come out, clean up some stalls, and learn some things," and of course I said, "Absolutely." I started hanging out with her a lot, and she pretty much took me under her wing. In a way, Kathy saw me as a daughter figure. She dragged me along to everything, and that was my first real introduction to a racetrack.

My mother passed away when I was younger. My parents had gotten divorced and my mother was taking care of all three of us. She got cancer and had three or four months to decide what she wanted to do. My aunts and uncles already had their own families and kids that were our age, and they didn't really want to take us in.

If we went to foster care they wanted all three of us to stick together, and it's hard to find one child a home, let alone three. And my dad at the time was not a fit parent. After the divorce, there were some red flags that said it was probably not the best environment for these children. My grandmother stepped up to the plate with my grandfather, and they took us in. They lived north of Spokane, Washington. So we crossed the state, and I had to restart. I went from being in more of a fast-paced city out to the country.

Before, I'd been riding my Arabian, doing all sorts of English saddle activities, but over there, nobody did any of that. All of the kids there were on these Western horses. I had this pretty little fancy thing, an Arabian, and everybody's got these quarter horses, Appaloosas, paints and mustangs—backyard horses that have been out in the fields, whereas my horse had been in a stall. It was a city versus country kind of a deal. That's when I got into a whole different crowd of people. These were country folk.

Everybody's sitting on the back of their horse trailers and trucks drinking beer, saying, "Let's watch a rodeo!" It was a completely different atmosphere, way more laid back. I was teaching my horse how to do barrels and things like that. I had all these kids teaching me, so it kind of helped me fit in at school because I had some people I could hang out with and talk to.

Every town in that part of Washington has a fair, a little get together, and usually it's the biggest event all summer. Some of the kids were talking about doing the Indian relay races at the fair. There's the Spokane Indian Reservation, and there's a lot of Native Americans all around there. "We have a horse and you take it around the track and then we switch off riders." There's no saddles, and they pull up on a dime and then they switch riders, and another person's up and taking off.

That's how these kids ride. They jumped on horses and rode bareback. They would just use twine and tie it around the mouth and just take off. They didn't even need bridles. It was kind of a Wild West scene. I thought, "Wow, I want my horse to be like that." English style is cool—being all fancy with your $200 bridle—but jumping on your horse with a piece a rope around its neck and taking off? That's 10 times cooler to me. They asked if I wanted to do it. I said, "Heck yeah!" I ended up competing one summer. It was so much fun.

That type of riding—riding a horse bareback, having no stirrups to use on a horse that's going full speed—helped me a lot with what I'm doing now. When you've been on something that you have no leverage on and you can get it to stop for the next person to get on, that's just an amazing feat. I've gotten run away with before—pulling back, trying to get a horse to stop, standing up with my feet on the dashboard—and it's not stopping. One thing that I've always taken with me, something I've done since I was a kid, is that any time I ride, I always have the mane. That's how the Indians ride and that's how I've always rode. Having the mane and knowing that I'm connected to the horse gives a better sense of balance for me. A lot of the trainers don't like it because you can pull out their mane a little bit. I never tell them that I do it. It's just how I ride and it works for me and that's how I feel most comfortable.

I got into some trouble in high school. It was pretty much as soon as my mom died and I had just moved over there to Spokane. A girl I didn't get along with kept calling me names and making fun of me, so I did the right thing. I went and told the principal, "I'm getting harassed. This girl's bothering me. I'm letting you guys know about it." Most of this was taking place on the computer. This was back when AOL Instant

Messenger was a big thing. They said, "Well, it's not school so there's nothing we can really do about it."

It kept going on and on and one day I snapped. I had a fit. I went into the art room, found the biggest pair of scissors I could find. She was down in the courtyard where everybody was congregating, so I went down there, punched her in the face, knocked her down, got her in a half-nelson, and pulled the scissors out the back of my pocket and cut her ponytail off.

I had just come over from the coast, where we handled things differently. I'm not going to take anybody's shit. I'm going to do something about it. In a way, that built up my reputation. Nobody messed with me after that. The scissors might have been a little excessive. I think I was trying to make a statement. Everybody knew who I was and heard the story. They all called me Chelsea the Barber. I got assault with a deadly weapon on my record. She said I was trying to kill her because I had scissors. I ended up going to juvie for a week and a half.

Juvie really wasn't that bad. My parole officer said most people cry or get upset about it. I don't think he knew what I had gone through. I had said to him, "I've been through a lot more that most kids have been through at this age in my life. I realize my consequences; I'm not denying my actions." It's been a long time, but I still keep in contact and say hi to him. He still knows me.

Prison's probably a completely different thing than being around a bunch of punk ass teenagers who have messed around and done whatever. But I took it, and I learned my lesson from it. I think a lot on what's right, what's wrong. I know the difference. I always think, "What are the consequences going to be?" I try to think before I act. I didn't think that fight was going to escalate that far. I'm not a mean person.

I love animals. If there's something I can do I always try to help. I try to be a better person. If I see some garbage I try to pick it up and throw it away. You have to be the change you wish to see.

Attitude is everything. You can take anything negative that is thrown at you and try to turn it into a positive, or you can sit around and mope about it. Dealing with the death of my mother, moving to a new place, I knew I had all of this anger and hate and it was not healthy. I needed to channel it somewhere. For me, stepping into the wrestling room and going up there every day for practice and just getting my ass kicked by all the boys taught me some discipline. It taught me to be humble. It taught me a lot of mental strength.

There were no other females on my team, and I only wrestled a handful of girls in high school. If I went to an event and there was a girl, it was often an exhibition match. At a tournament, there were only guys in there. At all the meets versus other schools my coach would tell me what weight class he wanted me in and I'd say, "Okay, I'll get to wherever you need me to be to wrestle at."

I had to deal with a lot of sexism and a lot of people who said, "Oh, a girl," and didn't see the things I was capable of. For me it was fuel. It was something I could use to prove a point. They'd say, "Oh, you do this like a girl," and I could say, "Well, look at these weak ass boys I've beaten. What's that say? What's their excuse?"

I'm a rough and tumble girl. I grew up on a farm. I'm tougher than your average city girl. It's like instinct. You either have that aggression or you don't have that aggression. You're either mentally tough or you're not mentally tough. You can't buy it. It's something you just have to have. And I have a lot of it. It pushes me forward.

I placed third three years in a row. My senior year I took state. I was Washington State freestyle champion at 119 lbs. In college, I ended up winning the collegiate national wrestling championship at 112 lbs.

A lot of the guys in my high school didn't get the opportunity to wrestle in college. You had to be really good. A lot of them, as soon as they got out, went straight to MMA, mixed martial arts. It was mostly hillbilly boxing. Some friends told me, "We found a fight for you. This girl's only been training for six months." I said, "Well I ain't trained at all. I don't even know how to throw a punch." I went on and took the fight. Even though I didn't know any submissions, wrestling's the strongest and best base to have in MMA. If you look at anybody who holds the belt titles right now, most of them are effective wrestlers.

I was just looking to take her down. You have four-ounce gloves on. Your hand is wrapped and then you have just a little bit of leather there for your gloves. So when you get hit, you can feel it. It hurts. They put Vaseline on your face, around your eyes, on your bones, so the leather doesn't pull and break open your face. I remember getting hit. It's one of those things where

you fight back, but the only way to not get hit is to get out of the way. So you're trying to circle out. You're looking for an opportunity, waiting for that person to step and then you think, *There's my shot.*

In wrestling, you don't get hit when you go in for a shot. I went in for a shot and then the girl punched me in the face. I thought, *Oh hell no.* I picked her up and slammed her down. The whole crowd went nuts. I held her down and had her pinned. She couldn't do anything and everyone was yelling, "Punch her. Punch her." I got her in a crucifix so both of her arms were blocked. The gloves we wear don't have any padding on the sides, so you can hammer fist somebody in the face. It's very effective. I sat there and did that. It ended up going into a decision because I couldn't submit her and she kept moving around and trying to get out. But I pretty much whooped her butt for all three rounds, and I won.

A bunch of promoters were there and they all came in like hawks. "What's your name? What's your information?" They were immediately interested in me. From then, it was like wildfire. I fought a couple of times in Washington and over in Idaho. I was fighting around. I was still training, but at the same time still wrestling and going to college. I got a scholarship to Yakima Valley Community College in Yakima, Washington. I wrestled there for two years, got my associate's, then transferred to Oklahoma City University, a private university that was very expensive but had the best women's wrestling team in the United States.

When I moved to Oklahoma, I was able to get fights there. I wanted to go to a good gym, and there was America Top Team, which is known to be one of the best gyms in the United States. It's a really expensive gym. I went in there with all the confidence in the world and said, "I really want to train here. I'm not going to be able to afford it, but I want to train here.

What can you do for me?" It was my time where I could have been turning pro. I wanted to get a couple more fights. The only difference between amateurs and pros is getting paid.

My coach, Juliano, was from Brazil. He was a black belt in Brazilian jiu-jitsu. He got me and a couple guys from the gym, all three Americans, on a card down in Brazil. I had my first pro fight down in Brazil against this giant, steroided-out girl, Juliana Costa. Brazil is known for steroids. I have pretty big arms for a girl, but this girl was definitely way bigger. I was the underdog. We were in the same weight class, but really I'm a 105'er. Because of the lightest UFC weight class is 115 pounds, I've always been fighting up a weight class because there's hardly ever any smaller girls. I've even fought up to 130 before. I've never even weighed that in my life. 120 is pushing it for me. It's hard for me to be up there.

I had never been to Brazil before my first pro fight. It was beautiful. It was awesome. We went down there for two weeks and trained on the beach. It was really nice. That's where my coach grew up. He speaks fluent Portuguese and was able to jump in his parents' car and was show us all sorts of things. We went to see Christ the Redeemer.

The venue was really big. I think it seated 20,000 people. It was on national television. They had a news crew come out in the morning to watch us train, film us on the beach. In America, I'm trying to post things on Facebook and get myself known, and nobody cares. I go down here and they're asking me all these questions, people want to take pictures with me. It was a really cool experience. They had a vehicle going around the city that they put a picture of me on, like a promotion. My coach said, "It's going to be a big fight." I'm thinking, *Oh, cool*. When he takes me to the stadium and it's this ginormous place, I said, "Oh wow.

This is a big deal." Costa had had one fight at the time and she had won it. She was Brazilian. Brazilian jiu-jitsu was her forte. This was the Americana versus the Brasilia. I wanted to submit her. I wanted to beat her in her own game in her own country.

I was the co-main event of the night. We had two other Americans come up that were fighting on the card. One got kicked in the balls, and as he went down in pain, his opponent kicked him in the face. It wasn't right. It was very unsportsmanlike. Both of the American guys ended up losing the fights and I feel like it was bad reffing, bad judging. He didn't win that fight and it was very unfairly judged. Seeing my team lose, especially in a cheap way, was upsetting to me and my coach came in enraged and said, "You don't have to fight. She didn't even make weight. They're being super unfair. You don't have to do this."

When we weighed in, Costa didn't make weight. She was already bigger than me and she didn't make weight. I said, "No, let's do this. I came down here. I'm going to do it. I didn't fly all the way down here and train this hard for nothing."

I think Costa was like two or three pounds overweight. My coach went ballistic. If you don't make weight, they give you an hour and you have to lose that weight and then come back and weigh in. My coach lost it. He said, "My fighter made weight. Yours didn't." She gets fined for missing weight. The ref said that if I lost the fight, I would get the show fee but also get 30 percent of her purse because she missed the weight.

In the first round, I got in a little bit of a boxing match with her. She got me once right in the jaw. I saw a little bit of stars and thought, *Whoa. This bitch hits* hard. I knew that, whatever training, she also had steroids behind her. When the round ended and I got on the chair for the break before the next round, my coach said, "You need to take her down. You need to

get a TKO or you need to submit her. Don't stand with her, she's way bigger than you. We don't know how much she weighs. You're smaller. If you're wrestling, you're going to be able to take her down."

I took her down within the first minute. I mounted on top of her. I was punching her in the face and she put both of her hands up to try to block me: the perfect set up for an arm bar. It's the most white belt, lowest level thing you can do to block like that and leave your arm open, so it was my perfect opportunity. I got her in an arm bar and she tapped the ground. In the video you can see her face where she knew she lost. She was not happy about it. The crowd went wild. I don't know why, but apparently not a lot of people liked her.

I had my Washington state flag with me that I'd sewn together with the USA flag, so one side was Washington and the other side was the United States. My coach threw it over and I just took off running with it. I was super excited and afterwards people were getting photos with me. It was really cool.

Before we went out that evening, my coach goes over to the announcer and holds his hand out, and this guy gives him a stack of cash. He comes back over and hands it to me. "Here's her 30% because she didn't make the weight." We rounded up everybody else and went out and took off to grab some dinner. I wanted to drink a beer that night because in training you don't get to drink or anything. I wanted to try a Brazilian beer.

I had some friends from Washington that were MMA fighters and they were living in Vegas. When I was going to college, we had gone to the same gym, and I just always kept in contact with them. They said, "Hey, why don't you come live with us? We have a fighter house and room for you if you want." I took the invitation, and moved to Vegas.

I ended up meeting my husband David at a club there. He was there on stag duty—one of his friends was getting married. We talked about horses and stuff. When me and him got married, he got me back into horses. He's the one who taught me how to ride a racehorse after so much time away from horses.

In January 2016, I got a job exercising at Oaklawn in Hot Springs, Arkansas. When I moved here after Oaklawn, our first year in Kentucky, I was introduced to a trainer named Karen Riddick. I was told, "You guys would connect really well because she does jiujitsu." I said, "Okay, a girl who does horses and jiujitsu. I don't really meet many people like that." They

either do one or the other. They don't really do both. She has her own horses and she's got her own stock. She trains them and runs them. She's an exercise rider herself. She kind of does it all. Sometimes she runs horses at Churchill. She mostly races them up at Indiana Turfway and Belterra.

David was going to be going to the track. I had talked to a friend who said, "You should go out to La Grange. Maybe you could find a job out there." I just called Karen and asked, "Hey, could I come and help you out?" She said, "Yeah, sure. I'm in barn number two. Get here at 7:00 and I'll see you." I get out there and it was my first time really seeing my vision of Kentucky.

Coming from Hot Springs in Arkansas and a little training center with a three-quarter mile track and old, rundown stalls, I thought, "Finally. This is Kentucky. This is horse racing. People take pride in this. This isn't some jimmy-rigged shackle barn. People have dropped some money and actually made this place beautiful."

Karen and David taught me to ride a racehorse. I have to give a lot of credit to her for taking the time and teaching me. I've walked hots. I've groomed. Now I'm an exercise rider. My trainer is Jinks Fires. I follow a lot with what he does to see his training methods. He's an old-school trainer and he shows me the ropes and tells me a lot of things.

Every single day when I go out to ride a horse, I know which ones have an issue here or there, and I'll try and do something a little different if possible. When I jump on a horse I don't go out there and think, *I'm getting $15 per head, per ride.* I go out there and make sure that the horse's needs are accommodated.

I might not have had a good day on this horse, but there's always tomorrow, and I can try this tomorrow to see if this works. One horse I ride, if she has a bunch of other horses going around her, she gets really frazzled and falls apart. If a horse goes whizzing past her, she wants to keep right up with him and loses her composure. She gets all stressed out and thinks, "Oh, race mode." But today we took her out later, and there weren't as many horses around, and she was relaxed the whole time. Now I know that, for her, if she has breezers coming up, or if there's people who are coming on the track, it stresses her out. So I'll give my note to the trainer and say maybe if we take her out later, she'll be more relaxed and be able to be trained better.

One horse that I got ready recently raced in the Clark Handicap. It's a big $500,000 race. The horse was a front runner. When he gets dirt in his face, he doesn't like it and spits out the bit and just quits, so he has to be in front. Not saying that he has to be leading the pack the whole time, but the moment he gets dirt in his face, he'll just sit back and he won't do it. Some horses are just frontrunners. There's a lot of things to consider with the horses, like knowing sprinters from distance horses. It also depends on the horse. Some horses don't mind the dirt. Some horses are stalkers. They'll just hang in there, hang in there, hang in there. Some horses have a turn of foot, which means they can all of a sudden pick up speed and move faster. Some are closers. They can use all their energy and go the distance but pick it up more at the end.

You have to have a really good clock in your head to be able to know the times. When you're out there in the crowd and you're watching, sometimes you see how fast they get to the quarter pole and the time comes up, and you say, "Man they're flying. Why are they going so fast?" Horses burn out. If they breeze ⅝ of a mile, they're just done. But you'll notice the horses hanging in the back: The jockeys are in their heads. They're going through the times. Those are the ones that you see come up from all the way in the back and win the race. It's important to know things like that, to be able to space it out.

My husband knew a girl who couldn't quite learn to count her time, so she was using a metronome. That's what my husband recommended to me. He said, "Why don't you get one? You use it in music to keep a beat, so why not use it in horse racing? It's a tool." I used to play piano a little bit when I was growing up and I used to have an old-school one. It went tick, tick, tick, and it helped with the bars and speeds of your playing. In your head, you're counting *one Mississippi, two Mississippi, three Mississippi.* I got a little clip-on metronome and I attached it to my helmet. When I am galloping in the mornings or breezing I have it on. The beep on the helmet, my metronome, tells me my times and helps me know what speed to keep the horse at. It doesn't spook the horse. It's very quiet. Only I can hear it. Even when I'm going to sleep at night, I can still hear this beeping going on.

Some horses are bullies. Some of them know their size and they will try to take advantage of you. There are reasons why you use certain equipment on them to control them. You are in control of the horse, but there are times where they get really strong and try to run off on you. There are some cases where the horse runs away in the wrong direction. That's why you have to look around and listen for the sirens. The other morning it was super foggy and that's kind of dangerous if there is somebody breezing, for example. And what if there was a loose horse that nobody had seen yet or had just gotten loose and darted into the rain? You're going top speeds coming in there. Things can go wrong. That's why it's very important for everybody to look after each other and do the things you're supposed to do—telling somebody if you are going on the right or the left of them, or pulling up when necessary. It can be a hazard when you don't do things the right way, like galloping really slow, which is like driving really slow in the fast lane. Or when somebody is breezing horses and somebody is on the rail, you yell, "Rail!" so that they know somebody is coming. But because you've got the wind coming in your face, you can't hear what's behind you, so you have to keep looking to see what's going on. It can be dangerous out there. There's no meetings where somebody says, "Everybody, let's review what we're supposed to do."

I've been up in the air about getting my apprentice license. I've had a lot of people who've asked me. I've said, "Yeah, I'd like to ride someday." Since I started officially riding in April 2017, I'm still fairly new to it.

I'd have to get a jock agent, somebody who'd be able to take me around to trainers and say, "Hey would you like to ride her?" I'm known out there, so it's not that I'm just a nobody. People have seen me. It's not like I'm coming in from California and people aren't that knowledgeable about me. But I've never gone up and asked my trainer, "Hey, if I took out my bug, would you throw me on one, would you give me a shot?" That's what it comes down to. You take out that bug and, once you do it, you have a whole year until it expires.

Some people try to progress so quickly that they were a groom and then, all of a sudden, they just jump on the horses and ride them, and then they're a jockey. But there was no way I would ever have been able to do that. I want to make sure I go about the right steps and find myself a good jockey agent, somebody who's going to work for me, somebody who's going to help me ride at a good track. You come here to Kentucky and you got all the big dogs. You got everybody coming from New York, California, Florida, and you're the minnow in the shark tank.

The whole point of you taking your bug out is for you to get the experience and to have the opportunity. I want that fair opportunity, just being around every single top-notch jockey. Why not? Why not give it a shot? I want to represent women. On Breeder's Cup day 2018, there was not a female jockey out there. I would've loved to just see one.

Nobody knows if I could become a top-level jockey, but I'd just like to be out there trying it and doing it. I'd like to set an example or even be an inspiration for other women. Same thing as fighting. There's a good number of female fighters out there, but a lot of my friends don't know about them. It makes me feel good when other women look at me and think, *Maybe I'll try doing a kickboxing class, or boxing, or self-defense.* It's not just boys who box, and it's not just boys who ride. /

Lee Lockwood

OUTRIDER

My whole life, Dad had one or two race-horses at home. He was a backyard trainer in Sallisaw, Oklahoma. Our place was very small, three acres or so. Racehorses were Dad's passion, so I grew up with racing. From the time I can remember remembering, Dad had a horse that he was taking out to the track to run. I tagged along and would stand there on the rail watching the horses race by. I loved everything to do with horse racing. I had to be a part of it somehow.

Dad's a pretty optimistic feller. He don't mind buying green bananas. He had a couple good quarter horses and a nice thoroughbred not too many years ago. I'm saying nice by Blue Ribbon Downs standards; That was where we used to run. He never had a lot of success on a stage like Churchill. He was a small-time guy and had mild success training a horse or two for outside people, but all horse trainers dream of having the big horse.

When we still lived in Texas, he took a string of horses as a private trainer for a season and I'd ride out with him on the weekends to the races. He qualified a nice little filly for a futurity. Her name was I'm a Jet Girl. She was an Easy Jet-bred filly; he was a very prolific sire, and there were a lot of good Easy Jet mares that came

out at that time. I remember seeing myself as a little kid in winning pictures at a little track called Maynard Downs, down by San Antonio. I'm smiling in the photo. I was always excited to be in the winner's circle. Winning cures all ills.

When I was young, Dad got a position with the railroad as either a conductor or a brakeman, and we moved from Texas to Oklahoma. We moved in the summer and I didn't have any friends. I was a shy kid to begin with—closed off and quiet. I'd sit over in the corner and let y'all talk, and if somebody spoke to me I was more than happy to speak back. I wasn't the person that was going to go out there and make friends easily. So I spent time with our horses and talked to them. Horses can be like big dogs. They can be your best friend or they can kind of give you the cold shoulder if they think something's up. They've got that personality. They're *this* close to being human.

I'd just get up on my horse and ride, head out into the ditches. We lived just far enough out of town that I could ride down the ditches on the highway to some dirt roads or some trails. Saddle up in the morning and ride all day long. Eastern Oklahoma is a lot like around here: a lot of trees and small hills, not mountainous by any means.

I was 12 when I first started galloping. We had a mare that Dad had raced and then retired. There was a training track just a few miles down the road from us, so we'd trailer the horses up. Dad would usually gallop the racehorse, and I would gallop the old mare, Foreign Starlet. Dad let me ride her to learn how to gallop, what to do and what not to do. I had a very limited skill set then. It was sort of a baptism by fire. You got to learn how to stay on. Where I came from, it was a lot more western riding—if you get on and stay on, it makes you a pretty good rider. Eventually, I got to ride the racehorses.

Dad taught me how to hold my hands and how to have rein pressure. You want contact with their mouth, but not pulling to where they're uncomfortable. When you're riding racing horses, you've always got a little bit of contact with the mouth. And as they want to run more, they pull you harder and harder. So you try to keep them as soft as possible early on so they don't get too strong too early. I can't count how many times Foreign Starlet ran off with me. She'd get to going a little too fast, and I couldn't get her to settle. She wouldn't go very far. She didn't need to run at all at her age. That horse taught me a lot. I think she lived to be over 30. She spent all her years on the place. Dad got several babies out of her, and then stopped breeding her. She just lived out her days there at Dad's place in Oklahoma. They buried her on the farm when she died.

When I was a kid I dreamed of being a jockey, but in high school I shot up about six or seven inches and that dream quickly went away. When we moved to Oklahoma, I met some people the same age as me who were bull riders. I'd seen a cowboy movie with this bucking barrel in it, and I said, "I've got to have one." So I went out and I built one out in the trees and I started riding it with my friends. I got an old steel drum, punched four holes in it and hooked four ropes up to it, found four trees that were roughly square to each other, and just tied one rope on each tree. I put garage springs on them—those big longs ones—and there it was. You had to have somebody pull it for you, and there were times we had a person on every rope and this thing would go 10 feet in the air. It was very different from a live animal, but it kind of ingrained in your subconscious the things that you do.

I was an adrenaline junkie when I was young. My friends were rock climbers, so I'd go rappelling and rock climbing with them—whatever it took to get the heart rate up. Maybe that's what attracted me to horse racing. I don't know what drugs do for people who are hooked on the dope, but bull riding sure gave me a high. When I started getting on live bulls, that was my replacement for my dream of being a jockey, and I figured I'd go for the rodeo dream for a while. It was all in good fun. I was never talented enough to go very far.

I was galloping horses at the racetrack and a jockey friend of mine invited me to ride up with him to Remington Park one day in Oklahoma City. He had a couple of horses to ride. On the ride he asked if I'd ever thought about going out east to one of the big farms or racetracks and seeing what it was like, and I said no. He said, "Well, I've always thought of it and I want to go try it out. If you want to go, it would help to cut the cost and what not." I said, "Yeah, I ain't doing nothing. I'll come see it." It's not like I was tied down there, so we split a place when we got up here.

We found a hotel that rented rooms by the week then came straight to Churchill Downs, which was a little intimidating at first. The hardest thing was getting through the security gate. They wouldn't let me through. Then I got to talking with a guy about the bull business. He loved the rodeo and was really into bulls, but he didn't have any. We got to talking about that and he said, "I'll take y'all around the backside and introduce you to

some people." So he got us through the gate and got us to where we could start talking to people.

I walked around the backside asking if anyone needed any help, but I didn't have any luck for the first few days because I was a taller guy and they all wanted the small people. There was a myth I'd heard out west that here in the eastern states, they like somebody who is a little bigger and stronger who can handle their big race horses. I was 20 or 21 and even skinnier than I am now, but they took one look at me and said, "You're too big." So I went over to Lexington and got on horses at the training center for a day, but I didn't like it at all. I didn't feel like I was going to be in a learning environment. I wanted to be around better horses and better people to learn from, people that you would look up to.

When I came out here, I wanted to see the other side of it. Back home, I was more interested in rodeo

and quarter horses because that was the environment I was in. You watch these big thoroughbred races on TV and these successful trainers, and I wanted to see what's the difference. The horse flesh is obviously the first thing you see: the size and the look. It's just a different caliber of horses. But I wanted to see how different people interact with them, and everybody has their own style; I found that out. There are people who are rougher or softer, but for the most part they're all good horseman—they can read a horse very well— and I wanted to observe what I thought looked like a better way. What are they doing to these horses that's different as far as training methods? I knew that there had to be a better way than being John Wayne.

Out west, people might train every third day. They might pony them a day, then gallop them two or three days later, and in between that all they did

was walk on a walking machine. But it's a different breed of animal from a thoroughbred. They're training them for two different routines. With a quarter horse, you want them to have that bottled up explosion. The average quarter horse race is 300 to 350 yards. They run straight away, stay in their lanes. It's over in the blink of an eye. It's drag racing versus NASCAR. It's better for quarter horses to do light work every day.

Here, I saw right away that people train every day. It was seven days a week. There was no weekend. There was no Sunday morning. Friday night didn't mean anything because Saturday morning you were getting up and going to the track. The biggest difference I saw was the consistency of the training. They don't miss a day. It seemed more professional. And the care these animals get, it's just two different worlds. It's like playing on a minor league team and being in the pros. In the minor leagues you're riding on the bus and you're lucky if you're able to wash your clothes in between stops, whereas in the pros somebody's handling your luggage from the plane to the five-star hotel room.

After I went to Lexington for a day, I came back to Churchill and met an assistant trainer, and we got to talking about quarter horses. I probably made a joke about how I like quarter horses more than thoroughbreds. He was a quarter horse guy too and he says, "Come back tomorrow and we'll put you on a couple horses and see what you got." So I started working for him, and I worked that spring here at Churchill.

I was making good money. I don't know if it was that much more at the time than I was making in Oklahoma, but it was certainly a lot easier on the body. In Oklahoma, I was getting on 20 horses a day; here I was getting on six or seven. I stayed in a tack room here at the track for a while. It wasn't even a private tack room. There was a set of stairs that led to the upstairs room. So when the guys who lived upstairs came down the stairs to go to work, that was pretty much my alarm clock. When they opened the door, it was time for me to get up. Later I moved into an apartment with the foreman on that job and stayed there for the rest of the meet.

A normal day for me at that time was get to the barn at 5:45 in the morning. Look at the set list to see what you're on, put on your helmet and vest. At 6:00, ride to the track on your first horse. Each horse takes roughly 20, 25 minutes. Maybe some more, some less. Back and forth for seven to eight horses. Then when you're done, clean off the tack. Hang the tack back up in the tack room. Usually before 10:00, you're headed home. You're done for the day. So it wasn't a bad deal. Got the whole rest of the day to do whatever you want. I couldn't stray too far because I had to be working tomorrow morning. The tough part about jobs like this are that idle hands are the devil's playground. When you got all that free time during the day, a lot of people turn to drink or other bad habits. I'm just lucky, I guess. I never had the desire to do a lot of it. I mean, I went out my share, for a weekend of partying or drinking or chasing women or whatever.

That's what you do when you're 20. But I guess I was just responsible enough to keep from getting into anything. I guess I was lucky and made the right choices at the right times.

When I was in Sallisaw all them years ago, there was a couple of times where one of the outriders there asked me to fill in for him. He wanted a day off from racing to go to a roping somewhere. He said, "I have a horse for you. All you have to do is show up and work the races," and I said sure.

So I filled in sometimes and that was my first introduction to outriding. When I got up to Churchill Downs and was working and ponying, I got to know the outriders here. It didn't look like a bad gig, and then I found out that if you got on full time, you had vacation time paid, you had health insurance, you had days off, which was huge at the time. I went for a few years where the only day off was when we were moving from one track to the next. There was no relief, no finish line in sight. A lot of people come here every day, never take a day off, and go for years. It's just day after day after day. I just couldn't see myself doing that. I didn't want to be one of these people who says, "I haven't had a day off in 12 years. I haven't taken a vacation."

Outriding looked like an opportunity and it was something that I enjoyed. It had a little cowboy aspect to it. You get to ride your own horse, you get that little bit of adrenaline rush when there's a loose horse or something happens. When an outrider job came up in New Orleans, at the Fairgrounds, I bought me a couple horses, put in for the job, and got it.

Outriding is kind of a niche job. You don't see it on Jobs.com or anything. People aren't just waiting to be an outrider. I heard about the job and I put in and gave my references. I had good references from all them years exercising and ponying. I'd kept my head down and showed up for work. After you've rodeoed awhile you've seen enough wrecks where you don't really get excited about too much. A couple of horses might have a little wreck at the track, but it just doesn't look as major compared to some of the stuff that I've seen in the rodeo. I'm a pretty laid back guy, too, and people like to have that in situations such as this.

Sometimes someone just gives you a shot. My boss here at Churchill, Ben Huffman, was the Racing Secretary down there at the time and he gave me my first shot. The guy who taught me down there, Kenny Lavergne, is really good. A legend. We are still really good friends to this day. He comes up and works the Derby with us every year because we need an extra man for that. He has been all over the country, outriding.

So I got my start in New Orleans. Then that winter, a position opened up here at Churchill as the third outrider. It was just a part-time employee. But I was lucky enough to get it, so I would work here in the spring and through the summer into the fall, and then I'd go to New Orleans in the winter. I got the full-time job in 2007.

When I first started, I couldn't wait for somebody to fall off. *Watch me catch this horse!* I was excited about it. Now that I've gotten older, I think, *Everybody just stay on. Don't do anything stupid. Let's get through the morning without any wrecks and I'll be perfectly happy.*

When there's a loose horse or something, I still definitely get my heart rate up. You start seeing all the wrecks you have to keep from happening while you're trying to catch this horse. I don't enjoy it as much as I used to. I enjoy catching horses, and back then I didn't mind if it was going to be tight. I'd say, *We're almost going to crash here, but I think I can get him caught before we crash.* Now I say, *I hope these people get out of the way because I don't want to crash this.* Now it's all about safety.

Before a race, we sit in the paddock until the horses are all saddled and they say, "Riders up." Then Greg, the lead outrider, usually starts walking out and all of the horses line up behind him. Then I follow the last horse out, and we make our post parade. We walk around to wherever the race is, wait until it's time to line up, then we hit post time. All three of us have certain positions on the track relatively close to the starting gate because that's where all the action is.

When you have a loose horse a siren goes off to alert people to pick your head up and get out of the way. We try to be up in front of them, and as they get closer to us, we sort of haze them toward the outside fence leaving just enough room for the racehorse to get through there, so you kinda grab them on the way by. Catching horses is not super technical. It's just something you can either do or you can't. It's all a timing thing. You have to be ready ahead of time. If a person is getting run off with, or a horse has dropped a rider, and it happens right there in front of you and you're at a dead stop, there's no way to catch them. You have to wait for them to come back around or go off the track. They're running, they have no weight on them, and they're bred to run distance, and you're sitting on a quarter horse who's bred to run for a couple hundred yards carrying you and your stock saddle: You're outmatched from the start. You have to take every advantage you can get to be ahead of them to start with and let them come to you. I compare it to merging on an interstate, stepping on the gas when the time is right. It's about knowing when to fit in. There's a little, small space, but you can time it right. You have to know when to step on the gas to make sure you come out at the right spot. If you get to that spot too soon, sometimes that horse will suck back, he'll duck, he'll do something that changes the situation. You have to do something different, or you mess up.

Or you get there too late, and you give him too much space.

We always have two outriders out there in the morning. One will sort of create the trap and the other will slide in behind and make a little noise, just slapping his hand on his leg or something. The horse will realize, *I have to get away from this*, and they'll come through and you catch them like that. It's a team effort.

There's so many situations. There's been times that I wish we could just rope them. Sometimes a horse gets loose and you can only get so close to him before he'll try to savage you or your horse. A lot of them have a tendency to bite and then run. We can't do anything with them. That's when I really want to rope them. But if you can get it to stop and stand and look at you like in a deer in the headlights, then somebody can get off on foot and catch it. One person will stay behind and the other will keep slowing him down and get him stopped.

If you have loose horses running, or a horse that has a broken leg and is still running, if they don't have the presence of mind to stop and stand there, some of them will keep trying to run, and you can't just stand out in front of them. You have to get somebody on a horse to get them because if there's a horse broke down, there's probably a rider down too. If we don't get those loose horses caught, they could run back around to where the ambulance is stopped and paramedics are checking the rider out.

Years ago at Keeneland, Patty Cooksey got dropped. She was down on the ground, they had her on a backboard on the track, and the loose horse got past the outriders and came back around. The ambulance people had to jump over the inside rail, leaving Patty laying there. The loose horse jumped over but never touched her. Nothing bad happened, but it sure could have.

Unfortunately, it doesn't turn out like that all the time. It's so dangerous if things don't go right. It's dangerous if they *do* go right.

———————————

If the Derby doesn't get you excited then you don't have a pulse. Something is wrong with you. You don't have to like horse racing to get excited about the Derby. They sing "My Old Kentucky Home," and then as soon as the last word's said, the crowd just erupts.

Half of them don't even know why I'm out there. We don't all get to be rock stars or movie stars where people are yelling for you, but it's fun to be out there hearing it, being part of it. It's not every day you see 150,000 people hollering and screaming. I have a radio that clips right on my vest, and on a normal day, the volume is turned halfway up and I can hear everything fine. For the Derby race itself, I turn it all the way up and sometimes still struggle to hear anything come out of there—and that's after the race is over. Nothing is said during the race; usually it's radio silence, unless something bad were to happen. Something like Eight Belles.

I was the one who held her down while they put her to sleep.

She broke down just behind me. I was 50 to 100 yards away at the most. It was after the race was over and she was galloping out. She was a pretty gray, dark sort of mixed in with the gray. She'd just come in second in the Derby. The horses were all galloping out, and we were set up to pull anybody up that needed help. The jock had her out wide, seemed to be pulling up normally. I was looking at all the other horses, seeing who needs help, and just out of the corner of my eye I saw a movement that didn't look natural. I turned back, and she was down. She had slowed up, was almost to a stop, when she broke a leg. Then she broke the other leg trying to catch herself.

When I got there, she wasn't laid over; she was sort of sitting up like she was thinking about trying to get up again. It appeared to be catastrophic, so we immediately tried to just hold her down. If you lay them on their side and sort of hold their head down, you can keep them laid down without a struggle. She was trying to stand back up, but she had broken both cannon bones in her front legs. She was standing on nubs, so I had to pull her over to get her to lay down so she was taking some pressure off.

There was a state vet there within seconds. By the time I'm holding the horse down, the state vet's there. He looked at her and made the obvious judgment that it was catastrophic and he needed to put her down. Unfortunately it was a no-brainer. As soon as you see a compound fracture in the cannon bone, the main thing you can do for them is to put them to sleep. The shot puts them to sleep pretty quickly.

Obviously it was heartbreaking. But at the time you have to be mentally strong. There's probably a better word for it. You do your job first and then you can be emotional later. We were trying to do the right thing by the horse quickly and safely. At that moment, you just do your job. It's a subconscious thing that takes over. You see the horse in distress, you get to her and hold her down so she doesn't fight and hurt herself even more. Try to make the situation as peaceful as you can for her. You get used to it. I never look forward to it, and you try to keep it from happening. You do your job. Somebody has to tend to that horse and get it loaded and out of the way because the next race is coming.

There's a picture of me that they made into signs and held up at the Preakness while they were protesting how horrible horse racing is. They're holding up this sign and there's me in my red jacket, holding her down. That was awful. What are you going to do?

You can let it bother you, or you can say, "Well, they're holding up their sign for a cause they think is right." It's on them; I know what was happening in that picture, and I'm okay with it. We were just helping hold her down so she didn't try to get back up and stand on her broken legs. I was trying to do the right thing, trying to keep her quiet and calm, and make it as un-stressful as possible. You don't want their last memories to be standing up on broken legs and making it worse.

I believe people are good, and for the most part they are. They're trying to get the best racehorse they can get, and do the best by their horses. They do everything humanly possible to care for these horses. If they had any inclination that would've happened that day, they wouldn't have run her. If there's anybody who suspects at all that a horse might not make it through the race, they scratch them. If the person doesn't do it themselves, then there's a vet who will say, "This horse isn't running."

I try to learn from every situation I get in with a horse. From watching one to riding one, I try to go through it in my head, what happened, what worked, what didn't work, what maybe could work better, and I hold that stuff in my memory.

When you're riding a really, really, really good horse, it leaves the margin for error a little broader. Just like it's hard to find a racehorse that's going to win the Derby, it's sure hard to find that one for an outrider that's exactly how we want it to be: They got to be fast, they got to be very catty—very handy is a good way to put it—and they also have to be calm, calmer than anybody else around. In a touchy situation, they can't be saying, *I ain't going in there. That looks like a bad idea.*

The horse I ride in the afternoon is great at catching. There are certain situations he doesn't like very much. Sometimes noise can get him a little dancy—

nothing bad, just enough to let you know he's on his toes. And I got a morning horse that I use that cannot stand the afternoons. He's a good catch horse and he's very quiet in the mornings. He can be a little more watchy than the other one, and he can really run, but I've tried riding him in the afternoons a couple of times and he just can't. I don't know whether it's the crowd, whether he just refuses to work after 10:00—I don't know what it is, but he will make your day miserable, because he just can't settle. He'll be in the paddock bouncing off the walls.

The morning horse's name is Roany. His color is roan, so it was pretty simple. He's getting older now. I've seen some jockeys I used to ride with in New Orleans and they'll ask me, "Is that still him?" and I'll say, "Yeah, that's still him." Then they'll say, "He might be faster than all of us!" There's a lot of exaggerations on the racetrack, in case you hadn't figured that out.

Usually we can tell if a problem is because of the horse or the rider. If it had been a horse that was that bad, and we thought the rider wasn't doing anything wrong, we'd have said, "The horse has got to go." Take him to a farm until you get him lined out, then you can come back and try again.

You can see when it's the rider's fault when something happens, even if it's a bad horse. A lot of people tend to blame the horse first off, and that's the sign of a bad hand to me. They say it's the horse doing this or doing that. From the outside looking in, you can say, "No, it's *you* doing that. You're allowing the horse to get away with it. You're causing the problem before it happens." Certain horses take certain kind of hands.

If there's a horse that's bucking the rider off or just so out of control that they can't be on the track, then that's on us as the outriders, and we'll put a stop to it. Sometimes it comes to the point where you can't have that horse here.

It's a personality thing. They're just like people. There's people you can turn around and get on the right track and there's some people that, no matter how hard you try, they're always going to go back to their ways. Horses are the same way. Luckily they're rare cases, the ones that cause too much trouble.

When somebody puts on a helmet and vest, they're portraying themselves as an exercise rider. But if they're not qualified, you can almost always tell. They just sit a certain way, and if a horse moves you can see that they're not in timing. Riding a horse is one of those things that people have a knack for or they don't. There's a time frame when someone can get better, but there's some people who reach a plateau. They think they're a good rider but no matter what you tell them or no matter how many more horses they get on, they don't ever get anything done.

Greg Blasi tells a story before I started outriding. Bob DeSensi led a guy out on the track on his horse, and as soon as the guy walks by, Greg says, "Hey, Bob? Is your workman's comp insurance paid up good?" Bob asked why and Greg says, "Because you're fixing to need it." You can just kind of tell about a person a lot of times.

One time this guy was trying to tie his knot—you always keep a knot tied in your reins so there's no loose ends dangling for something to get hung up in—and he couldn't even tie the knot properly. Sure enough here he comes around the turn, and the kid is wrapped around the horse's neck, hanging on, and the horse is running down the outside rail. Greg had to go catch him and tell him, "You're no longer allowed out here on the racetrack because you can't gallop." That was pretty funny.

Just this last year, I had a girl come to the racetrack. She was friends with an owner, and they told me she was going to gallop a horse in a few days. First they let her jog a couple of days beside the pony. Just long trot. I could tell by the way she held her hands that she probably rode English or dressage or something. A lot of people come from that and some of them are very good. But you could see just by the way she held herself and her hands that she had never galloped a racehorse.

They finally said, "We're going to let her gallop today." Here she comes around the turn, and you can see the horse picking up steam, and I'm shaking my head because I could see the situation playing out. It's just one of those things you see coming. The trainer behind me said, "Could you go pick her up?" I said, "Yeah, I'm going to have to. I was just giving her every shot I could first." By the time I pulled out on my horse to get in front of her to pick her up, she was screaming bloody murder. "Help! Help me!" The panic was starting because she was out of control at this point. Once you panic on a horse, you're done. You can see it when they're picking up speed and the horse is doing it on its own. The rider doesn't move, they freeze. Panic never leads to anything good.

Luckily, she rode well enough and was riding with her stirrups long enough where she had no trouble staying on. I was just trying to calm her down. I said, "I've got you, I've got you." She was still screaming for help. Afterward, of course, we politely said, "You don't belong out here. You need to find some place else to learn how to gallop." I like to tell people that outriders are like the lifeguards at a pool. There's no running at the pool. If you're doing something stupid like running around the deck, we tell you you can't do that here. And if you see someone who obviously can't swim, we say, "You need to go to the shallow end." Well, here at Churchill we don't have a shallow end. /

William "Catfish" Smith

GROOM

PHOTO BY JOE MANNING

I grew up on Iowa Street, up on The Hill. Mostly racetrackers and L&N railroad workers over there. Half of their sons worked at L&N, others were rubbing horses. Growing up, we met all kinds of race-trackers. I grew up next door to Willard Pinkston. He was the best exercise boy on the track at that time. He was a good dude. He could handle a mean horse. He could really handle a rough horse. Willard was a good horseman. Uncle Willard always kept some hound dogs. He liked to go hunting all the time with Tommy Long and and my stepdaddy Roy Dixon. They would go out to Newburg. Sometimes they'd go way out Florence. They'd come back with plenty of rabbit. Roy Dixon would bring that rabbit home and my mom would cook it with grease—fry it up just like you would chicken.

I came into Churchill Downs with my uncles and my stepdaddy and everybody. When I was six years old my stepdaddy would bring me back there. All the barns had coal stoves back then. They brought me inside and taught me how to work with horses. Everything I learned came through all those old timers: Scotland Yard, Willard Pinkston, Houston, Red, and Uncle Smoke, who was an assistant trainer for Spendthrift Farms. All them. Tommy Long brought all of us through the gap. Old Man Long was Doc Harthill's man.

Tommy used to make up leg medicine and sell it around here. He mixed his own and never let nobody know what was in it. Doc was crazy about him. I think Tommy Long might have come up with Harthill's daddy.

When they brought you around, the first thing they did was show you how to roll a bandage. Then you'd start raking the shedrow. Then they'd put a shank in your hand and get you in on walking horses. Next you start rubbing horses, starting with a pony. You didn't get on a thoroughbred until you earned your badge on a pony. I loved it! They'd make me take them bandages off and put them back on until I did it right.

First horse I ever rubbed was Seneca Chief for Dave Vance. When he won, he was so sore he'd lay down for a week. But he had heart, and he'd get up a week later, and Vance would run him again and he'd win again. They know when you take care of them. They know.

I tried to go to Ellis Park when I was 15, but they denied me my card. I wasn't old enough. I started hanging out at Miles Park, and then the next year I went to Ellis Park when I was 16. The tracks didn't run at the same time. They would run at Miles Park, then Churchill, then go to Ellis Park, then Latonia. I loved traveling because I met a lot of people. I enjoyed that.

When we come around, we enjoyed doing it. We tried to do better than each other. Set up there and tried to outdo each other. It was a contest to see whose horse looked the best or who put on the best bandage or who had the horse's mane lookin' like it was supposed to or who had a horse shining with big dapples on them. You have to get into a horse, get the hair off of them, for those dapples to come in. You were doing something then. When you put on the bandage it looked like you painted them on. But not too tight. You could bow a horse if you didn't know how to put on a bandage. You had to know how to tuck it; you had to lock it at the bottom, up under the ankle. If you didn't know that, you were in trouble.

You could tell who was taking care of the horse the best by which horse looked the best.

And when we went to run a horse, we bet on it.

We took care of the horses back in the day. We'd be up under that horse all day. Up in the shed, walking back and forth, seeing how many times the horse would take a shit. We did all that. We loved to do it. That's what we got paid for and what we loved to do: taking care of the horse.

We loved what we were doing back in the day. When the trainers see that they start giving you good horses. Start rubbing those top horses. I rubbed Dogtooth Violet, Nelly Pilot, I rubbed a colt called Angle Light who was Secretariat's stable mate. Work-house Red. I rubbed Midway Magistrate. I rubbed a whole lot of good horses back in them days.

Back in those days we drank; we didn't mess with that other stuff. You could drink on the job and

the trainer wouldn't mess with you, and they'd win races. We did our work and that was what was the most important. We didn't ever leave the barn. We took care of their horses and made money. That's what we did. We enjoyed it. We'd be up under those horses all day, clean until feed time, then wake up the next morning in the barn with those horses. When we were with horses we would feed, maybe start drinking, maybe have a dice game or a made up card game up under the barn. Everybody would be walking up and down the shedrow; every time the horse shit we would pick the pile out and smooth the stall out and everything. We drank and took care of the horses and sat around there. We enjoyed it. Only time we left was when we got ready to go to town to party.

There was a joint called Emma Pearl's—that was Paul Goffner's auntie. Right on The Hill half a block from Churchill Downs. She would cook a lot of food and we would go in there and enjoy ourselves. She specialized in wild greens. They would get them at the track and she would bring them in and cook them up. And she would cook chicken, pork chops, and all that. When everybody would be through in the afternoon, they would go out there and eat. They wound up making The Chippy Joint into a house and my family ended up living there. Then there was June Ray's. It was a joint. She had cold beer. John Lee Robertson had a place right up the street from Emma Pearl's. He sold beer. They had a jukebox up in there. We'd leave from Emma Pearl's and go up to John Lee's. It was a neighborhood thing. The Hill was a good neighborhood. /

Merlin Cano Hernandez

HOT WALKER

PHOTO BY JOE MANNING

My family is from Casillas, Santa Rosa, in Guatemala. We're from a village called Barrera. It's in the countryside, not a city like here. It's more like the forest. We don't have any neighborhoods. It's just my house and trees. It was all green, away from the city. Peaceful.

Where we lived, we had a lot of space to plant stuff. My parents had plantains and coffee plants. They used to grow plantains in the middle of the coffee because the coffee plants liked the shade. They owned a coffee plantation close to the house, and Dad also owned some other land about an hour away from our house in a colder place that was really good for plantations.

My parents used to hire workers to harvest the coffee when it was ready. They'd hire workers who came from places like Las Flores, Los Pocitos, Buena Vista—places that were really far away. My dad already had connections with them, so he would call and say, "This job is going to start and we need people." They would bring their families and everything. Young people my age would come, too. My parents would have a house prepared for them to stay in. They owned a big house near the road that they would give them to stay in while they did the work.

Sometimes the workers would teach me how to harvest. It's not really hard, but your hands get dirty and you get tired. They used to tie baskets on their waists and cut and fill their baskets until they weighed 25 pounds: that was my goal for the whole day. Older people used to do like 100 pounds of coffee or more in the day. They would cut it, stock it, and get it on the car. I used to go back to the city with Mom and Dad to sell the coffee. They had to get the car full, then take it to the city and see what the price was. My parents had a person who they took it to all the time. They would make exceptions sometimes, because other places were paying more money. Coffee is a big business. My brother still owns some land over there, and I heard him say the prices are going down. It's not good. Last year was kind of bad and sad for a lot of people because prices were really low. That's how some people get their money, and it's a lot of work. It's not because people aren't drinking coffee. It's the economy going down.

In Guatemala, there were four of us. I'm the baby of the family. We all came to America together with my mom. My dad was the one who got his green card first and did a petition for us to come here and took the responsibility to come here and provide for us.

My mom was really happy about coming here to the U.S. because my sister and two of my older brothers were already here. She went 15 years without seeing them, so she was excited to see them and they were excited to see us, too. My brothers here didn't even know me, since I'm the youngest.

I wasn't sad to leave Guatemala, and I wasn't happy to come here. I didn't know it was going to be really different. Then meeting my brothers was weird, too, because I didn't know them at all. They have a video of me when I came to the airport, and one of him said, "Are you going to hug me?" And I didn't want to hug them, because I thought, *I don't know you. So why am I supposed to hug you?*

That was in April 2012. The first Monday here in Louisville, my brothers took me to the chapel on the backside at Churchill Downs. I've been a member since then. They help me a lot, and I learn a lot there. That Monday, they were giving out teddy bears and I got one. I think it was a panda. I love pandas. They are so cute.

I always say if I could adopt a panda I would do it. Maybe I can work with one someday if I go to veterinary school.

There was this girl there that first day. She was the same age as me. She talked to me, but I couldn't understand. I just looked at my brother as if to say, "What's she saying?" He said, "She wants you to go play with her." But I didn't, because she couldn't understand Spanish and I couldn't understand English. I didn't know how to communicate. I was really shy. I was really scared when I got here and I couldn't understand people.

I try to go to the chapel every Monday when there are services, but sometimes I can't make it because of work or homework. But my mom goes every Monday.

The services have changed a little bit. Two years ago the English speakers would go to one room, and the Spanish speakers would stay in another room, but now everybody is all together. That's a good thing. When I came here, the chapel was a big help because I got to interact with other kids and that made it

easier for me to learn the language. We also did a lot of coloring and writing. They did different activities in the room.

They usually have a clothes closet open for the people who work there. If they need anything, maybe a jacket or shoes for the cold weather or something, they can have it. That's mostly for the workers, because they need more stuff usually.

Every Monday night, a different church donates food and gets together for the service. They bring food and give it to the people who go there. A lot of those people live there on the backside. I think they're not allowed to cook inside their rooms above the barns, and that makes it kind of hard. That's a good thing that they get to eat something healthy and good on Mondays. They prepare maybe chicken, mashed potatoes, beans, rice, and fruits like apples or oranges or bananas. You can take fruit home if you want to. They have a table in this room and everybody eats together there. They usually do it before the service.

On Wednesdays there's a Bible study just for women. They didn't have one until a woman named Daisy showed up two years ago. She announced it and my mom wanted to go. I was still kind of young for that, but I went with my mom and I liked it. I liked to hear the conversations. I would say about seven to ten women show up. All of them work on the backside.

My mom likes to go because they come up with different topics. I like it. I usually don't talk a lot, but I like to hear the other women talk. Sometimes they say, "Men are this and that." Since I'm the youngest they say, "Focus on school. Follow God more than anything." Sometimes they ask me how I'm doing in school. Daisy especially. She asks, "How are you? How's school? Do you need help with anything?" She always tells me, "If you need something, let me know."

Sometimes Daisy asks me about what I want to do in college and how this school year is going for me, since it's my last year of high school. I always tell her it's been really hard because I have five Advanced

Placement classes and I don't know how to keep up with all of them. Sometimes I give up for a little bit, because it's a lot of work. There's all these things going on––applying for college, thinking about how I am going to pay for college. Sometimes I realize I'm having a hard time right now in school, so I think about how it's going to be in college.

I tell her all of those things. She just tells me if I need anything, she's available to help me. I think she has a degree in psychology. She's really good at listening, and I feel really comforted to talk to her about things.

At the beginning of the Bible study, they have a small talk about things that are happening in the world. Then they study some things in the Bible. At the end, prayers.

Last week they talked about all these migrants coming together to the United States. They talked about how some of these people are coming with children, risking their children's lives and theirs.

They're bringing kids with them, knowing it's not going to be easy. They may not make it. How bad is the economy in their countries for them to bring their kids, risking their lives and everything? The life they have back there is poor. Maybe they don't have food or something, and people tell them there are a lot of opportunities in the United States. But it's not really easy to just come. And they're just coming and they don't know. I'm pretty sure some of them have family here. Others maybe not, and that's really sad. I understand that the economy is really bad back in our countries, but I don't think I would risk my kids' lives. I would maybe just come by myself, leave the kids, then maybe later on try to bring them here. Right now, it's a lot of people coming in together. I don't think Donald Trump will allow all of them in, and that's that. It's just sad and crazy, all the things that are happening.

The women in the Bible study like to talk about real things that are happening. A lot of times they compare what's going on to the chapter in the Bible about the apocalypse. They put it in prayers, hoping that things will get better. Daisy has told me that she likes to read that chapter of the Bible because, if you compare it, it's similar to what's happening now, and it's really sad. Daisy's call is to get all these women, including me, to be more into God's stuff. To learn more about it. To believe in it.

I think that's a good thing. Being in a church is way better than partying or something. I like to go there and learn. I won't say I'm a strong believer, but I like to learn and get to know more because I know I'm young. I don't know a lot of the things that are going on outside of my house and school, so I like to learn how they really are, and not just picture something in my head. I usually have a lot of questions.

––––––––––

I came here when I was 11 years old. I'm 17 now, and I'm currently a senior at Iroquois High School. I've gone back to Guatemala once, two years ago, for a month. I felt weird. It didn't feel like the same place it used to be. I didn't know a lot of the people that were in my village anymore. And a lot of people don't see you the same. They talk to you differently. That made me feel weird. When you live in the United States, if you don't take a present to them, they get mad. They think that here you have the rich life, but you really don't. You have to work for it. When I was little, I used to think it would be easy to get money here too.

Back in Guatemala, even if you get a degree, it's really hard for you to get a job. And if you get a job, you will not be getting paid a lot. This friend of mine told me she already got her degree. She's working in a bank, and she said whenever she started, she worked for a

Merlin's five brothers, all of whom are exercise riders

whole month and she didn't get paid until two months later. It is really hard to put food on the table if you're not getting paid. That's why I feel like it's better here. The money I'm making working part-time at Walmart and at the racetrack is as much as a professional would be making in Guatemala. I'm really lucky to be here and have these jobs.

All five of my brothers work at the track as exercise riders. You can get paid a lot as an exercise rider. Sometimes like $800 a week. My older brother Rogelio has been riding for 18 years, and he says, "I don't do it because I get paid better. I love horses." He's really passionate about it. My other brothers have all followed him. They've all gotten hurt before, but they still don't quit. They keep riding, even though it's dangerous. The two oldest ones have been sent to the hospital after they've fallen off a horse. My mom worries because she knows it's dangerous.

Once, I was sleeping on the couch really early one morning when a friend called and told me that an exercise rider had just died in an accident on the track. I got really scared when they told me it happened because he didn't tell me a name. He just said it was a rider from the same stable where my brother Jose works. I said, "Why are you calling me?" My first impression was that he was calling me to let me know that it was my brother. He said, "I don't know who it was." So I had to call one of my other brothers. I said, "What happened?" He told me it was a friend of theirs named Cuba. "Cuba just died in a horse accident." He said that when the alarm went off, my brothers who were exercising horses at the time had to get out of the track. When they heard it was from Jose's stable, they all ran to find out if it was him. When they found out it was Cuba, they were really heartbroken because he was one of their best friends.

I knew him. If you see pictures showing him riding horses, he was always smiling, sending kisses to the camera. He was a really happy person. He was a really funny man. One time I was walking with one of my brothers, who stopped to talk with him. Cuba looked at me and said, "You must look like your mom, because I know your dad and your brothers, and they're all ugly. But you're beautiful, so you must be like your mom."

My brothers are really sad about the accident. All my family was really good friends with him. He used to have cookouts and everything. My uncle was like his best friend. They used to hang out a lot. My brother who used to work with Cuba said he was thinking about retiring next year.

I work in the same barn as my dad. He used to be a groom but says, "I'm too old to be grooming." It's a hard job because you have to do everything. Now he's a hot walker. We get up at 4:30 and get to the barn by 5:00. In the barn, there's a list of the horses. The horses that are not going to the track that day we call *caballos frios*. You walk them first to get them some exercise. While you're walking them, the groom gets their food and water and stable ready, and maybe they get a bath after their walk. You want to walk the *frios* so you don't get behind and have to do it at the end. The track opens for training at 5:30, and you're not going to have time to walk the cold horses out if you don't do it first thing.

The horses that are going to the track are divided into different sets that go out at different times. An exercise rider gets up on a horse and takes it to the track to exercise while the groom is getting the stable and food ready. When the rider comes back, he gets down and takes the exercise tack off the horse, and the hot walker is ready with the halter. You put the chain through the halter so you can walk the horse. You're supposed to be the leader. If the horse acts up, you pull the chain to calm them down. If they don't have the chain on, they'll run off.

A lot of times they come from the track *amarrado o pegado*, they say; it means they're sore. So you can stop them for a little bit until they cool down some and then you walk them around the shedrow for about 20 minutes.

If they breezed on the track that morning—that means to run as fast as they can—you have to walk them for 10 minutes, give them a bath, walk them for 15 or 20 more minutes, then you put the horse in the stable and whistle a little bit. This is to train them to pee because after races sometimes they have to go to the detention barn to be tested. Then you take him out and give him a couple more turns.

You have to be careful they don't hurt you. Some of them are really nice to walk, but a lot of times it's a pain to walk them—the whole time you're walking them they're bothering you, pushing you, or trying to bite the chain. I'm thinking, *Can the 20 minutes be over so I can put you back in?* Other horses are just nice. I like those horses. Sometimes I like to pet them and say, "Good boy. You did good." But then other ones, I say, "You were mean to me. I'm glad I'm putting you back in."

Last summer, Walmart was scheduling me to do eight-hour shifts, and I worked every morning at the racetrack. I would say I worked 60 hours a week. My goal was to buy a car, and I got one. I reached my goal. That was the main reason I was doing the two jobs at the same time. I got a 2012 Nissan. I'm currently paying for insurance for my car and everything. I'm proud of myself, because my parents didn't have to help me. I'm trying to help them instead since my mom is 60 and my dad is 64.

My dad drives, but his vision is not that good and he has diabetes and high blood pressure, so it's dangerous for him to be driving. Since I'm the one that is at home the most, I take my parents to buy food for the house, or whenever I have free time, we go out. Sometimes they're at home all the time, and I don't think that's really healthy, so sometimes I ask them if they want to go somewhere and do some stuff.

We go to Iroquois Park. My dad likes to walk, and my mom just likes to be out of the house. So we go and have walks. Or sometimes my mom says, "I didn't cook today. We should go out somewhere." Usually, we go to Mexican restaurants, or there is this restaurant called La Guanaquita. I like to get pollo con tajadas—chicken with plantains.

My mom is a believer. My dad is a believer too, but he's more to himself than going to church and interacting and talking about it. He's just to himself. He came to the U.S. 30 years before me. He used to come here for like four years, visit us back in Guatemala, then come back and do another four years. Since he has been coming here since before the 1990s, they gave him a permit to work here. Then he applied for his residency and got it, and that's how he brought us here. After he got his, he applied for ours.

My parents have struggled a lot because they didn't have an education. They know how to read in Spanish, and write some, but they don't know a lot. Many people don't have much education or opportunities before they come to the U.S. The Backside Learning Center helps the people that live and work on the backside a lot. They offer classes to people interested in learning more English. My parents wanted to try those English classes, but didn't want to go by themselves. I already knew some English and had been going to the Center, so I said, "I'll go with you." So I

went to class with them. I even was a little helper to the teacher sometimes because I knew English.

A lot of the people that work in the stables—especially the elders—don't have an education, so they need help with filling out papers for clinics or other places. Sometimes they just give you a paper to fill out, and sometimes people don't know what to do. They don't have family here to help, but they're welcome to go to the Backside Learning Center. It's really good that they do that. I went to the BLC for some help with applications for college and my FAFSA. It's like a family thing, too. People who don't have family here can go to BLC to socialize with other people and with the BLC staff. It's important because being lonely isn't fun.

When I got into National Honor Society in school, I needed to do some volunteer hours, and they told me I could do my volunteer work with them in the Family Program at the BLC. I did that when I could, but it was kind of hard because of my work schedule. Then they called me and asked, "Do you want to work with us? Quit Walmart and and come work with us." I said okay, and now I'm the Youth Activities Leader for the Backside Learning Center. They said I was a good fit because I'm still young and because I have these perspectives as a student and a youth and also as a stable worker.

I told them that I wanted to apply for my citizenship as soon as I turn 18. They've been helping me with my application for U.S. citizenship. They gave me some resources to study for the citizenship test, and that's what I've been doing. I don't have the specific date yet, but I got an email saying that I will be able to schedule the citizenship interview soon. It feels good because when I'm a citizen, I'll be able to vote. I feel like I'll be counted more here in the U.S. as a citizen than I am as a resident. /

LIZ SCHLEMMER, WFPL NEWS

Sherry Stanley

EXECUTIVE DIRECTOR, BACKSIDE LEARNING CENTER

I admired the work Sherry Stanley has done at the Backside Learning center before I started working there. I wanted to interview her to know more about how the BLC has grown and how working with people on the track with their different stories and problems has changed her. Sherry is always working hard to make the BLC better for the backside community and to support the workers and their families. She's honest with people, and nice. I like her strong attitude. She's tough. She would not let anybody mess with her. Also, I love her Spanish. Her accent is perfect.

—Merlin Cano Hernandez

When I was in my early 20s I was a bit lost, trying to figure out what I wanted to do with my life, what my purpose was. I was interested in exploring the world and learning about other languages, other cultures. I really wanted to work abroad for a period of time. I had never lived outside of Indiana. I was a naive Midwestern girl, and in 1995 I had an opportunity to go to Guatemala on a volunteer trip for a month. I absolutely fell in love with the country and the people. I felt like it was where I needed to be and I knew I wanted to go back. So, I applied for the Peace Corps and, one year later, I was assigned to El Salvador. That's how I ended up going there in early 1996.

I lived in a rural coastal area with no running water and extreme poverty. It was an eye-opening and transformative experience for me. I really learned the value of community, and what brings happiness. You may have a lot of challenges and a lack of opportunities, you may have no money or material goods, but that does not necessarily determine your level of happiness or fulfillment in life.

There was a project funded through the health ministry to build these above-ground composting latrines because there was no sewage system. People didn't even have latrines on their properties. My job was to educate people on how to use those latrines and talk with them about basic healthcare: treating your well water, and issues around drinking water. Dengue fever was a really big problem at the time. During the rainy season, you'd have huge puddles of water just sitting there with a lot of sickness and mosquitoes.

My job gave me the opportunity to visit every single home in that entire community and talk to people. That's all I did. My job was to go house to house all day long. I had never been exposed to that level of poverty before. It became apparent to me how much of a bubble we live in within the United States. It can be easy to close our eyes to the realities of poverty within our own country, but it's a whole different level in other countries.

By the end of my time there, I knew every single person in that entire community of 3,000 people. They took me in without expecting anything in return. They would constantly bring me food and other things. It was such a meaningful experience for me, the way that people can be so generous. It was probably the best experience of my life. I learned a lot more than I ever taught anyone. That experience has guided the rest of my life.

I was there just four years after the civil war ended. The war caused a lot of detriment to the society, to the environment, and to the economy. I learned a lot about the impacts of immigration. During the war, a lot of people were leaving the country, many young people. Probably three-fourths of the homes in that community had sons, husbands, or fathers who weren't there because they had immigrated to the States.

I saw what that meant for the families back home. It is a true sacrifice to leave your home, children, and family behind to go to a country you have never been to before, not knowing what's going to happen to you, what you're going to do, or even if you're going to survive the trip there. Just so your family can have a better quality of life and not have to suffer.

The important thing to understand about immigration is that people don't *want* to leave their country, their culture, their language, and their family. They feel forced to. It's really a matter of survival. It's not easy to be in another country where you don't know anyone, you have no support system, and no one who speaks your language. That's an enormous sacrifice.

My goal in the U.S. was always to get some job experience here and continue my education so I would be able to go back to Central America. So I got a master's degree in sustainable development, received a fellowship for a couple years back in El Salvador, and then stayed there working for another six years.

My first daughter was born in El Salvador in 2006, and we ended up moving back to the States after she was born. We moved back in with my mom, who was living in Southern Indiana. I had just started looking for jobs. Louisville was the next closest city, so I started looking for jobs in this area and got a position with the Kentucky Office for Refugees. This is a department of Catholic Charities that administers federal funding for refugee resettlement programs throughout the state.

The Spanish-speaking population has definitely grown here since then. There weren't a lot of jobs that I felt would fulfill me like the work I had been doing, so that was the first job I accepted that was working with an international population. It was an amazing opportunity to learn about the state of refugees in the world

and in this country, but then this job at the Backside Learning Center came available. It just seemed like my dream job, and that ended up being the case.

The Backside Learning Center (BLC) began in 2004 as a collaboration between the Kentucky Derby Museum and Churchill Downs. As the population of backside employees was transitioning from more U.S.-born workers to a greater reliance on immigrant labor, they realized there were a lot of safety concerns. Due to a language barrier there were issues concerning communication and cultural norms, and both entities believed that it would be great to open a school on the backside to provide educational opportunities.

The partnerships with the Derby Museum and Churchill Downs continue to be very important; we work together on a regular basis. But it was important for us to have our own organization and identity. I started working at BLC in 2013, and in 2015, we applied for nonprofit status and became a stand-alone organization in early 2016. It's been a great experience to build our own independent organization and take another look at our role and value in this community.

When I first started, the organization was a lending library and we had some English classes. People would come here just to hang out. We had that community aspect to an extent, but people were intimidated since they thought that we were just a school. For me, it was really important to make our building feel like more of a community center, so we made a lot of aesthetic changes. We painted the whole building. All the rooms are different colors. We put up art and got new comfortable furniture like sofas and chairs so it didn't feel so much like a school. Now it feels more like a home, where people come to hang out, watch movies, do puzzles, art, play music, and just be around other people. Details like that make a big difference.

I worked really hard when I first started at the BLC to get to know the population and figure out— from the perspective of the people that work here—the role the Backside Learning Center could play. We're here to serve them and help better the lives of the community here, so we need to figure out what they need us to be.

One of the first things I realized was that there wasn't any programming geared towards youth. I had no idea how many families were back here, how many people had children in public schools but weren't really accessing any after-school programs or homework help. It's extremely difficult when you don't speak English fluently or you're working every single day without a break. You might be a single parent trying to help your child with their homework, in English.

The reason most people come here from other countries is because they don't have access to education in their home countries, and they want to make sure that their children do. A lot of times, our parents might only have studied up to third grade, sometimes even first grade, or maybe never went to school at all. Maybe they were working on coffee farms from the time they were six years old, which is not uncommon. Most of the people that work here are from rural areas, agricultural-based societies. So education and support is really important for these parents. That was number one on the list.

We had to figure out how to offer support to families and especially women, because it was mostly men that were coming into the Center. Women have more responsibility to their families—getting their kids off the bus, making dinner, taking care of the house—so we didn't see a whole lot of females in here that had children. There were a lot of women who didn't have kids or mothers whose kids weren't here with them. So that was a really important population.

The mothers are the ones that are the most motivated now. We have had our family program for almost five years now, and our mothers are incredible. It's so clear that their number one priority in their life is to ensure that their kids are successful and do well in school. They want their kids to go to college or have a profession, which wouldn't be possible if it weren't

for them and the sacrifices that they make every day. Supporting families is important, in addition to continuing to support the population of workers here. The families are part of the larger Louisville community and give so much to the community and this industry. We need to give back to them and provide the support that they need to fulfill their dreams of their children's success and a better quality of life.

The beginning was crazy, because there was a point in time when I was trying to do everything as the only staff person with a whole crew of volunteers—providing services, setting up programming, working with community partners, and raising money. It was great, though, since the organization had and still has so much potential for growth and impacting people's lives in a meaningful way. The important thing was just going barn-to-barn and talking to people. I can't remember exactly when I came to the realization that, "Oh wow, there's a whole community of families and children out there. We need to figure out how to serve them."

We ended up doing a focus group with some mothers. I identified three or four mothers that seemed like they were really motivated people. These mothers, by the way, are still in our program. They've been our most loyal attendees. Bertila. Maria. Marta.

From the start, we wanted to run a pilot program over the winter. In the past, the Center was just serving backside employees, so staff was really busy serving people and working from April to November. But during winter months, we weren't seeing a single client or providing any services. Part of this was talking to people and realizing that there's this huge population of people that don't travel over the winter. They stay here in town. And we needed to take advantage of these months when the track is closed and we have more down time to create some sort of a program for them.

Churchill Downs gave us permission to run a pilot program in the backside chaplaincy over the winter for three months. We started running that out of the new wing of the church on the backside.

We had two rooms: one room for all of the children and one room with the moms learning English. It was really difficult, really loud, and chaotic. We didn't know what to do exactly, but we had to do something. We had a volunteer teaching a class at that time, and when the horses started coming back we had to look for some space off the track because they don't allow kids on the backside. We ended up moving into a space at a nearby church in South Louisville, where we continued the program.

We probably had three or four mothers with six or seven kids. It was connecting with this core group of people who were these super moms who work at the track every day, dedicating each day to supporting their families in every aspect. They're here at 4:00 in the morning, raising kids, and attending our program

in the evenings with their kids—all while trying to learn English. I really don't know how they do it. Just by word of mouth, they started bringing their friends and other mothers and kids. "My neighbor has three kids and they want to start coming." That continued to grow and grow and grow. And four years later, we sometimes have 70 children at our program. It's been incredibly successful.

Now we have a staff of six that is doing an outstanding job of formalizing our programs. Our programming is now structured. We have two adult classes for parents. Our students Maria and Bertila are two people that really stand out who have been here since day one, especially in Maria's case. Bertila is a little different, because her daughter Evelyn is in high school, and is a wonderful kid in all AP classes that doesn't need help with her homework. We've used her as a tutor many times for our younger kids. She's been a volunteer here a lot, and we're going to be sure she gets the support she needs to go to college.

English class at the Backside Learning Center.

In the case of Maria, her son was probably eight when he started. Now he's 13, and they've barely missed a day of the program in the last five years. The progression in Maria's and Bertila's English and their sense of self-confidence has made them community leaders within the backside. Marta, who is equally outstanding, is actually the forewoman of her barn, a leadership position. And her kids are also outstanding children.

From what we've heard and observed, it's the friendships and community aspects of the Learning Center that impact everyone the most. Anyone that is working in the industry and living on the track is probably not from Louisville and therefore may not have a support system here. They don't know their way around, where to go to the grocery store, where to go to the police station, the park, or any kind of need

they might have. The Learning Center provides the backside workers with a support system of people who can orient them to the community, make them feel like they belong here, and do fun activities together so their life is more than just work.

I've never seen a group of people work harder than the people that work back here on the track. I have the utmost respect for everyone that works on the backside. Maybe what I've learned the most is about sacrifice. Seeing the level of sacrifice that people make for their families has changed how I understand what brings meaning to life.

These are really down to earth people. They have great attitudes. They're really happy to have the opportunity to do what they're doing. To have jobs, to be outside and work in this community of people. And I

think that the community aspect is what keeps people here on the track. It's very different than working in a factory. That's one of the toughest adjustments for people that come from other countries that are much more community based. We live in a very individualistic society—very competitive. You don't know your neighbors, and people keep to themselves. That comes with economic advancement. You don't need to rely on your neighbor. You can rely on yourself because you're making money and have a good job, so you don't need to go to your neighbors to ask for any kind of help. That is very, very difficult for people from a developing country or from rural areas, where, if you ever need anything, your community is there to support you. That happens all the time. That's the nice thing for the immigrant population and non-immigrant population

that work back here: They have that sense of community and family just because of the nature of the work.

That's what I think is really fun and gratifying about working here, because so many lifelong friendships are formed at the Learning Center by people who are going to classes together or come here just to hang out and talk. We try to introduce people to each other, especially when they're new. Maybe they just arrived in the country or they've never been to Louisville or Churchill Downs before. They don't know anyone. Inviting them to anything and everything that's going on is how we form our relationships with them. Seeing these friendships blossom between people who are maybe from different countries, maybe speak different languages, is really a beautiful thing. /

Daisy Bàez

CHAPLAINCY ASSOCIATE

I met Daisy when she was new to the chapel. I remember seeing her walking around the barns early in the morning talking to the workers. It was really nice to see how fast people started to love her. She seemed to know everything about the church and us, but we didn't know much about her and her family back in Dominican Republic, and that's why I wanted to interview her. I wondered how she handled being away from her family and why she made the choice to come here. I really admire her self-confidence and attitude towards the people on the track. Daisy is a really happy person with a positive attitude, and she's a really strong believer.

—Merlin Cano Hernandez

When I moved to Louisville in 2016 for a master's program at the seminary, I had just finished college in Dominican Republic. Before going to college, I wanted to do Christian missions. That was the desire of my heart. But my parents said, "You have to study, you have to study, you have to study." I said, "Okay. I'll study." I got my college degree in psychology, which I loved. I don't regret it, and I think it has been very helpful. While I was a student I worked with children in very vulnerable communities, kids that had learning disabilities and functional limitations partly due to poor socioeconomic conditions. When I finished my degree and the Lord opened the doors to go to seminary, I was very excited, but I was sad about leaving the kids. I learned so much from them.

Before going to seminary, I got a scholarship to move to Canada for a four-month English language immersion program. I've now been speaking English regularly since 2015. They give you a test when you arrive to measure your level: English I, II, and III. Somehow I got into level III. I didn't grow up in a bilingual school. My mom always tried to make me and my siblings go to English class in the afternoons, but I did not like it. I did not feel comfortable at all. It was embarrassing. I never finished a full program. I did grow up listening to English language music all the time at home in the Dominican Republic. I sang Fergie and Britney Spears way back then, and all of the songs in English that sounded so nice. I would go online and read the lyrics and memorize them. Then I would translate using a dictionary to understand what I was singing. Music in English helped open up my mind to language.

After Canada I moved here to go to the seminary. When I first came, I started praying and asking the Lord to provide a ministry or a place where I could work and serve. I worked with refugees for a little while, trying to find something. Then a friend of mine called and said, "Hey, are you interested in doing a Bible study with women at Churchill Downs?" I said, "That sounds like an answer to a prayer." I didn't know about horses or anything related to the industry. I came to visit at the end of May 2016 during the Horseman's Picnic. That was my first time coming to the track, and I fell in love with it. Even though a great number of the workers are Hispanic just like me, the culture is so different. I realized I had so much to learn. Their desire to overcome limitations and their cheerful attitude just captured my heart. Eventually their hard work awoke my respect and admiration. I started volunteering every week, and then they hired me full-time after I graduated from seminary, and here I am.

One of my goals is to walk around the racetrack every morning while people are working. The first time I came here, I was a little overwhelmed by the number of people. It seemed impossible to actually remember all the names and know everybody. They were transitioning all the time. Sometimes they'd seem to disappear, especially the people who don't have families here. They move around all the time, or they just stop coming to the track. There didn't seem to be an interest from the people to engage in a relationship or a friendship. So it was overwhelming in the beginning, but I learned that consistency and presence are key.

If you really want to know the people, you know where to find them. You walk around, you say hi. You give a smile and they'll give a smile back to you. You just have to say, "Hey, how are you? Can I pet that horse?" It's not hard, and if you do it every day, then people just get used to seeing you. Then they know you, and you know them, and you start remembering who is in which barn. "Yeah, she works in Barn 14," or, "She works in Barn 20." When people see you consistently, you become trustworthy. So it's just a time commitment. And of course, genuine presence and care. You want to make sure people know you're there if they need you. Not just sometimes. So I try. Sometimes I have other things going on, but I try, even if it's just 20 minutes just walking around so that people can see me in case they need help with something.

The chapel opens every day. We have multiple services, but we also like to have the doors open for people to walk in, get coffee, and talk. We have worship services and free meals every Monday evening. We have a food pantry that provides emergency food for workers in need, mostly non-perishable items. They are also welcome to use the kitchen to prepare their meals. We also have a Clothes Closet, which opens from 10:00 to 12:00 on Mondays and Thursdays. The Closet provides clothing, bedding, toiletries, shoes, and much, much more. It is a wonderful resource for the workers. All our services are run by awesome volunteers and funded by many churches, families, and individuals who love the Lord and the industry.

We try to have whatever we know the workers will need, especially those that have no family here and live on the track. A lot of the people on the racetrack don't have family in the U.S. There are a lot of lonely people here, and it's an honor to have the opportunity to get close and talk to them. "Hey, you can have a friend. We can watch a movie together. We can hang out." The chaplaincy exists to help them and provide for their needs, both physically and spiritually. We want to gain their trust. But ultimately we want them to know that they need Jesus, not us.

When the horses are gone and the racing season is over at Churchill until the end of March, we open the doors for the moms to come and learn new skills, or to further develop old skills. They come to do crafts here in the chapel. Some of them sew, some of them crochet, some of them knit, some of them cross stitch. It's amazing. They always say, "I don't know how to do this!" But then I see them using a sewing machine, or putting together a beautiful blanket, and I say, "I thought you didn't know how to do this?" They say, "Oh, well, just a little bit. Just enough to make my clothes, and my tablecloths, and my curtains." They are great!

So I'm trying to help them take ownership of that, and develop their skills even further. They learn really fast. It's amazing. During the winter, they come every Monday, Tuesday, Thursday, and Friday for sewing or knitting or decorating jars, or whatever project we find on Pinterest that we can do. They are good—they don't need anybody else to show them—but sometimes a teacher comes and teaches them a specific project. I'm

Women's Bible study group

still trying to crochet, but I don't think my fingers are smart or fast enough.

On Wednesdays they come for Bible study, which I only do with women. Before I started doing the Bible study in 2016, I thought, "That would be so awesome, but I don't think I'm necessarily the person for it." I thought someone else could know more or do it better or have more experience and more background. I was hoping that an older woman would show up and say, "I'll take care of it." But that never happened, and I think that was God's plan. He has taught me so much in the process. I hope it has been a blessing to them as well.

I enjoy the Bible study. It is a smaller group. I'm a little younger than most of them. We are going through the parables of Jesus. I really enjoy the time to just go through Scripture and try to understand together what the message is. And I don't mean a weak interpretation or whatever comes to my mind. I like to look deeper: *This was the context, this was what was happening, this is what it means, and then there must be a response from us to what that is saying.* Once you know, you decide what you're going to do after. It's a gift to see how God's Word works in their hearts.

I have learned a lot from the people on the track. They have expanded my small world view and changed my cultural limitations. They have taught me to value life in a different way and enjoy the daily little things. They know so much that is not necessarily valued in U.S. culture. Here, you may pay someone else to make food, or you buy food pre-made and just have to bake it for 10 minutes. You don't necessarily need to make it yourself. But these women do things with their hands, they value even the smallest thing. They make a flower out of an old piece of paper. They put time, effort, and heart into everything they do, including their work with the horses. They raise their children, *closely*. My mom was very much like that, so they remind me so much of my own roots. For them, community and family are king. If all they have is $10, and that's all they have for a month, they will share it with you if you need it more, or they will work together to help you get what you need, even if it means to sacrifice their time and resources. That, to me, is amazing and beautiful. I just love the opportunity to know and share with the people on the backside, and I am thankful for it. They are awesome. /

Butch Lehr

RETIRED TRACK SUPERINTENDENT

PHOTO BY DARCY THOMPSON

When I went to work at the racetrack after I graduated from duPont Manual High, I did all the sign painting—the lettering, all the names on the trucks, the barn numbers. That's what they hired me for. I wanted to be a commercial artist at the time. I was good. But I was draft age and I think that's why I didn't get any work in design.

You didn't make a lot of money at Churchill, but you could work all the hours you wanted. They couldn't find people who liked to work all the time, so we'd work 80 hours a week sometimes. I think that's why I got promoted, because they could count on me being there. We got ahead financially by working weekends.

I later had an opportunity and signed up to be a carpenter because I got about a dollar an hour raise. Then I worked my way up through the track crew. I drove water trucks and tractors. I did pretty much everything.

It was a big gamble to go into management. I left the Local 576 Hod Carriers Union in March of '76 when Thurman Pangburn made me his assistant. From that day forward I was on my way to the management level, and all the jobs that I was in charge of I'd done myself. The Board of Directors promoted me to Track Superintendent in 1981. It was a big honor. I was in charge of all the barn area, all the backside facilities and buildings, and all the track surfaces.

Racetracks that care about what they're doing are going to have pretty consistent racing times. Each one of those trainers knows if his horse can run a particular time or not. If they run exceptionally fast, that trainer is going to bitch because it could possibly injure his horse. It's a legitimate complaint. So I charted every race, every day. I looked in the *Racing Form* for the times to see what the horse's average time was. They should run somewhere close to those times on our track. Before a race, I'd average out the times and say, *If I've done my job today, they ought to be running about this time right here. And if I'm running faster than that, I might not have quite enough cushion.* That's the only way I could judge.

The difference between a hard track and a fast track is that on a hard track, there's not enough cushion. A fast track has just the right amount of moisture, just the right amount of cushion. It's not muddy, it's not too deep, it's not so wet that it's heavy. Some tracks might have a lot of lime dust. If you let it get too dry, it'll get hard like concrete. The material that we used, I believe, is the difference: 75 percent sand, 23 percent silt, 2 percent clay. That's the key. Keep it about 2 percent clay.

Butch Lehr receiving Best Track Superintendent Award from the Jockey's Guild, 1997

If it got any lower than that on the track, you would see the times slow down. The horses have a hard time holding on to it. So as far as I was concerned that was the standard, but there's still not a book that says this is what it should be. It's what worked for us here in Kentucky. If you try to copy that in California, it's a whole different environment and it doesn't work the same. In California, it doesn't ever rain. What they call bad weather is 56 degrees and rainy. The year Smarty Jones won the Derby, we had four inches of rain in one hour. One section of the track surface actually washed out and we had to go out there with shovels and repair it. We were only 15 minutes behind schedule for the Derby. When we had the first Breeder's Cup, it was like 30-something degrees that night, and we had rain. And that's not too bad. At least it didn't freeze. Our

track has always handled the rain well. At least in my tenure. I believe my formula worked.

We always had to make sure we had the right amount of water and the right material. If the track's too hard, you water it more. Some people don't water it enough. We usually put between 80,000 and 100,000 gallons a day on the track. If it was real windy, we'd water between every race. Those are the things that I had to watch for. I didn't do it from the office. I'd go down there and walk on it. I always graded it myself so I could feel the track as I was doing it. I did that for 33 years and came to those conclusions. I could tell. I lived and died on that track.

There's not a book you can open up that will tell you how much material to put in your racetrack. Mine was all trial and error. I'd work on it, I'd add a little bit of this and add a little bit of that. I was the first one at Churchill who took soil samples. I did it once a year. We were going to start racing in the summer in '83 and '84. Churchill had never raced in the hot months, so I was a little concerned about if we were going to be able to keep enough water on the track. That's when I got curious and started taking some soil samples. When I got the samples back the first time, it was 99% sand. The horsemen always said the track could be cuppy at times and if it got real hot, it was hard to keep it wet. the 99% sand was the reason. It was too much sand. We needed to put a little more clay in there.

I'd have samples taken, usually right after the fall meet, because then I could make any changes that were needed when there was no horses in January and February. If I added material to the track, that's when it was.

We have to add material because some of it goes off down the drains from hard rain, some of it the wind blows it away. The horses carry it off. Trucks carry it off when it sticks to the wheels. And I had to pick my time for weather being good. I used to add material to the track when it was frozen. A lot of the guys were spreading things out there and saying, "Why's he wait 'til it's so damn cold?" It's because the track won't change. It's froze solid, and you can spread material on there real uniform because it's harder and won't fluctuate. So I used to do all my resurfacing in the winter. That's how I resurfaced the racetrack.

I always got the material from soil in our area. We were fortunate that it was a native soil. I had enough stockpiled to last me 10 years. I kept it in a big pile and that's still over there at Churchill. Anytime I saw it, I'd buy it. I got guys that I worked with in construction projects, and if someone was digging a construction site somewhere, they would call me and say, "You need any sand?" I'd say, "I'd like to look at it." If it's good, I'd

Butch Lehr in the grader with his grandson Andrew.

stockpile some at Trackside Training Center and some at Churchill.

Every racetrack I ever went to—and I went to a lot of them—when I come home, I had little bags of sand in my luggage that I took from each track I visited. All these guys would say what their tracks were made of. I'd have it sampled and keep it on file, then I'd know whether they were lying or if they knew what they were talking about.

I've been retired for seven years and there's still no book standard for racetrack surface, and until someone puts a roof over a racetrack to control the elements, the weather dictates what people like myself must do. Weather in the Ohio Valley is hard to predict. I always said my favorite TV show was The Weather Channel. /

Henry Osorio Hernadez

GROOM

*B*efore coming here, I lived with my parents on their farm. My village in Guatemala is beautiful. It's far from the city, far from everything. I love it. I took courses at the university that qualified me to be a teacher's assistant, and then I was chosen to give adult education classes—not for my experience, but because of the relationships I had with people from my village.

I'd been helping elderly people in my village who couldn't read or write. Many people really appreciated that, since many people couldn't add, do multiplication or division. They would say to me, "Before, in order to do calculations I had to ask someone to do it for me, but now I can do it!" And that fills you with happiness, to know that you helped these people carry out their work, if only just a little.

I got that job in adult education, and at first I wasn't very convinced and neither were the students. But then they started to realize that they were learning, and they started liking it. They started coming to my house to ask, "When do classes start? When can I sign up? I want to learn." It is really nice when people come to look for you at your house for something good.

Like everyone, I had always wanted to have the pleasure of seeing the United States. Even though I haven't seen all of it, I hope to one day know all of the United States. I have family here—aunts and uncles and cousins. My father is here in Louisville. He's also a groom. I would like to continue to improve my work each day. My job as a groom is not difficult. I like it. The only difficult part is when I have to take care of babies that don't know anything. You must teach them. It can be very dangerous teaching them. They can kick you, bite you, or hit you because they aren't used to having a saddle put on them, or having their feet picked. They come from farms where they were running around free.

Sometimes on the job you make little mistakes, and you become disappointed and then you get sad, but I've learned that it's not good to get sad. You must learn from your mistakes and keep improving every day.

My dream is to continue my studies and graduate with a degree in an area of study that I like. Then have a good job and travel after that. I think that's what everyone desires—to have a good job and see new places. There are many parts of the world that I would like to travel to. But first I would like to know my own country. There are many beautiful places in our own countries that sometimes we've never been to—beautiful places without a lot of people, where you can have fun and relax.

My greatest struggle right now is learning English. I think that if I apply sufficient interest I can learn it pretty quickly. This is what I would like to do. After learning English, I would like to help people—people who are like I am right now, who don't know English. I have realized that it is very necessary. There are many people that—due to fear, or because they don't know how to read and write—don't understand English. I would like to someday help motivate these people. I like to help people whenever I can. It makes you feel good. /

Carla Grego

SOUTH END NATIVE

I work as the Membership Manager and Horseman Relations Liaison at the Kentucky Derby Museum. Horseman Relations is a new position. My job is to build relationships throughout the thoroughbred industry. Not only with the past Derby winners, the owners, trainers, jockeys, but also to keep a lookout on the next Derby winners and make sure they know that the museum is there to always protect and preserve their stories.

When the Derby is over, that's when we take over the connections. Once the winner has been crowned, it's our job to build a relationship with those people, to get their story and make sure that we have it correct here in the museum, that the story is always available to people. In recent years, we've started an oral history program. We interview the people connected to the winners: the owners, trainers, jockeys, and track personnel. At some point in time, we want to be able to show all those interviews that we've done and for the public to be able to hear those stories in people's own words. I think that will be an amazing thing.

I was raised on Southern Parkway, so I haven't gotten very far from the neighborhood or the track. I spent all my life in the South End. I went to Holy Rosary Academy, which sits at the entranceway of Douglas Park. I'm the great niece of Roscoe Goose, who was a jockey that won the Derby on Donerail in 1913. In that same year, his brother Carl Ganz—the German word for goose—won the Oaks on a horse called Cream two weeks later. It was always in my DNA, I guess. It was natural that I would gravitate towards 4th and Central. My first job out of high school was at Wagner's Pharmacy. I met my husband on the track, and in the drugstore at breakfast time. At that point, the deal was sealed. I wasn't going to go too far. We've raised three kids in the thoroughbred industry.

Horses have always been a central part of my life. I grew up with horses, riding up and down Southern Parkway. My parents owned a riding academy located in an alley off of Southern Parkway. They leased horses to people for an hourly rate. They would go out and buy horses, then make sure they were amenable to have all types of riders ride them. Their barn wasn't huge, probably 10 or 15 horses. My mom gave lessons. They didn't run the academy for very long, a couple of years I think. My friend Neil Huffman would know better than I would, because that's where he hung out. That's how we know each other. He came to the hospital when I was born. Him and a guy named Izzy that my mom said was tall and wore a cowboy hat. They hung out quite a bit there. Neil was around

15 or 16 years old when he started coming around. His brother Blackie was younger and they dragged him along too.

At the time, you could leave Southern Parkway and ride all the way down to Iroquois Park and around the park. There was even a watering tank at Southern Parkway and Taylor Boulevard that ran fresh water all the time for the horses. When you rode down into the first part of Iroquois Park, there was a little restaurant called Parkside. It was on the same side of the street as Colonial Gardens, where AutoZone is now. There were hitching posts at Parkside where you could tie your horse then go over and get a hamburger or cheeseburger. Quite a few people did.

Because my parents lived on Southern Parkway when I was a kid, it was not unusual to see horses going up and down all hours of the day and night. There were still people that drove their buggies up and down there. There was a lady that rode her horse every single day. She had flaming red hair. She'd stop, tie him up, go to Parkside and have a beer, then get back up on him and go home.

They had moonlight rides. We would even ride our horses to Easter service at the top of Iroquois Park. They would have an Easter service there at the lookout. We did that for quite a few years growing up as a kid.

When I was five or six years old, I would just take off on Southern Parkway. The horse that I had would actually stop at the cross streets. I could ride all the way to Taylor Boulevard but I couldn't cross. So I always turned around and went back, because I would've gotten in big trouble if I hadn't.

My mom told me I could only walk and trot. It was a four-lane road, and on the side were carriage streets. We'd have to stop at the cross streets and start again. One day, a little kid came up on a pony and wanted to race because I was a girl. I had a decent-sized horse.

She was old, but she was a good size. So we raced for about three blocks. When I took the mare back to my mom, she was wet. Oh my gosh, I got in so much trouble. I had to give her a bath and walk her until she dried out, cooled down. That was the last time I ever did that. I refused all racing offers after that.

I didn't know anything about the racetrack then. When my mom was growing up, it was taboo for women in the Goose side of the family to race horses. She mostly rode saddlebreds. You were supposed to enjoy riding horses around the Parkway, but women weren't allowed on the racetrack. My mom enjoyed the races, but it was just ingrained in her that it wasn't what a lady did, going on the backside of the racetrack. But there were ways my mom would sneak around the barn area and ride. Her greatest fear was that Uncle Roscoe might see her and tell her dad. She would be in big trouble. Growing up, my mom and her friends spent most of their time riding up and down Southern Parkway and through Iroquois Park. She could probably tell you every inch of that.

My dad grew up around the Taylor Boulevard area and wanted to be a vet. He trained saddlebreds for a while and found out there wasn't going to be any money in that. He was going to go to vet school, but the Navy had other plans. When he came back home, my parents met and married. That's when my father started the riding academy. Then he became a real estate agent. In fact, he sold a house one time and got a horse for his commission. That's how we got a lot of them back then, when we moved down off Old 3rd Street. We bought a little land there, had horses, showed quarter horses mostly.

We raised some horses, we bought some, we'd show at the quarter horse shows around town. My dad was in the sheriff's posse. He'd ride in the Derby parade. We went on vacation and took our horses. We

Riding on the carriage path on Southern Parkway

Roscoe Goose

would spend one week, two weeks in Hodgenville where we'd camp and take the horses. Then we'd go to all the county fairs and show our horses at night.

I was showing quarter horses at the time. My mom let me take off. I didn't have to go to college right away because there was a big American Quarter Horse Congress. I was on the Kentucky youth activity team that showed at the Congress. It wasn't until October, so I got to take a semester off. I didn't have to start college until January. During that time, I needed a job after the horse shows.

I went to Wagner's Pharmacy and started working there. It was the old location at 4th and Central. When they widened Central, they took that building down. We'd go into Becker and Durski's across the street to get horse supplies back then. I found Wagner's fascinating.

When they opened the doors in the morning, it was the same people in the same stools every day. If somebody strange walked in, everybody knew it.

When the races came to town and the jockeys and the trainers were coming in, it was just fascinating to me. I was working there during Open City, when they were cracking down on bookmaking and prostitution. That would've been '71. I think they busted two of the girls that worked behind the counter at Wagner's for bookmaking. The girls would call the bookmakers and lay the bets off. At the time, you could walk outside and there was a phone booth on the corner. They busted one of the regulars for bookmaking out of the phone booth. It was way before cell phones and computers and all that stuff. They couldn't reach bookmakers at any time. They couldn't go online and place their bet.

I'm sure the bookmakers had people all over that somebody could call. That phone was there at Wagner's at all times. They would check in with the girls at the counter and get their bets. "I want a cheeseburger, dressed, with a side of fries, and five on the three horse in the fifth race." The girls had to be getting a cut. They wouldn't risk it without a cut. That phone had to be tapped during Open City. There was a whole lot of things that had to go on for them to get busted.

I grew up knowing that my grandfather and two of my great-uncles were bookmakers. I don't think that it was a shock to me. Bookmaking has always been around. There's always people that want to bet and don't have the money to bet. So you call the bookmaker. And that goes on today. It's calmed down quite a bit because now the platform wagering can give you a rebate, where the bookmaker doesn't. It goes through the windows, more or less.

The guy that sat closest to the telephone, and the guy that sat beside him at the counter at Wagner's were some of the biggest bookmakers in the city. That was their morning hangout. Those were their chairs. If somebody came in unbeknownst and just happened to take one of those seats, they really stared them down and made them feel uncomfortable. When they would open up at 8:00 in the morning, probably half of those seats were taken by regulars. It was pretty cool.

Lee Wagner Jr. had horses. I got to the point where I was going over and walking horses in his barn. He had a trainer named Joe Rodriguez. I would work for Joe in the mornings and then work at the drugstore in the afternoons. Then the next step was working on the backside. It was a great time in my life. I really enjoyed that. It was a lot of fun. I was 18 or 19 years old.

My mom and I fought about college all the time. I never wanted to go. I didn't like school. When I found the racetrack and knew how to support myself, I didn't need it. That was back in the '70s. College wasn't as mandatory as it is now. I chose not to go. My mother wasn't very happy at all. She kicked my dog out of the house. She kicked me out too. She was really upset because for her whole life, she was told, "You do not go on the backside of the racetrack." That was a no-no. And here I went and worked on the backside of the racetrack. So not only did I not go to school, but I did

this as well. Looking back, it was probably a hard pill to swallow for my mother.

I met my husband Donnie about 1975. Donna was born about 1977. Donnie had had horses down in Miami before coming up here. I think he was getting low on horses and decided it wasn't worth it and came up here with another trainer. He was galloping horses. He was a really good exercise rider. He did that for a couple of years and then he decided to go out on his own and get horses. He probably had nine or ten horses to start. We had breeders that we knew that gave him some horses. His horses ran pretty good. He had a pretty good career. He cashed a lot of bets, and back then betting was a source of pride.

Betting is not the same as it used to be. Not at all. A trainer doesn't make enough on the daily rate, even back then or barely now I would assume. Back then, you didn't have workman's compensation, you didn't have to have all these other things. You could pay a lot of people in cash. It makes it a little harder now. You had to make opportunities for yourself. One thing you could do was take a horse that you thought had some talent and run him in a race he wasn't ready for so that his odds would be longer the next time. Then, when you were sure he was ready, you'd run him, bet on him, and maybe make some real money.

Some guys claimed unknown horses that were ready to run and moved them up into better races. You'd see something in a horse that maybe the trainer before was overlooking, or maybe he didn't have the resources to help the horse. It didn't always work, but sometimes it did.

Donnie galloped his own horses so he could feel them out. He was really good with the young horses, getting them ready for the first time. One time Donnie had these two three-year-old fillies. He worked them together here at Churchill in the fall and they were both pretty well-bred, talented horses. The owner wanted to keep one filly in another trainer's name because he was well known, a leading trainer. So Donnie ran the horses in this other trainer's name with Pat Day on it. She went off 6-5 and won. The other filly was just as nice and talented and Donnie ran her in his own name with a jockey named Leroy Moyers on her. She won and she paid $45. She ended up being a stakes winner. He had worked both of them together and he knew they were good. You just take advantage of situations like that. You take advantage of opportunities.

When Donnie and I were about I have our first child, Donna, we were sitting on buckets talking with Tommy Long, Beetle, and Paul on a Saturday morning. I'll never forget it. They were the ones that told me, "Buy the Pampers. Don't go for the cloth diapers." They were the first ones to give me any parenting advice. I hadn't even read the pink book yet, *What To Expect When You're Expecting.* They told me about formula, they told me about all kinds of stuff. Then they watched my kids grow up.

I'd come back and water off the racehorses when Donnie had his stable. Every time I pulled in the gate to get into the backside, I'd have to stop at the guard station. George Ralston, who had always worked for Doc Harthill, was security on the backside then. He would say, "Stop that car," and come out with candy for the kids. He'd want to look at them. He'd say, "Let me look at them babies."

I'd go back at 10:30 at night and never think a thing about it. I was protected back there. No matter what situation you're in, the way you handle yourself is the way people treat you. I treated them just like I

wanted to be treated, and they respected me. I never had a problem at all.

Women were starting to come around then. I wasn't the only one for sure. There were tons of people back there. There were tons of girls starting to shift that way. It's a very transient lifestyle, so you get all different types of people. The way you act is the way you're treated. I never had any problems. Some did.

When I worked with Joe Rodriguez for Lee Wagner, we left Arlington Park one year and we went to Hawthorne. Usually we got apartments and stuff wherever we would go, but this time I lived in a tack room. I thought it was going to be such a lark. Donnie and I were just dating back then. When I first told him I wanted to do this, he was really ticked. He said, "You're insane." The more he said I was insane, the more I wanted to go and do it. I wanted to know what it was like. I had my mind made up I was going to do it.

We were just supposed to be there two weeks, but we ended up staying over a month. At night, I had my tack room upstairs with my little hot plate. You had to go two barns down to go to the restroom or shower or anything like that. I'd been taking ballet lessons for exercise when we were in Chicago, so I had these ballet pictures hung up in my tack room.

I worked with an older guy that was the biggest bootlegger on the backside. His name was Big Skin. Like all the older grooms, Big Skin taught me a lot about the horses. My room was upstairs and Skin's was downstairs, so he could hear everything at night. We'd sit on the steps and I'd read to him, because he didn't read. I would tell him what was going to be on television that night and what channel it was on. I couldn't make a move upstairs that he didn't hear. He'd make sure I was okay.

I was very ill-prepared for it. About the first two weeks it was okay, and then after that I was wishing that I hadn't done it. I finally got to the point where I was calling Lee and saying, "Lee, you've got to get me out of here. I can't stay much longer." I was terrified. It was scary. We're talking Chicago. It's downtown. You're right by the incinerator. It's nasty. It's really scary. When you drove out of Chicago, there was Little Mexico, there was Little China—all these different areas—and you didn't go into an area you weren't supposed to be in. I was a hick from Kentucky. It was way out of my lane. And then living in a barn was a little scary. It wasn't my kind and gentle Churchill Downs on the backside, where I knew everybody. It was a different ball game.

I could have got the heck out of there, but I wasn't going to leave my horses. I wasn't going to leave. I just had to stick it out. I never stayed in a tack room again.

Big Skin would sell half-pints. When we went out of town, he never drank a drop. But when he drove his big old white van to the backside, they'd be lined up on payday for Big Skin. Every half-pint he sold, he broke the seal and took the first drink. He was amazing.

People like him and Scotland Yard were great. If they thought you really wanted to know, they would teach you. I've always had a passion for the horses and wanted to know everything. They were super to me.

It was as much about life as it was about the horses, really. One time I was in the barn with Scotland Yard. There was a trainer who locked up his tack room everywhere we went. The minute he would step away from the barn, he'd put the padlock on it—even if he was just going over to the restroom or doing whatever. I was sitting there with Scotland Yard one day and I said, "What is wrong with him? What do you think? Why does he do that?" And he said, "Let me tell you something. He's a thief. People always think that everybody else is out to do what they're thinking." I found that to be so true in life. There's a lot of times when people give you a tell sign if you're quick enough to watch it.

Another important lesson he taught me was about the mud that grooms make. There was a particular type of clay that grooms mixed with water and some salts. You use it to pack the horses feet. It's hard to do, to get it just to the right mixture so it doesn't squish out, so it's not too watery, but it's not too hard to pack down in there. Scotland Yard was the best at it. When I first started, he told me, "I'll tell you what. You can borrow anything I got, but don't ever touch that mud. I put stuff in it that nobody else can use, and it'll really hurt your horse's feet if you try to use it." At first I thought it was some kind of secret potion. There wasn't anything dangerous in there, though; he just didn't want me using up his mud.

My racetrack family taught me to have pride in your work, in the way you took care of a horse. The grooms would brush the horses, and as they brushed, they would click the backs of their brushes together. It would make the dust fall out so the next swipe would be a cleaner swipe. Little things like that. Never take them over dirty. The horse reflects you as much as it does anything. And they took a lot of pride in it. They brought their kids into the business and taught them as well. If they knew you really meant it, that you really wanted to learn and that you were serious, they'd show you anything—except what was in their mud.

They were showing me as much about life as they were about the horses. For me anyway. That's how I felt. And I really appreciated that. /

Kenny Luckett

OWNER, LUCKETT'S TACK SHOP

I grew up on Denmark across the street from Eleanor Churchill Semple School, but we went to the Catholic school. Holy Name had 400 kids: two classes for each grade, first through eighth. People came from all over to go to Holy Name. They had a good football team.

Father Tim was the pastor when I first started going there. He was a heck of a guy. When I went to work at Wagner's Pharmacy later in life, Father Tim would call up and say, "Hey, I'm sending a couple people down there. You just put their bill on my tab." Tim was a heck of a guy.

Sister Martina, on the other hand, could be good one day and evil the next. They had cloakrooms in the back of the classroom where you kept your lunch and stuff. One day Sister Martina hung this little boy named Donnie up on the hook in the cloak room. My brother had her for the seventh grade, and at the end of the year he said, "Thank goodness: no more sister Martina." Then they moved her to the eighth grade, so he had her again. Just a couple of months ago my brother said, "If I ever get an evil bitch dog, I'm going to name her Sister Martina."

You went to church every weekday morning back then. I was an altar boy too, so I had to do mass on Saturday. They had a mass at 5:15 in the morning, and if you served the 5:15 mass, after you were done they'd send you to the Downs Bakery. It was where El Molcajete is now on 4th Street. They had these trays of chocolate and caramel cinnamon rolls. When you came in early, they were still hot and the guy had just put the chocolate or caramel on them. You got three cinnamon rolls and a milk for doing the early mass. Otherwise, you could buy three of them for 12 cents.

There used to be this board in the basement of the church where all the altar boys' names were listed. If you served all your masses you got a green star. The only person that ever got a red star—the bad star— was me. I got it for taking a halo off of a statue. We did what they called 40-hour devotion around Easter where there was somebody in the sanctuary at the altar for 40 hours straight. It was just something they did every year. I don't think there was a priest there but there was people out in the church and altar boys up at the altar. I was standing in the vestibule, and I took this halo off a statue and put it on. A nun came through and caught me.

When I was a kid, One of the guys in the neighborhood worked at Wagner's delivering prescriptions. He said they need another delivery boy and that

I should go up there. Lee gave me a job just like that. I delivered prescriptions around the neighborhood on my bicycle. We delivered prescriptions until 9:00 at night. We went as far as Eastern Parkway and Bardstown Road, and over to Shively—all on a one speed bicycle.

Wagner's was on 4th back then. On the opposite corner from where they are now. There was Tollie Miller's tavern, the Downs Cafe was next door, Uncle Miltie's Pawn Shop, Jimmy's Grocery. There was a little bitty liquor store, Scoby Brother's Hardware. Then, there was a bank building with a doctor's office above it. Becker and Durski Turf Goods was right next to it in that same building where Churchill just built a new entrance. They had a store and their leather shop was in the basement. Becker owned it and the guy that ran it was Ray Griffith. He started working for Mr. Becker when he was 14 years old and wound up owning the business later. And then Wagner bought it from him.

When I was 20 years old I got drafted. I went to basic, then went to advanced individual training. Then I went to NCO school at Fort Benning, Georgia. I was

in the Army seven months. I was E5, a sergeant. My wife Dede and I got married in November and I went to Vietnam right after Christmas.

I got deployed to the Bien Hoa Airforce Base and took a helicopter ride right to my company in the field where the war was. When I got to Vietnam as a sergeant, I was in charge of 12 guys. I didn't know shit. These guys had been there for a while. I just showed up. The first thing they asked me when I got there was, "Sergeant, do you smoke?"

I said, "Yeah, I smoke these Marlboros."

"That's not what we're talking about." They were talking about smoking pot. They said, "Do you mind?"

I said, "Listen, fellas. I'm new here. I don't give a shit. All I want to do is make it through my time and go home." They never smoked it in the field, but when we were in the rear area they smoked the shit out of it.

We had a guy with us that they called a Kit Carson scout. His name was Prin and he was he was a Montagnard, which is a Vietnamese mountain person. Like an aboriginal Vietnamese. He spoke English and was out in the jungle with us as a guide. He stayed out with us for two weeks and then went back to his home for two weeks, and every cigarette that we didn't smoke he took back with him. Each of us had to dig a hole every night to get in. If Prin helped you dig a hole, we knew there was Viet Cong in the area.

On my first night in Vietnam, we got in a firefight. We shot all we could shoot. And then it was shit all the time. All the time. We were on a North Vietnamese supply route from Cambodia into Vietnam. The ones we got into firefights with were the ones we ran into by accident. We'd be positioned at these trail intersections waiting for people to come in, and we would work on the trails setting out claymore mines. There'd be four or five of them in a line along this trail and we'd put a trip wire attached to those mines with two pounds of

Kenny and Prin

Kenny with his fiancé Dede at Fort Knox

C-4 and these big BBs and other projectiles. The worst night was when some of our guys walked into their own trip wires. It didn't kill them, but it fucked them up. On my third night there we had a guy get killed.

We had been out for 35 days and they brought us back to Bien Hoa Airforce Base where we were able to get cleaned up. You know the first thing they did when they brought us back? Took our ammunition away from us so we didn't go get stupid and shoot somebody.

The prostitutes were in the barbershop at the base. There were 12 of us in the squad, and seven of them got the clap. We had to go back out and when they all start showing symptoms of the clap, we had to send them back and go out with five people instead of 12. We just had to carry on.

I'd been in Vietnam for 75 days when I shot myself in the foot. I had my M-16 sitting on my foot. I don't know if I grabbed the trigger or what, but when I went to move, it fired. They airlifted me out and send me to the hospital in Saigon. That doctor said, "I know you didn't do this on purpose." I said, "How do you know?" He said, "Everybody who's ever shot themselves in the foot on purpose shot up in those bones

right in the middle of their feet and fucked themselves up." I was very lucky. They were having trouble with people getting infected in the hospital in Saigon, so they sent me to Japan. A great big black guy put his arm over me so I wouldn't get up out of the bed. I said, "What are you doing?" He said, "You're going to Japan. That was your ticket home."

In Japan they worked on my foot. I had a damaged nerve. It must have been something serious because they gave me a spinal block. I was depressed at this time. There was a whole lot of people in the hospital who were really fucked up. Had been hurt bad. Here I was: I shot myself in the foot. I felt like a fool.

I was in Japan for a week, I guess. I still couldn't walk. I was in a stretcher on the airplane flying back from Japan. I couldn't walk until I got back to Fort Knox, where I was in the hospital for two weeks before they let me actually start doing stuff. They gave me a job of filing the paperwork for all the guys who came to Louisville and got the clap and had to be treated.

I still had 11 months to go, so I was a platoon sergeant in the clerk's school for a while. Then I graded proficiency tests and PT tests.

Then I ended up driving a front end loader at the rock quarry at Fort Knox for the last six weeks I was in. It was in January. A guy showed me how to operate the loader to fill trucks with gravel. Then he said to me, "You know what, it's pretty goddamn cold. Don't come back 'til it gets warm." So I didn't have anything to do for the last six weeks. We had to raise and lower the flag, and we had to do some kind of guard duty, but that's all I had to do. By the time I got out, I had long hair.

I was a sergeant. Once you came home, you never got sent back unless you wanted to. It's not like now where they can redeploy you someplace else. They didn't do that then. They called me in to see if I wanted to reenlist. I said, "Fuck you. I'm getting out of this man's army."

————————

After I came out of the Army, I learned to do leather work above Wagner's Pharmacy. They did silks and had the leather shop up there. I learned some from Henry, the guy who worked up there, but I learned more by doing it myself: hand sewing, cutting leather, making blinker straps, running all of the halter parts

and the shank leathers through the creasing machine. They had an electric creasing machine up there. Mine is hand-cranked.

Dr. Harthill built this building across from the backside, and when Wagner's bought Becker and Durski, Lee moved it here to Harthill's building by Gate 5. It was all fixtured out real nice. In the back was drawers with blankets and displays for saddles. It was really cool. Harthill had his practice next door and the Kentucky Racing Commision was on the other side.

I worked for Lee Wagner, sewing above the drugstore and working at Becker and Durski for a couple years. Then Lee said, "I'm gonna let you run the turf goods store." The guy who ran it, Ray Griffith, was going to retire, and I was going to run the store. But then Wagner hired another guy to run it. He knew nothing about the business. A big fat guy. I had to go to the bus station and pick him up! I said, "Lee, I quit. You promised me I was gonna take over the store." I said, "I don't trust this guy."

So I went and did other things for a while. I worked construction. I worked with the Army Corps of Engineers at a thing called the Louisville Repair Station. It was a gift job for being a veteran. If you're traveling on I-64 going toward Indiana from downtown, over on the right is a bunch of big cranes across the canal. That's where I worked.

Then another time, I hauled water to people with cisterns who didn't have city water. One of the jobs was to water the show ring at the Rock Creek Riding Club over by Seneca Park. On the day our first child was born, my wife Dede was riding around in the truck with me while I worked. She was in early labor, nothing intense, and she was back there turning the valve on the back of the truck so I could water the ring.

We didn't ever really plan on kids, but we had three. They were each four years apart, so that was good.

We had two of them at home. The first one, our son, the midwife was late. But we had a lady who worked in the delivery room at the hospital who rented a room upstairs in our house. She was there when Berry was born. She helped us with the birth at home, and then we went to the hospital. She was there for all three of the births of our kids: Berry, Leigh, Kate. We bought a house on Southern Parkway 40 years ago and have lived there the whole time.

I went out on my own in 1984. Started a shop in a little two-car garage down the street. Didn't have a garage door, just had a window and an entrance. I started out paying $300 a month rent for this little thing, but it was air and heat, all paid. I rented that little building and started out as Leatherhead Tack Repair. I was affiliated with the Leatherhead on Bardstown Road.

They had a big sewing machine and I did the big sewing up there. I did that for maybe five months. Then I became Luckett's Tack Shop. Jerry, the leather guy that worked at Leatherhead, came with me. We've been working together for 32 years. I made money from the first day we opened.

It costs a lot of money to start out in horse racing. I had a guy who came to the U.S. and was starting a stable from the ground up. He started with nothing and had 20 horses at Skylight. He needed some saddles, bridles, girths, saddle pads, feed tubs, water buckets, and everything. Receipts were $20,000. I gave the guy who sent him my way a finder's fee.

When we first started, we were still making exercise saddles. I couldn't have done them without Jerry. He had the patterns all down and knew how to make them.

We copied it from a guy who made saddles in Arizona, a guy named Bob Ross. Jerry improved on it a little bit to make it easier to deal. Ross's were hand-sewn together where ours were put together with screws. When we were doing them, it would take a couple days to finish one. They were probably $400 apiece. Now if we made one we'd have to get $800. But we don't make them any more.

A guy brought a saddle we made in here the other day. It was wore out. He wanted to see if we could do something with it. It was too far gone—the leather was dry rotted. But he was still using it. I remembered that Barbara who works for us had bought it for her husband. It still had his initials on it: JPB. He worked for Rick Hiles and he let Rick use it. Rick's had it for years and years. They last a long time. Must be 20 years old at least.

I was in that shop in the alley for seven and a half years, and then a place in Dr. Harthill's building came open. I came over and said, "Doc, what do you think about me coming in here?" He said, "I'm gonna give you a chance." He was kind of stern. He said, "If you do good, I'm gonna raise the rent." I said, "Doc, that sounds good to me." The rent was reasonably cheap, $650. I've been there 30 years.

Harthill was a great landlord. Never bothered me, ever. Not once. Somebody asked me one time, "How do you rent from him?" I said, "I stay as far away from him as I can." He was very good to me. He still had his vet practice next door. Had the Churchill vet, and made all the medicine downstairs.

I guess I was in competition with Becker and Durski. But they didn't have anybody going around the racetrack picking stuff up, and I was going through the barns and picking up tack to repair and then delivering it back. Wagner didn't have anybody doing that. I don't think they wanted to do that. They had enough to do.

He didn't say much when I opened up my own shop.

I first moved here for a fall meet. All we did was leather. I just did leather repair, and made halters and reins and things like that. I wasn't selling any other supplies or liniments or anything. But people kept coming over and asking me for that stuff because it had always been here when it had been Becker and Durski. So the next year I started carrying stuff that people needed for the stables. Then gradually I kept getting more over the years.

In those early days we were fans of the band Riders in the Sky. They were always singing, "Do it the cowboy way." Well on the back of my truck, I had a sticker that said, *Do it the cowboy way*. We all thought that was pretty funny. I still say it. I had a guy come in for some work the other day. He wanted to watch me do the stitching. I said, "You want me to do it the fast way, or the cowboy way?" He says, "Well, what's that?" I said, "It's the right way." /

Wanda
Mitchell-Smith
HIGHLAND PARK NATIVE

There was just so much excitement in the Highland Park neighborhood when the horses were in. The community would stir about. You saw the grooms coming in, boarding in people's houses, so you knew that the races were starting and Derby was coming. It was just phenomenal. Derby was a special time. It was work and yet it was play too.

You had bookies in Highland Park. People would play the horses because they knew the horses. They knew when the horse they had cared for was going to make it across that finish line. They knew if the hip or leg was going to be able to handle the pace of the track. They knew whether a horse was a mudder and could run on a sloppy track.

Derby time was employment for a lot of people in Highland Park. A lot of the women, including my grandmother and my great aunts, would work on the track. My mother would take off from her job to work there, because she would make more in tips working in the restrooms for those two days of Oaks and Derby. The economic power of those two days was enormous for Highland Park.

It was really an awesome time. You saw the fruits of it even down to when you went to church on Sundays. You knew that the tithes and offerings were going to be at a higher increase than the norm because of the Downs. We had two Holiness churches.

We had a Methodist church, Lampkins Chapel. And we had a Baptist church, Highland Park. My family went to Highland Park. But the great thing is that we didn't look at denominations. We knew what they were, but we were intertwined. For instance, when it came time for the church Sunday school picnic, Lampkins Chapel and Highland Park always hooked up so that we would be able to have our picnics. The community was dead on those days, because everybody went on the picnics together. That's community! That's the part that the economic developers missed out on when they decided to tear down the neighborhood to expand the airport. The land has yet to be developed to this day.

When the Bass family were going through the loss of their mother, they were very young. The community didn't want social services or anything to come and split up that family. So Plummie and his sister Sharon lived with Uncle Jack and Aunt Lou. And I think Dumplin, Toby and JoAnn lived with Miss Katherine, next to Mr. Grady. They were not splitting up that family. It wasn't happening. They made sure that the kids were well taken care of. The older women had a network of knowing who needed what and when. Someone would say, "You know that they need a little bit of money for whatever," and by the time they got to the corner, it was done.

The men were there also. They worked two, three jobs. I mean, they *worked*. The women would come back home and say, "Hey, I need $20."

"What do you need it for?"

"I'll explain later, just let me have the money. We have a family in need, and we got to help out."

He'd say, "Okay, my wallet's in there on the dresser," or, "Go and look in my pocket."

If there was a need for something, the community made sure that the need was met. Because we are our brother's keepers.

Like our community alcoholic. He did what you were taught to do and worked his whole life, but then he lost all his money in the stock market crash because he had put his money in the bank. That's when he became an alcoholic. Sometimes he'd come home, sometimes he wouldn't. He had a wife who loved him dearly and worked nights at a restaurant. The sisters in the neighborhood would take care of him. They'd yell to him out the door, "Have you eaten today?" Then tell us, "Here, take this sandwich down to him and make sure he gets it."

Then the neighborhood was just taken away. It was gone. And it was devastating. When that defining moment came, when they took all the homes for the airport, it was appalling. We had lived with the noise, we had lived with the air pollution, we had lived with all of that, and we were fine. Our church had bought properties and had been looking to build and expand.

When the government and the city came in and were acquiring the properties for the airport, we lost approximately nine older members of our church within a two-year period. It really took a toll on the lives of the older people. That sudden change shook them up. *I'm in my twilight years and now suddenly, I'm having to move?* Aunt Lou was bold to tell the media, "This is my home. I've been here. I'm not moving. I'm not moving." It really took a toll on all those seniors to relocate them at that age. There were funerals left and right at our church because when you abruptly interrupt someone's life to that degree, they throw in the towel. They don't know what is going on, don't understand what all is being told to them. Many of those people's homes were their life savings.

We had vacant lots at that time, we had houses that were empty, but to the community's credit, they were kept clean. There were some people in the neighborhood who had issues with substance abuse, but you could say to them, "Hey, I'll give you five dollars if you clean up this lot." They'd clean it up spic and span and go and get their five dollars. They'd be lit the rest of the day, but the job was done. They took care of each other.

There had been a community in Highland Park for a long time. There was sharecropping on that land even to where the airport is. My great, great grandfather—they called him Papa—had land over by where the airport is now, and they would farm all of that and eventually owned the property. They worked the land. They tilled the land. They had gardens. They lived off the land. And from that was the creation of the community of Highland Park.

My grandmother's name was Winifred Lucille Ford. Everyone called her Gram. Even the adults called her Gram. Our pastor called her Gram. She was my heart. I went everywhere with Gram. They used to call me her shadow. Little bitty statue of a woman. But so humble, meek and loving. And my, how she could cook! Gram had a cast iron skillet, and that was her skillet. The flavor had to be in that skillet. Someone in the family got that skillet. I wanted it so bad.

My grandmother was just a wonderful woman and a woman of faith. But quiet. She knew a grandmother's role and she epitomized that. She made sure that everything came together for our family, for my mom.

Wanda's neigbhor, Mrs. Margaret Conwell.

In those days, we didn't know that we were poor, but we were.

My grandmother and my great aunts did day work when the track was closed. We called my grandmother's oldest sister Big Auntie because she was the oldest of the family. Dot was the other sister. Her name was Evelyn Brutley. And my grandmother, Winifred Lucille, was the youngest of the trio. They would all come together at 426 Nevada. They would call my mother and say, "Okay, school is getting ready to start. What does this one need? What does that one need?" And they would write it all down.

So, when they would come home from work with shopping bags filled, it was a great day because we knew they had clothes in there for us. And when we went back to school, we had school shoes, we had book satchels, and we were some of the best dressed kids in Highland Park. Our hair was together because my mother was a licensed beautician. So, we were looked upon as well-to-do, but we were still poor. Our family

knew how to do for others as well. Mama would say, "Well, Wanda's outgrown this, that, and the other." And she gave them away. There was no consignment. You gave them away so that everybody would have clothes.

Big Auntie and Uncle Odie—Susie and Odell Livingston—did very well. She didn't have any children, but we were her children. Odie worked at International Harvester. A lot of people worked there. Big Auntie and Uncle Odie knew how to save and how to make their money work for itself. They owned real estate.

Uncle Odie also bought horses and trained them on the side. He had a trailer for the horse, and he had a truck, and he would go up to Turfway Park, and the Downs, and race his horse, and he had some winners. Jerrywood was one of his winners. Another one was named Susie Q. He named it after Big Auntie.

When he was in Louisville, he would keep his horses stabled on the backside of the Downs. But there was one thing that he never wanted for us, especially the girls: He did not like for us to be on that backside. Because he didn't feel like that was an appropriate place for young girls to be. He said there was all types of things that would go on on the backside that he did not want to introduce us to—drinking and cursing and just all different types of things. He did not want us to be around any of that, even though there were one or two times that I happened to be in the truck with him when he would have to stop at the Downs. I would have to stay in the truck. I'd say, "It's hot in here. I want to go out." He'd say, "You better stay in there." By the time he would get back in there, my hair had reverted, I was tired, I was hot. But he would make it up to me by getting me a soft drink or an ice cream cone or something like that.

During Derby season, they would work at the track. They would work in the restrooms making sure that the ladies' rooms were spic and span. They had to wear black uniforms with white collars. Phyllis Knight and Jim Walton would do their interviews for WHAS not too far from the paddock, and when Phyllis Knight would need rest, she would come into my grandmother's restroom, change her hats, rest, and go back out. My grandmother would keep all her hats for her in her restroom there. She did that job for years and years. The tips were so good. It was a good income.

Jockeys' wives would come in my grandmother's restroom. Miss Brumfield was a jockey's mother, and she would come in and show me her program and ask, "Which horse do you like in this race?" I'd say, "I don't know." She'd say, "Do you like that one?" I'd say, "Un uh." She'd say, "You like that one?" I'd say, "Well, I like these colors." I'd pick a horse because of the color. I'd pick a horse because of the name. I didn't know anything about odds or anything like that. And

if the horse won, I got money for picking the horse. We would be there with my grandmother all day. Just posted up. She would let us go out of the bathroom and look at the races.

We would go over to the paddock and watch the horses come out because I knew I might see my uncle Dinky walking a horse. My uncle Dinky was a hot walker, then he was a groom, and then eventually he moved up and he was a foreman of a stable. He worked for the Thorntons who own all the filling stations. It was amazing to me to see these people that I knew—I mean, I really *knew* these people—walking these big horses. I remember seeing Uncle Dinky take a horse and just snatch it by its reins, really rattle that thing. And I thought, *Oh my goodness, he really knows what he's doing.* Especially Derby time, we would look for all of the people we knew on TV: "Look! There's so and so and so! Oh, there's Uncle Dinky! Look!" I was so very proud of them. And then to see them in person when we were able to go was exciting.

To be able to go to the track with Gram, we had to behave. Gram would lay it out: "If you do this, this, and this, then I'll ask your mother to see if it's okay for you to come to the track with me on Saturday." So, during the whole week, you were making sure that you did all your homework. Whatever your responsibilities were in the home, you were making sure that all those things were met so that we could get a chance to go to the track. We didn't realize that some of those Saturdays, our mother was working too, so Gram had to take us with her anyway. We had absolutely no clue.

When we went, we were always very well dressed, and our hair was immaculate. It had to be, because we wanted to have an appearance. It taught us to look well, and feel good about ourselves, and mind our manners. Make sure you say thank you, please, yes ma'am, yes sir, no ma'am.

I remember this one time in her restroom when I heard my grandmother saying "yes ma'am" to a Caucasian lady that was much younger than her. I said, "But Gram, *you're* a ma'am. Why are you saying *yes ma'am* to her?" Because for me, it was about age. For her it was race. It troubled me, but she said, "Shhh." And I said, "But I want to know: Why are you saying *ma'am* to her?" She said, "Well, it's my job. It's what I do." It was hard for me to try to understand and digest. I thought that this manners stuff was about age and respect.

It was much later, when we moved from Highland Park to the West End, that I got my answer. In Highland Park we got along with everybody. There was a part of Highland Park that was primarily Caucasian. But we would still pass by their houses walking to school in the morning, and it was cool. The same kids were in my class. When we got to the West End, I was in for a rude awakening. That's when I figured out, *Oh, it's because I'm black for real? Oh, okay.* But it's not okay.

In the West End, we were the second or third African American family to move in on our block and had encounters about race. It was just horrific. My brother was chased from the bus stop home from school. We encountered things like that. I didn't get called the N-word until I came to West Louisville. I mean, I had heard it. I knew that people used that language, but for a Caucasian to call me that? I didn't get that until then. It was alarming. It was an adult that said it. What I didn't know was that white flight was happening—because we had moved into the community to better ourselves, we were one of the reasons that people were moving out.

––––––––––––––

I didn't know my father until about a year and a half before he died. His name was Skip. When you had a child out of wedlock, you were marked.

But this guy over the years would look at me and smile. He knew that I was his child. But I never knew him as my father. I thought, *There's something wrong with this guy.*

One time when the horses came in, one of my friends came and said, "Your father's here to see you." I thought she was talking about Daddy, my stepfather, and I said, "Okay." She said, "No, no, no—your *father's* here to see you." She said to my sister Bev, "You can't come. He just wants to see Wanda." I was scared, but I went. And Bev went with me anyway. I got in so much trouble for slipping off. He was standing on the porch. He wanted to hug me, and I wouldn't let him, because I didn't know this guy. He gave me about $50. In those days, it was a lot of money. I said, "But I don't want the money." He said, "That's okay." From that point on, I would hear things.

Later, I was sitting down and talking to my mother. I said, "Mom, I'm not judging you. I know that you did the best thing for me." She said, "He was just so good to us." She told me that when I needed something, she'd send word. She had a friend whose husband was on the track with Skip. He would see Skip and tell him, "Hey, I got word that your little girl needs glasses"—or whatever the need was at the time. And that was the communication line that he kept open for me. When I was around 28, I finally got up the nerve to find him and to have the conversation with him.

We spent almost two years together. It was amazing. For Father's Day, I baked him his favorite pie—a lemon chess pie—and we had Father's Day dinner. He took my husband's dad, my husband, and me to the backside with the horses. I just went crazy, and he thought that it was the best thing since peanut butter and jelly. He said, "You like horses?" And I said, "Yes, I love horses." And I said, "And one of these days I'm

Wanda's father, Skip

Wanda

going to get my own horse. And it's going to be a filly." And he laughed profusely.

We had quality time for a year and a half. He was very proud of me. He'd say, "You're very articulate. You've gone to college. That is something I wanted for you to do." He told me, "Your aunts were mean to me." He said that they would not let my mother see him. They would not let them bond or spend any time together.

When I married and became a mother, I gave her his name. Erin Elisabeth Harden-Smith.

Skip retired from the track, but later he went back. I'd call him and ask, "Where are you?" He'd say, "Well, I'm in Florida." And then, "I'm here in New York." He got back to Louisville and I said, "Why are you back on the track?" What I didn't know is that he was saving money to buy a horse. He came back to town and bought the horse. Her name was Shimmy's Flowers. One day he walked that horse to cool it down,

then sat down in a chair and had a massive coronary and fell over, dead. I got a call from his lady friend. She said, "You need to get to the hospital." I said, "Okay, I'm on my way."

I wish I'd had more time with him, but we had a year and a half of blissful times, which was a blessing.

I had to sell the horse. I ended up selling her to a close friend of my father's for a dollar. Whenever she ran her first race, he called me and said, "She's going to win this one. I got a really good feeling." I was able to watch it on television. And that filly *ran*. And it was a decisive win—it was not by a hair or photo finish. She stretched those legs across that finish line. /

Highland Park

The neighborhood of Highland Park was established in the late 1800s and was home to hundreds of families and employees of the L&N repair yard and nearby industries. The neighborhood was also home to generations of Churchill Downs employees, racetrackers, and horsemen, some of whom authored this book.

In 1987, the city government of Louisville announced plans to incrementally relocate residents of Highland Park and demolish the neighborhood in order to accommodate the expansion of Louisville's airport. The plan was alternately met with acquiescence and strident resistance from the communities of Highland Park. By 1993, the neighborhood was entirely demolished. To date, the airport has utilized only a portion of the land acquired. The images in the following photo essay were taken by Pat McDonogh for the *Courier-Journal* in 1988 and 1989.

Sam and Ruby Jones have a lot on their minds as they contemplate leaving their home in Highland Park after almost 60 years. They eventually moved to a new home on Smyrna Road that costs $28,000 more than they received for their Highland Park house.

Gary Holt stands in front of his home on Park Boulevard as a jet lands at Standiford Field.

Bill Thomas, far left, has operated a barber shop in Highland Park for 34 years. He's shown cutting hair with Bill Polston.

Ella White sat alone with her memories in her house on Adair Street. She had intended to spend the rest of her days there.

Residents of Highland Park, Prestonia and Standiford neighborhoods protested at government meetings as the fate of neighborhoods was being decided.

A young girl runs to her Highland Park home after being dropped off by a school bus, as shadows cross the street.

The tidy Highland Park home of Alvin Walters, shown cutting grass was hardly an example of blight, as deemed so by urban renewal.

Highland Park prospered as the L&N Railroad prospered.

Residents of Highland Park, Prestonia and Standiford neighborhoods protested at government meetings as the fate of neighborhoods was being decided.

Myrtle Bishop, with her dog, Tiny, wept at the prospect of moving. Urban renewal offered $26,000 for her home. She settled for $31,000 and $5,000 for relocation.

A man carries a counter top from Mohawk Drugs as the store's furnishing are auctioned off.

A elderly woman left the Highland Park Neighborhood Association building after learning by way of a flyer dropped in her yard that the city of Louisville and urban renewal would be acquiring her home.

Leonard "Plummie" Bass

SECURITY GUARD, RETIRED GROOM

Ain't nothing left of Highland Park. The city bought all them houses and bulldozed them. The airport expansion took the whole neighborhood. They gave me $38,000 to relocate from my grandmother's house in Highland Park. I thought it was worth more than that, but they said, "Take or leave it." You either had to take the money or get the fuck out. I took all of that and put it down on the house I'm in now. I live about a block and a half from the racetrack.

Highland Park used to be right where the railroad tracks are by Cardinal Stadium. It was a small neighborhood. "Highland Park? That little country ass town?" That's the way people talked about it. We had one grocery store called Brown's Grocery Store. I was 14 years old when my mother passed. Mr. Brown sent for me and said, "I always loved your mother." This is a white guy and his wife talking. "I want you to come down here and get any amount of food you want and you can just pay us monthly until you get on your feet."

I'm the oldest and there was seven of us. After Mom passed away I rented a house with four bedrooms, and my brothers and sisters all stayed with me until they graduated high school and moved off and got married. I had a lot of pressure on me, but I didn't know it. The old people in the neighborhood knew, though. They'd cook for us. I didn't know what I was doing.

I just didn't want my family to go to a home. The church people and the people in the neighborhood took care of us—Highland Park Baptist.

There was a tight relationships in the neighborhood. We weren't segregated in Highland Park. Two streets might have been black, but whites lived in the same area. The rest of it was together. You know, people say "niggers" and "crackers" and all that, but we were never raised up like that. We didn't know what that shit meant. We lived right next door to each other, white and black. We played together and we fought together. We had a boy's club where we played baseball. Highland Park was so close to the airport it looked like these airplanes were coming down on us when we played football.

Over on Crittenden Drive is where a lot of people worked. Wood Mosaic, PepsiCo, International Harvester. Around the corner was Winn-Dixie. The L&N railroad was over there. Lots of people from Highland Park worked at this place that made telephone poles that was owned by J. Graham Brown, who also owned horses. He couldn't mess with horses himself because he was allergic. He had people train for him. He had guys like Tommy Long working for him. He'd come to the barn in a limousine with a white poodle. He never got out of the limousine.

The trainer and grooms would come out and meet J. Graham Brown. He just loved the game. He died and didn't have no people, so he left all that money to help the state of Kentucky. The J. Graham Brown Cancer Center, that's his money.

Everybody respected Tommy Long. White, black, whatever—everybody respected him. Tommy was just a hell of a guy to be around. Just a pure horseman. Me and some friends started working with him when we were around 11 years old. He was more like a father to us than our fathers were. Tommy would come through the neighborhood and say, "What're y'all boys doing? Let's go. Get in the truck. We gonna go see some thoroughbreds." Mom would say, "Where y'all going?" And we would tell her we were with Uncle Tommy. He took us over to a farm where thoroughbreds were, showed us how to ride, showed us how to handle horses. It was exciting. They had a pond on that farm where you could fish. It was just a lot for an 11-year-old to do. We worked for him and Tommy never gave us shit but some bologna and crackers and a lemonade, but he taught us how to work! He did the shit my dad couldn't do. We were happy as a lark. We got a chance to get away and go see some horses and ride.

After a while he'd take us to Miles Park, a little bull ring track down in the West End. We'd go down there and walk like eight horses a day for two dollars each. Sixteen bucks was a lot of money back then. This Jewish guy named Jimmy Levitch owned car lots and stuff. He had maybe 60 head of horses at Miles Park. Every day he come in he had $3,000 in his pocket. He'd say, "Keep track of how many horses you all walk, son."

Tommy Long would say, "Jimmy, these boys are well schooled. I taught them myself. These boys can handle a rough horse." 10:00 came and we'd walk in the office. "How many horses you walk?" I'd say, "Eight."

And he'd say, "Hell, take $20." That was a lot of money when you were 11 years old! That's how we got stuck with being around horses, and guys like Tommy Long, Bates, Smoke, and Scotland Yard taught us everything. They taught us how to be a groom, how to take care of horses, how to make a horse run better.

You start from the foot up. You always kept that horse's feet sound. That's what makes them break down so quick. You got to keep the feet clean. Wash them out. Not every day, but every other day you got to use reducing. And you got to use mud to keep his feet packed. Reducing and mud draws the fever out of the bottom of him. Reducing is this black stuff you heat up, and when you put it in there, it draws the soreness out. You wash his feet out first, and then you take a towel and dry it. You put the reducing in the palm of your hand, and then you go around to the outside of the hoof. You put mud in it, pack it with mud, then you put a sheet of paper over top of it. You leave it in there overnight and do that every other day when you think they're sore.

Laying bandages on was an art, and Tommy was the best. I remember one time, we was over in the barn, and Doc Harthill was going to run this horse in Lexington. Big red chestnut horse. Back in the day, Keeneland was known for being a speed track, and horses would burn the skin on their heels. This horse was running so fuckin' hard he was burning the skin off the back of his legs, burning through the bandages.

The horse was ready to run, and Doc went to Tommy because he knew he was the best. Doc said, "Tommy, he's been burning through everything. If you can stop him, I think he'll win. I know he'll win." Tommy was the best bandage man that ever lived. He was just that good. He had a technique. He was unreal. Doc told Tommy, "I'm gonna give you $500 to lay those patches and put bandages on this horse. If we win, I'm gonna give you $500 more."

Tommy Long

Tommy said, "Plummie, go get me an inner tube off a bicycle. It don't have to be new." So I brought him an inner tube. He took some scissors and cut a band out of it about three inches wide and wrapped that inner tube right over the horse's heel. Not the hoof, but the back of the heel. Then he put silicone tape around them. And then he laid another patch straight up on the back. He took tape and went around it, then he turned around and put the sealtex on, then he put another bandage on it. So when the horse hit down it wouldn't burn up his heel.

The horse won easy, and Doc came back with a stack of $100 bills and gave everybody money. He said, "This son of a bitch did it. I bet $20,000 on him. Goddamn, it's a good day." Tommy got $3,000. All he did was lay the bandages.

J. Graham Brown left money to help bury Tommy Long. He told Doc Harthill, "I'm gonna outlive Tommy, but I want you to make sure he's laid to rest. I'm gonna leave this money back here. Give him $500 every week." That's true.

Doc Harthill was a world class veterinarian. He was a great guy. If you had horses back here and needed help, he'd do it free. People tried to pay him and he wouldn't accept it. He'd say, "I get my money from the rich people. I'm not a poor veterinarian. You need the money and you need my help to keep going and I'm going to give it to you." I was talking to a dude the other day who said, "Doc did work for me 20 years and never charged me a penny."

Dr. Alex Harthill

His dad was a small animal veterinarian and his mother was too. They came from Germany but Doc was born here. He was an only child. Doc started working with his dad when he was 11 years old. His dad was a hard working man. He said, "I want you to be successful and be a millionaire one day," and Doc did all that.

He graduated from Ohio State vet school. This guy that came out of vet school with him was over there at Rock Creek Riding Academy once. Dude's parents bought him a brand new Chrysler for graduation, so Doc and Warner Jones got a pig and let it loose in the backseat of this Chrysler for a joke. Pig shit all over the back seat of his car. Maybe they didn't like the kid because he had more than they did. Anyway, they had to take the car to get all new seats and everything redone.

Doc Harthill was known worldwide. He was always so much smarter than the next guy. Most big outfits got one vet. To be successful you need a good veterinarian. A groom named Bates got Harthill the job at Denmark Stables right after he graduated from Ohio State University. Bates had influence on them because he was just that good of a groom. Bates got Harthill the job and he got a horse to run third in the Kentucky Derby.

He had 40 patients right then and there. From there it went on and on and on. They called Harthill the Derby Doctor. All the Derby horses would ship in there and he was the vet for all of them. He was just that good of a veterinarian. He also owned and trained horses himself, of course.

I met Doc Harthill when I was catching the bus to school. Right on 4th Street. The bus went up to Broadway then I went down to Central High School. I was working for Jim Padgett walking hots at 4:30 in the morning, then got on the bus at 6:00 to go to Central. Two hours of work in the morning, got out of school at 3:00, and worked four hours in the evening.

Doc seen me catch the bus. He told me, "Tommy Long told me about your mother dying. He thinks you're a hell of a kid. You got six sisters and brothers?"

I said, "Yeah, and I'm the oldest. I got a lot of weight on my shoulders right now." When your mother dies, you think that's the only love you ever had. It's over, you know? In the back of your mind, you think, *What am I gonna do?*

Doc said, "I already talked to Padgett. You come work for me. I'm gonna pay you a good salary, and help you get through school." Back then, if somebody had a lot of money, they would see something in you and they'd pick you up and carry you along. Maybe he picked me out because he knew I was going through a hard time.

A view from the Wyandotte neighborhood. The 15,224-square foot 4K screen at Churchill Downs is one of the largest in the world.

So I started working with Doc when I was 14. By the time I was 18 or 19 years old I'd travel around with Doc. I loved going to Gulfstream in Hallandale, Florida. Pretty girls saying, "Okay, look at these Kentucky guys here." They knew we had a bankroll. Back then, they called grooms from Kentucky "hardboots" because we was hard to fuck with. We went everywhere and they knew what the Kentuckians could do. "Here they come. Here come them hardboots."

It was a trip. It was cool. From Louisville to Gulf-stream, and from there to Oaklawn in Hot Springs, Arkansas. I didn't want to go to New Orleans. Fair-grounds was a nice track, but it's fucking spooky. Grave-yard right behind the racetrack. When it rained you'd see the caskets floating on the back of the racetrack.

You think that ain't spooky? Fucking casket floating down the track?

I worked with Doc until I got out of high school in '75. Doc told me, "They're hiring at the International Harvester foundry. Leave this place and get you a job with a pension. One day you'll need it." So I left the track and worked 16 years in the hot-ass foundry. It was like 150 degrees. We built motors for John Deere. Pouring iron and everything. We had to be there at 7:00 and got out at 2:30 and you got a half hour to take a shower. It was a rough job, but it wasn't bad. $27 an hour. That was a lot of money in 1976. I was saving $200 every week. In six months, I saved my money and bought a Lincoln that had 6,000 miles on it. I got a four-bedroom house. First year at Harvester, when I was 17, I took my family in. And I kept them all until

Volunteer cleanup in Highland Park

they all graduated high school and got married. Where there's a will there's a way. That job was so good. It was a blessing, man.

When they shut down the foundry, Harthill called me up that night and said, "Come back to work for me." This was '91. We worked up until Doc passed in 2006. I came back and started rubbing horses with Tony Montano, Gayle, JD, Bates, Eddie Bonefont. It was a good crew. People think a trainer will make a horse win. That ain't true. It's just like a team in basketball. If you ain't a team working, it ain't going to work. Anytime you working seven days a week, you've got to be a team. A lot of people can't do it. You've got to love the animal, and love what you doing.

I was making about $700 clear a week from Harthill. Ain't no joke. Derby week I'd make $5,000. I'd go home and give my wife $2,000 and she'd ask, "How much did you *really* make?" I'd say, "I ain't telling you." Nobody never left. We never left that job. And the money wasn't no object. If you got in trouble, Doc would get you out of jail. He was just a hell of a guy. He was just loyal.

He had a lot of pressure on him, being who he was. He might go off on you one minute then come back five minutes later and ask if you want $3,000 or $4,000. I don't know that many people who would do that. He would say some shit and I'd think, *Damn, I don't believe that's Doc.* An hour later, we'd be working and he come back around. He'd ask, "What y'all doin?" He'd know he probably had stirred us up. He'd say, "Hey, I probably had some stuff on my mind and I probably used you all for a scapegoat to get it off my mind." We'd say, "Doc we're letting it bounce off us. Don't worry about it." He'd say, "What do you all need? Here, take your families out to dinner tonight."

He had his faults. He always told me, "I'm not an angel, but I believe in winning." He would do some things a normal vet wouldn't do that helped the horse win. He knew what the horse needed to make him run. A lot of vets don't know it, but he knew.

Doc would put horses in black trainers' names because when they led them over, he knew white people wouldn't bet because they were prejudiced. "This black guy. I ain't bettin' on this fuckin' horse." He knew he could get a better price with a black man taking it over. That's how racial it was back in them days. He capitalized on that. He said, "I know how they think." Doc knew people were prejudiced.

He showed me a wall the slaves built. It was over 100 years old. It was something to see. If you ever seen it you'd never forget it. Close to Georgetown College. Doc said, "Look at these bricks. Can you believe they ain't moved in all these years?" Some people never seen things that slaves did. It impressed me. He said, "It's something people need to think about, how fucking good they were. I wanted to show you how good your people were. If it wasn't for the slaves, the U.S. never would have gotten the jump they got." I was young, I didn't know all that. Just for him, being a white guy, and showing me that, nobody else ever showed me anything like that. It was unreal. It was so much history. I never would have known about it. He wanted me to know it. It was very special to me.

But we had a bad ending. Doc started to go downhill. One day he got into a car wreck and he tried to blame it on me. I was standing there with Kenny Luckett, and Doc came back and blamed the wreck on me. I knew it was time to go. So I said, "Doc, I'm leaving and I ain't coming back. You've been good to me. I love you and everything, but you ain't gonna call me no nigger and all that shit. I'm gone."

Everybody came to me and told me, "Go back to the old man. He can't do without you. He ain't gonna apologize to you for what he did. But he's suffering right now." It was a bad ending.

My wife's mother told me, "Plummie, he's been great to you. Now it's come to the end. Crazy shit happens. Put it behind you and move on."

It hurt me. It really hurt me. And everybody at the track heard about it. But beyond that, I still loved him. He was hard to love, but he was the greatest. He was generous in his heart. People loved him. They'll never be able to duplicate it at Churchill Downs. He was one of the best that ever did it. /

Maria Sol Aller

ASSISTANT TRAINER

In nature, outside in the wild, horses are prey animals who are hunted or eaten by bigger animals. Their instinct is to run, to get away from predators. It is very important that you understand that instinct, because this is what is going to keep you safe, and make them feel safe around you. You can tell right away when a person has been around horses for a long time; they look like a fish moving in the water, so natural. For the person who does not know how to swim, it seems amazing. Even the way they approach the horse, the way that they look at him. If you look in their eyes, sometimes they get scared. They are so massive, we have to understand and not forget.

Horses teach you more about yourself than you will ever in your life be able to learn. Horses are your mirror. If you are scared, the horse is scared. And if you feel safe, the horse is going to feel safe. And if you believe in them, they will run. That is why horses are so amazing to me, because it is a process of trying to know myself a little bit better. Every time that you are scared of something, you face it, and you just try to swallow the fear and keep walking. Something good comes after that.

My horse Stoptalkingmaria is the one that made me feel that.

She had an accident at Keeneland. She was inside the stall, reared up, and broke a metal screen with her front legs. She cut her tendons and had severe bone damage as well. Blood all over. It was bad. We checked with three vets, and one of them said, "Put her down," because she was so severely damaged that they did not think that they could even save her life. Another one said, "Look, she's not a racehorse anymore, but she may have a chance to live." It is a really tough decision. You do not want them to be in pain, but if you believe that she has even a one percent chance of making it, you have to take it. It's the way I feel. You just have to give them the chance.

I told the trainer, Murat, "I think I can save her life." So he put the horse in the trailer and brought her to my friend's farm. After being in the stall for 90 days, not being able to walk outside, she was terrible. We could not touch her, we could not come inside the stall, we could not hold her—we could not do anything. Every time she saw us, she was making an association between us and pain. They tranquilized her, but she was in so much pain that every time she saw us, she went nuts inside the stall. Nuts.

She was crazy, and she was in so much pain at the beginning that it was hard for me to make her forget it.

Giving her the medicine and changing her bandages gave her so much pain that she was scared of me. So I would buy hot chocolate at the gas station and let her lick it out of the cup. That is how we started. I would bring a chair and a bale of straw and put them in the front of the stall, and I would just sit every day and roll bandages, talk to her, and give her chocolates. I would spend all day with her. It took at least six months for her to heal from her wounds. She still has scars.

Then winter came and it was really cold. Horses are meant to be outside. They're free animals. She was getting better and stable enough, so we decided to turn her out so she could walk around a little bit. I remember seeing her legs covered up with snow. It worried me at first, but I realized it was helping her a lot. It seemed like the cold was kind of helping her handle the pain better. It acted almost like an anesthesia. So we turned her out in the field and just let her be a horse.

The next spring, we were with Murat, checking the horses out in the paddock. We saw Stoptalkingmaria running up and down the hills, so we decided to give her a chance. We decided to create a partnership and put her in training.

She had a name, but we didn't like it, so we decided to change it. We never thought she was going to be a racehorse, but I thought we should name her something fun and happy. At that time there was a horse from Pletcher that I loved the most. Her name was Stopshoppingmaria. It reminded me of when I was growing up, and my father would always tell me, "Stop talking, Maria! Please stop talking, Maria." We were all thinking, and Murat was kidding and said, "What about 'Stoptalkingmaria'?" And I said, "Yeah. That's the name."

Nobody wanted to ride her. Nobody wanted to break her. She was a tough horse. She threw six riders.

One brave Peruvian guy showed up, and he stayed on the first day. Then he stayed on the second day. And then he just stayed on.

When we arrived in Indiana for one of her races, I knew Maria was crazy, and that I had to be the one to take her out of the trailer. So I went inside, grabbed the shank, looked at her eyes, and said, "Look, this is between you and me. If you take off, or if you do something crazy here, you will have to kill me to run away from me. But I am scared to death, and you have to know it. So you better behave, because it's either you or me."

Even before the race, my adrenaline was so high that I could not see. I am not kidding. I was burning and my eyes were completely blurry. So when she was running, I could not see the wire and did not see her going across it. Then everybody was screaming and telling me, "Congratulations! Congratulations!" I did not know what happened. I was like, "We won? We really won?" I could not believe it. We didn't have much money back then and we had spent our savings trying to train her. And now she had won.

We came back, and the first thing I did was buy straw. I put so much straw on the ground that you could not tell if the horse was standing or lying down. She had straw all the way up to her chest. I could not even open the door. I could not even express how thankful I was.

After that, Stoptalkingmaria went to Keeneland and started to improve, run better races, and face stronger competition.

She helped me overcome my fears. When I started to work with her, I could not even walk her. She was insane. She was strong, and I was scared of that. She taught me to that even if you are scared to death, even when you have it in your heart that you are not sure, you just have to face your fears; if you do it, it is heaven

after that. You just have to be willing to do a little bit more. That is what she taught me.

Some people take everything for granted, but it was never like that for me. I have always had this feeling that life is short, because when I was eight or nine, back in Argentina, I had an accident. I got electrocuted. I came out of the swimming pool all wet and was playing hide and seek with my best friend. I went to unplug a lamp. The house did not have breakers, so I got completely stuck to the electricity. My friend did not scream or anything. She got scared, so she hid under a bed.

I was completely conscious of everything that was going on. I remember how it felt when I had the electricity running through my body. I felt like somebody was setting my legs on fire, and all this fire was just running down my legs and all the way up.

The lights started flashing, and my family came in. My father was the one who found me, and he kicked me a couple of times. I'd been shocked for a long time and was completely purple and black. My arms were purple all the way up to my elbows, and my legs were the same thing. My aunt gave me CPR but had no luck, so they took me to a hospital. The doctors told my parents that I was dead. But then they did some electroshock and I came back to consciousness. They were able to reanimate me, but I was so severely damaged that they believed I would have brain damage and was probably going to be in a vegetative state.

I woke up later that night and wondered, *Why can't I move my hands? Why can't I move my legs? Why is everybody here? What's going on?* They had tied my hands and my legs to the bed because I had been jumping and shaking. Then I said, "Mom, why are you crying?"

It was a huge deal for my parents, especially for my mom. It was really hard for them. Even today, I cannot talk to them about it. There are some details that I would like to know, but every time I bring up the subject, everybody starts crying. It is really hard for them to talk about.

Since then, I have always lived with this feeling that life is short. You have to enjoy, you have to do your best, you have to live your fullest. You have to be one hundred percent fully present today because today is the only thing you have. If I feel that I can do a little bit more, I have to do it, because you have to live to the limit—live until you can say, "Well, I've done everything I wanted to, I am everything that I could ever be. I am happy. I have no regrets. I have nothing left behind that I wanted to do."

I went to law school, and then from law school I switched to agricultural engineering. I had a good life. I had a house, parents who loved me, friends, and I was studying at one of the best universities in the country. But there was something that made me feel like I could do a little bit more. I wanted to find something bigger outside. I was not 100 percent happy. I realized I was doing a lot of things just to make my parents happy, but I was not 100 percent myself. I wasn't sure if I was able to choose between black and white. It was kind of gray.

I told my parents I wanted to come to America. I wanted to have an experience working in a different country—different culture, different language—for a couple of months. Just to see how it felt being on my own. They said, "No way. You finish university first, then you go." I was 22 years old.

I told my parents, "This is what I'm gonna do." They were not very happy at first, but then they said okay and they supported me a lot.

I called my best friend and said, "Hey, why don't

we go to the States? Let's just go and spend three months working and vacationing." She said, "Let's go!"

We went to New York and worked in a fast-food soup restaurant. That day I realized that I had never really worked one day of my life.

I was so spoiled. In New York during Christmas time, everything was so expensive. We had fun and spent money for a month, then ran out of money. My friend said, "This is not for me." She went back to Argentina, but something told me that I had to stay.

I called an American friend I knew from Argentina. She was from Ohio and she told me to go stay with her parents, so I did. I ended up in Columbus working the night shift at a Subway. The only thing I ate for three months was Subway turkey and cheese subs. I ate to try to stay awake on the night shift. It was terrible. I gained 20 pounds.

The whole time I was asking myself, "You're in a different country. You learned the language a little bit now. You're able to communicate. You're able to move around. So what now? What do you like to do? What is your passion? "

Horses. I wanted to go to a place where they have horses.

I literally went to Google: *What place has the most horses in the world?* I didn't even know about Kentucky. That's how I learned that Kentucky is the horse capital of the world. So I started to save money, and I started telling everybody, "I'm gonna go to this place, Kentucky. I think I'll like Kentucky." And everybody was like, "Kentucky? What are you going to do over there?" I said, "I like horses. I'm gonna try to go over there and do this." I just put it out in the world.

At the end of my shift one night, I counted the coins in the cash register and 25 cents were left over. It was a Kentucky quarter, with horses and fields on it. I kept that coin, and still have it.

It took me two days to come from Columbus to Lexington on a Greyhound. It was a terrible Greyhound, but I didn't care. I just wanted to come to Kentucky. I came to Lexington because my friend from Ohio had a friend there who picked me up at the Greyhound station, and then took me straight to her house downtown.

I was introduced to a horse trainer, and he said, "If you want to start working here, I can teach you some stuff. You can just help me out, and you can learn." He was just a small, crazy Argentinian trying to do it.

So I started to work with racehorses. The second or third day, I tried to walk a thoroughbred. It was jumping and kicking the walls, rearing up, and making a show. It was hard for me because his barn was a mess and his horses were very aggressive. I was going back home every day crying and thinking, "I'm not gonna make it.

I love this so much, but I'm not gonna make it." I was so scared.

With horses, you are not in control of anything, actually. When you have huge and strong and powerful horses going crazy and jumping and rearing up and kicking, you feel that you have no power whatsoever to control anything. I felt so useless around horses.

My friend R.J. told me, "You need to start being around horses in order to understand how they work, how they act. If you want to learn about horses, come with me. I'm gonna teach you little by little."

So I moved to Midway and rented one floor of a big three-story house on a friend's farm. I started to work with R. J. every day. He taught me everything little by little, taking it easy, helping me understand the horse's conformation, the horse's attitude, how to read a horse: the things that you need to learn just to know how to act around a horse.

Then in November 2009 we bought Stoptalking-maria. She was less than eight months old. We spent so much time together that she became my soulmate. The horse is a reflection of who I am, completely. We are one. It is myself in the form of a horse. She is my everything, my whole world.

We started at a very little farm which was falling apart. Now we've moved to Elmendorf Farm, one of the most historic farms in Lexington. It was a lot of work to get to this point.

Maria is at the farm now. She is the queen there. When she got hurt, I took care of her. But then she took care of me so much that I promise myself that, even until my last breath, that horse is going to have the best possible life that a horse can have. She is going to be the happiest horse on earth. I have been doing everything I can to make her happy. She is in the field with another mare, she is in stall number one in front of the office, with cameras everywhere. Every

time I go to the farm and see her, I always give her candies. I always go and hug her. I always touch her back. I always tell her, "Maria, you own everything. All this is yours. All this belongs to you. Whatever you want."

I live my life for her. That's the way it is. I cannot tell you how thankful I am, really. She is who I am. Murat and I started 50-50 with one horse, and thank God we were able to grow and increase our business together over the years. We were able to keep the glue, the queen who put it all together. And we are about to run her first baby already: Joe Benjamin, named after my grandfather. /

Matt
Bizzell

HORTICULTURE DIRECTOR

I was a nature boy as a kid, always in the creek and in the woods. It was just inside of me, so I always moved in that direction. I remember planting vegetable seeds as a young kid and being moved by it. One of my grandmothers had a big vegetable garden, the other had an ornamental garden. My mother always made a big deal out of planting stuff in the spring, and she always involved me in it. I spent my teenage years on a family farm in Milltown, Indiana, and that taught me a little about everything.

When I went to college, I got into the Indiana University Southeast biology program and I really loved it, but I didn't want to go to graduate school. When I found out they were hiring on the grounds crew at Churchill, it was more money than I was making at the nursery and garden center where I worked, so I came on and started in 1998.

I was 22 when I first got here. Five of the nine current crew were here when I started, and they are all 20-plus years older than me. They kind of think of me as their kid. So there's a weird dynamic between us—I'm their kid and their boss—but that makes me respectful of the work they do because I've done it and know how hard it is. And hopefully, that gives them some respect for me because I was in that position. I think we have a good working relationship. I've always felt very comfortable in the position.

We're our own department. We work on every area of the track. We skirt the front side and the backside. We also take care of the Derby Museum's landscaping. We'll take large areas and re-landscape them in wintertime. Anytime there's a water leak or a tripping hazard or sinkhole, we fix the bricks in those areas. There's more than 12 acres of brick on the property, so it's an enormous amount of brick to maintain. Because the place is a year-round facility, we never stop. We have a variety of deciduous evergreens. Perennials, grasses, tropicals, annuals. We have a mix of a whole bunch of different stuff, try to have layers and textures and things that are of visual interest. I love unusual stuff.

It's very difficult to get everything planted and watered in time for Derby. It takes a lot of planning, hard work, and luck. We do have irrigation on quite a bit of stuff, but a lot of stuff we water by hand. I'll have one person hand-watering. Four people are planting centerfield, our largest planting area. And then Mary takes care of the greenhouse and boxes up stuff for the planters. My crew does an incredible job, and I am proud to work with them every day.

The greenhouse is kind of an island in the sun at Churchill. It's definitely a neat place. We have 20,000 annuals there. Not counting the tropicals that we hold over year-to-year. For the fall, we did 8,500 mums. The swiss chard, the kale, the cabbage, and the giant mustard—we did probably about 10,000 or 12,000 of those. We also did pansies.

It takes probably two weeks to get everything in the ground for the spring meet. The springtime is very difficult, because the last frost-free day is normally considered Derby weekend or the weekend after Derby. So we need to have pretty much everything in the ground the week before Derby, when we open. We wait and watch the weather really closely, and as soon as it looks like we've had our last frost or the weather's breaking, we start planting and we plant like hell.

We do hire one or two temporary people that help us, and we work a lot of overtime. The rest of the year, we normally just work 40-hour weeks. But the prep for Derby and Derby week, we work quite a bit of overtime. And it's all weather-dependent.

For years and years, we used the same varieties of mums, and they bloomed when we wanted them to. Then when the lights went in, the mums didn't bloom when we needed them to. Chrysanthemums are light-dependent. So they've been accelerating to open in the greenhouse under normal light conditions. But the lights on the track come on at 5:30 or 6:00 in the morning and this makes the flowers actually slow down. The lights will slow them way down. It triggers them just like the sun. So we started buying varieties that bloom at a certain time of the year. We used to buy ones that were considered the latest-blooming varieties of mums, and then when we put the lights in, they slowed down too much. So now we put in earlier-blooming varieties.

The turf track is seven-eighths of a mile, so there is seven-eighths of a mile of the burning bush hedge. That has its own crew, the turf crew. They do a great job. You can see how chewed up it gets where the horses run on the track. So, during the September meet, they keep a temporary rail out there to keep the

Vicky Hutchinson and Cindy Levett

horses off the inside track so that it's in better shape for the November meet.

The turf crew tries to maintain what they have. If there's a bad section, they will cut it out and put sod down. But normally, they try to maintain what they have, which is the establishment of the root system. That's very important. They'll top-dress with a sand and dirt mixture to fill all the holes, then reseed and fertilize like hell. It's mainly a turf type called tall fescue, which is coarser and grows better in the hotter season, but it has some bluegrass in it, which is better in the cooler season. So when it's warm most of what you see is the fescue, but the bluegrass is in there, and it will start to grow during the cooler weather.

Not a lot of people get to come out to the Kentucky Derby Winner's Circle because it is only used once a year, for the Kentucky Derby winner. It's also the final resting place for a lot of people. Their ashes are sprinkled here. So the Derby Winner's Circle is sacred for multiple reasons.

We always do red geraniums there. It's traditionally always been red. Years ago, when you look at the pictures, they were red begonias. But since I've been here, they've been red geraniums. Sometimes we do an outline of white dusty miller around them. It's roughly 400 red geraniums. We always grow double the amount that we need, because if there's a particularly rowdy winner's party, they'll stomp it down. Under normal circumstances, the back area will get beat up and we'll replace it. But some years, the whole thing's wiped out and we have to pull everything up and replant it.

I do the landscape design. I just learned as I went. The person that installs it needs to be the person that designs it, because it's so difficult to get things right and there are always a lot of last minute adjustments. I started planning and purchasing all of my stuff for the next Derby in July in order to get the early-order discounts. I'm definitely in a routine, and I'm the type of person that likes to plan and think four or five steps ahead. I try to do things for myself and the crew that make things easier on us. I try to do it the right way the first time and not have to backtrack and do things a second or third time.

So you try to have a good plan, but then when things actually start growing and you see how things look, the plan normally gets flipped around. We're always kind of chasing stuff. We never finish. /

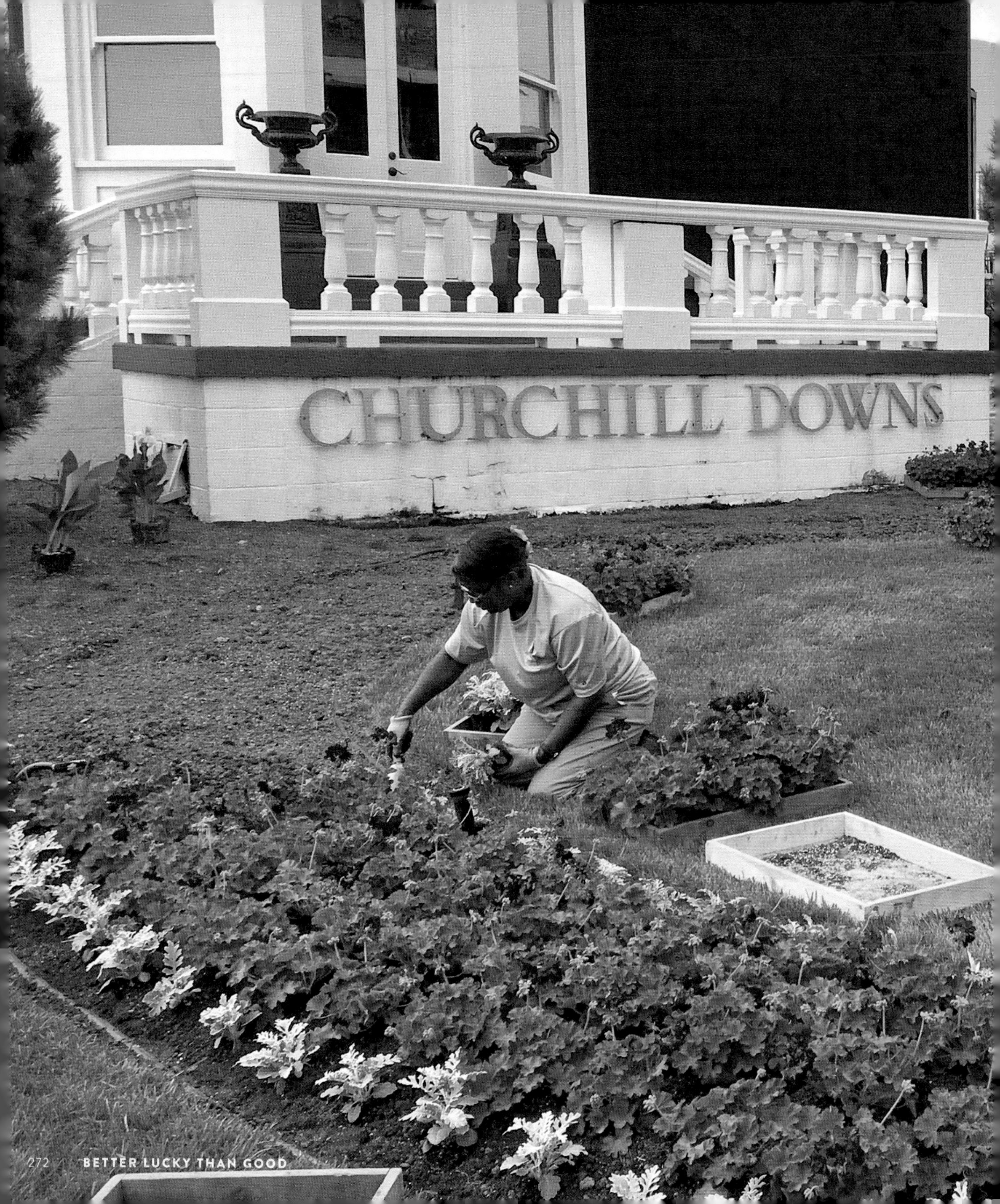
CHURCHILL DOWNS

Monnie Goetz
PONY PERSON

I think my mom rode when she carried me in her belly, if you want to know the truth. I grew up in this industry. I grew up on the racetrack in Beatrice, Nebraska, 40 miles south of Lincoln. Horses were my life. Dad had me on Pepper, a little dappled Shetland pony, when I couldn't hardly walk. I rode him all the time. I wasn't any bigger than he was. I was galloping race horses on Dad's farm by the time I was seven or eight years old. He bred a lot of mares and trained a bunch, too. Me and my dad were together all the time. There's seven of us kids, but I'm the only one that stuck with the horses.

Dad had racehorses that he'd run on the circuit in Nebraska. When I was going to school, Dad had horses at home and I'd gallop them. I'd come home from school and meet the horses in the back of the pasture. Because I fed them all the time, they'd come up to me and I'd just swing up on them and ride them straight to the house like they did in *Black Beauty*, where that kid rode that horse bareback. Oh, I'd beat my sisters home all the time. Those horses loved me. I'd leg them up while Dad was at the racetrack running horses. A lot of times I rode by myself. All I wanted to do was ride. I wanted to ride a different color horse every day. I'd ride him a couple miles up to the Dairy Queen and A&W.

I took care of horses on the farm. I grew up working. I learned how to muck stalls when I was five years old. I had responsibilities when I was 12 years old. I'd go out feeding the horses, legging them up, exercising them, and training them. We grew up working. That was just part of it. I would get up and feed the horses in the morning, go to school, come back, gallop horses if there were some that needed galloped, work until supper time, and then start over.

When you're in it, that is your life. It takes years to get there. You learn by watching other people who know what they're doing, and they teach you as you're going along in the routine. I learned to put bandages on horses, how much to feed them, how to put a shank on, how to pick their feet, how to put a saddle on right, how to put a bridle on right. In anything there's always an easier way to do it and the proper way to do it.

In the summers I worked at the track galloping and taking them to the gate. You had to be 16 to gallop on the racetrack, but I galloped for my dad, so they never said nothing. I could gallop as good as the others, so the outriders always left me alone.

There was a circuit where they'd run for weeks or months, and then everybody would pack up and move to the next track. We'd all travel together, all the trainers. They'd shut one town down, go to the next.

Monnie and her dad, Tom Hawkins

It was like a family thing. Everybody knew everybody real good; we all grew up together. Mom wanted to be with Dad, so we left the farm and rented it out, and us kids travelled and changed schools for two years. We lived in a trailer. They'd have trailer parks on the backside for the trainers and owners, so you'd park your trailer and live on the racetrack and take care of your horses and run them. It was a big gypsy operation.

We traveled and changed schools about four times a year. We went to Grand Island, Lincoln, Columbus, Madison, Sioux City. First and second grade we were doing that. Seven kids in a big trailer. I liked it because I was on the racetrack. School was never a thing for me. I couldn't wait to get out of school so I could be at that barn.

When we didn't have to go to school, I wanted to get up early to help out at the barn. I'd tell my parents before I went to bed, "Make sure you wake me up. Make sure you wake me up!" They wouldn't wake me up. Dad would get up at 5:00 in the morning and go out to the barn, start taking care of horses. I'd wake up, and everybody would be gone taking care of the horses. I'd be so mad. I'd start grabbing wheelbarrows—I couldn't even hardly lift them—and dumping them.

We did that for two years, until Mom said, "This ain't the way to do it. We'll just stay on the farm and go to school in one place." Then we'd come to the racetrack on Friday night after school. We'd leave as soon as school got out. We'd drive and it'd take us a couple of hours to get to the racetrack. Then we'd come back Sunday night, or get up real early Monday morning.

My first racehorse was Grand Patrol. Big old bay horse, 16 hands high. Dad bought him for $375.

I broke him on the farm. I wasn't old enough to gallop yet. He bucked everybody off. They were falling off of him right and left, but I never fell off that horse. I was the only one who ever messed with him. I fed him good. We wound up running him in races. He ran seven seconds in a row, and then he won. Then we had him in an allowance race at Atokad Downs and Fred Eckiphree was on him. He was the leading horse and he was in the turn and got clipped heels and went down to his knees. The jock almost fell off. He gathered himself back up, and still came back, and ran like fifth or something. He chipped both knees real bad that day. We wound up selling him.

I used to go to them farm sales they'd have once a month downtown. And I'd go to the horse auctions all the time. I bought me a couple babies. Six month old babies, for like $40, $50. Dad would be at the racetrack, and I'd find somebody at the sale to haul and drop them off at home for me. I wasn't 12 years old, and I was going to the sale and buying me a quarter horse baby. I'd make Dad feed him until he got big, and I'd break him. I sold one of those horses to a friend, sold one to my teacher. I went and bought a big old fish tank with some of the money. Bought all them Breyer model horses. I have a whole collection of them.

Grand Island, Columbus, Omaha, Lincoln. They're all shut down. Atokad shut down. Madison shut down. The best thing I could've done was leave and come here to be in the horse business. It's sad, but this is a tough business. You got to love doing it, too, because it's seven days a week.

I left in '85 and traveled around, went to Chicago, Minnesota, and Florida. I looked up a trainer named Rusty Arnold and galloped horses for him, and my first husband ran the shed for him. We went to Florida every year, and it sure sounded better than going to Grand Island in Nebraska, in January, to break 30 babies a day. That's what we used to do all the time in the wintertime, in the cold—it'd be 70 below with wind chill and we'd have to get on 30 babies a day.

It's better to break horses when they ain't been messed with or spoiled. They're hardly ever handled out west. They're turned out in tumbleweeds and the pastures and brought to us in stock trailers and we were breaking them at the racetrack. We could have horses galloping around the racetrack in three days; a lot of people around here wouldn't believe it. We'd drive them, get them in a stall, put a halter on them, put a saddle on them, then let them get used to the saddle, then driving reins. Then we'd take them out in pairs, ride them out of the stall, ride them in the arena inside the barn a little bit, and then go to the racetrack. They ain't very fit, and they'll get more tired than you will. That was the way they broke them in Nebraska. They do it different in Kentucky. They probably don't move them quite as fast as we did.

Horses coming from the sale learn to have their bath. They're walked and showed in front of people in the public, they get x-rayed and get their feet picked. They are so much more handled in this part of the country than they were where I came from. When we get them in Nebraska, they've never had their feet picked, barely ever had a halter on. They're pretty much wild horses. They turn out good if you know what you're doing and break them right.

Growing up as a kid, I'd watch the Kentucky Derby every year, and I always thought, *Man, some of the greatest horses in history are in the Kentucky Derby. I'm gonna be there someday*. I wanted to be where the big horses were. I knew in my heart I was going to make it to Churchill Downs.

Rusty Arnold wanted me and my first husband to come to Kentucky. We'd never been anywhere and didn't have kids, and we thought, let's go for it. Here I am ponying horses at the bush tracks in Nebraska. When the opportunity came with Rusty Arnold to pull me to Kentucky, it was a no-brainer. Didn't think twice about it. We came from cheap horses to good horses, and then we had the opportunity to go with the good horses—to go to my dream of Churchill Downs. Why not? *This is my opportunity to go to Churchill Downs. This is my love. This is what I want to do. Why not go where it's the best?* It was the biggest thrill, driving through Louisville, Kentucky, and pulling into Churchill Downs and saying, "Wow, I made it. I'm here. I'm really at Churchill Downs." I was as good a hand as anybody around me and I knew it. I had confidence in myself. I was galloping for Rusty. For years, I never ponied in the morning at all. I just galloped. I worked on salary for Rusty for seven years, and I would freelance a little bit on the side when Rusty would let me because people knew I was a good hand.

There's a lot of people who can gallop horses, but there are very few who are good at it. I galloped a lot of tough horses and made them look easy. The biggest key to galloping horses is what's called "being in your hands." When you're grabbing hold of a horse, you don't grab them right away. You let them grab a hold of you—your balance will hold you. You just take your hands and keep them down low on their neck, and you just don't move your hands too much, don't try to ride

their mouth and irritate them. Just sit still on them and try to start them off easy, to let them break into the work. It all falls together, just like a puzzle. You want to be relaxed on a horse. A horse senses all that. It's just this natural thing. You've got to have that feel, and a lot of people don't. You want to do what's right for the horse. Sure, you have to correct some of them, but you don't want to be mean to them. You want them to enjoy being out there.

A lot of people would say, "They're so tough." And the first thing they want to do is cram up on them, grab hold of them, and then they take off. They're already making them tough because they're grabbing at the bit. As soon as you reach and grab, they're going to reach and grab and they're going to be tough. You have to just relax on a horse, let them have their head, let them just go out there naturally with you sitting on them, have a little control, but don't ride their mouth. And then when you start them off, just leave their mouth alone and just try to keep them calm.

But then you get some, all they want to do is run, and you have to take hold of them and pull on them. Or you get some that want to bolt. I've had better luck when I've galloped horses bolting if I don't dramatically keep jerking on them—if I just take that rein, use that hand, and gradually start pulling them over more, rather than just jerk and jerk and jerk and get it worked up. You don't want to jerk horses and flip horses around.

A thoroughbred is at a racetrack in a stall 23 hours a day; they only get out for an hour. Think about it. They only get out to train, take a bath and walk 30 minutes and then back in the stall. You want them to go out to the racetrack and enjoy what they're doing, make them happy. It's easier to take a happy horse over there to run than one that don't want to go run. They'll run harder for you if you treat them right.

———————————

I loved galloping racehorses, but my pony business became so big, by the time people were quitting and retiring and moving on, that I had to take care of pony horses in the morning. The pony business was where the money was, and it grew so big that I had to pretty much stop galloping in order to take care of my pony business.

I'm self-employed. I got eight ponies at the racetrack right now and a bunch of people who ride for me, some riding their own ponies. I usually have three-fourths of the horses at Churchill. Like Derby Day, I'll have 90 or 100 horses that I have to make sure are covered. There's other pony people here. We all work together. I help them and they help me. It costs $25 for a trainer to get a lead horse during the races. The trainers pay us. We bill them by the month. It just

varies, it depends on what the card is, how many times during a regular day we will do that.

My job as a pony person is to make sure the horses get warmed up and to the gate properly. A lot of time we don't see the trainer in the paddock, so we mostly do what the jocks tell us to do unless we know the horse. Sometimes horses don't come out the way you expect them to; they get upset or nervous. You don't want them that way. You want to calm them down, and you don't need to warm some of them up that much. Some of them are very high strung. You want to get those away from other horses and away from people, and just try to pay attention to what you got with your horse and let them take that deep breath. And then there's some that are stiff and a little arthritic. You need to loosen them up and jog them and reach on out and gallop, then come back and calm them down before they go in the gate. This is all between the paddock and the gate. Usually between seven and nine minutes.

We grab hold of them and do the post parade. We start off jogging them, then break them into a gallop to warm them up. Sometimes you can see them coming out of the paddock being silly or nervous in the post parade—you get one wants to flip over, or be goofy—so you break post parade and get them away from everybody, to calm them down. It's your job to settle them back down. Get their heads straight and take a deep breath.

I'm there to help the jock. It's better if the jock has a little more control because you don't want the racehorse banging on your pony horse. It's harder on both horses. You want everything as smooth as can be. You do not want to jerk on your racehorse. You don't want to set him off. You want the horse to be free, relaxed, and calm. You don't want to clam them up or be fighting with them. You're out there to get along with them.

Sometimes you get an old bitchy female, or a mean stud horse. The jock or the trainer will let you know about it, "'Hey, this horse could be really bad." You just want to pay attention to them because they'll kick your pony, or bite at you. Our ponies take a beating sometimes. That's why we have bite guards on their necks and hip guards on the stirrups. When you've got a bad horse, you want to always make sure you have a good pony to go with that bad horse. I know which horses I can snug up. I can have a really bad, rank, mean horse beating up my pony, and he's going to stand there and take it and be there for you to do your job. When you hand them off to the gate crew, you want to make sure you get your pony back out of the way. Go forward and then go to the left, because otherwise they'll spin around and kick at you.

My horses that I call ponies are not ponies; they're 16, 17 hands. Most of them are thoroughbreds. I even use Perfect Drift, a thoroughbred who made almost $5 million. He was probably the only horse that's run five times in the Breeder's Cup. He ran in the Derby as a three-year-old and came in third, then I turned him into a pony horse. His first Derby he took California Chrome to the starting gate when he won, and the next Derby he took Firing Line to the gate and he came in second. I always called him "Perfect Drift Who Ran first, second, and third in the Derby."

You've got to teach a lead horse to do their job. You don't want them sailing out from underneath you and running away. You don't want them scared of horses; you want them to hang with you when you have a bad horse. They need to be babysitters. They need to have a little guts in them and get up and go. Thoroughbreds are the easiest ones to break because they already know the routine of the racetrack and being next to horses. You just put different saddles and bridles on them and you put a handle on them, teach them how to turn

Western Style and in response to leg pressure and they'll fall right into it.

I used to use my legs to control them, and a collar around their neck. It's easier on them big heavy horses because they're using their rear ends better. A lot of my horses are broke with my legs, and I got them with my legs. I don't ride them with my hands as much. You can guide them with your legs and no bridle, but our lead outrider here doesn't allow that.

I've ponied in every Kentucky Derby since '85. Never missed one. My first Derby was exciting. I had a beautiful pony. I called him Jesse. Beautiful horse, just as pretty as any pony out there, and did his job like you wouldn't believe. I had a long shot, sure. They're not going to give me a favorite. But that didn't matter to me. I was taking one in the Kentucky Derby. The best part was standing in front of the grandstand for the first time for the Kentucky Derby, on my pony horse. To this day, it still gives me chills. Each Derby, when you're sitting there and they do "My Old Kentucky Home" when they're coming out: what a feeling. It was always my dream to be at the Kentucky Derby. I made it. I'm here.

Every year, on Derby Day, I've gone out there with flowers. The other pony people always said, "You gotta have flowers on your pony." That's just a tradition. I usually have about 10 or 12 ponies in the Derby, out of a 20-horse field. And I get to pick whoever I want to take. For many years, I used to pick the favorite. We all want to pony the winner. I've only ponied one Derby winner in that time. Sometimes I have an idea who I'm going to take in the Derby beforehand. People always ask me who I'm going to take to the gate. They know I get to pick from quite a few, and that I see them train every morning and I'm out on the racetrack with them.

Like Zenyatta, the filly. When I led her out to the racetrack, there were thousands of cameras taking

pictures of her. aIt was unreal. It was the Breeders' Cup Classic. She was probably my favorite horse, Zenyatta. She was like Oprah Winfrey. Everybody loved her. Everybody knew who Zenyatta was. She was unbeaten. She had won 19 in a row. Never was beat until she came to Louisville, Kentucky, and run in the Breeders' Cup and got beaten by a nose. She got left at the gate and got so far back, but she only got beat by a nose. And that was the only time she got beaten in life.

There's nothing better than to have the love of horses in your life and sitting next to or being on one of the best horses in the world. What else can you ask for? If you love animals, it's just a great feeling to be in my spot. People would give their right arm to be able to just walk up and put their arms around her and pet her and love her.

I've been around long enough that I've got a lot of business and I've been blessed by that. And the good Lord has watched over me and took care of me and has carried me this far. Nobody gives you nothing for free. You've got to work for it. The business on the track is seven days a week. You got animals to take care of. /

Sylvia
Arnett

NATIVE OF THE HILL

I grew up in South Louisville on M Street, three doors down from the African American elementary school, G.G. Moore. We've owned the house for at least 100 years. Hard to believe, but it's true. When they bought the house it was four dollars down and four dollars a week. When integration came along and they were going to combine the black and white schools, they demolished G.G. Moore and bought the rest of the houses on the block to build a playground. The city bought the houses and would give them away, but you had to have it moved. My mother was a very shrewd woman and she decided she was going to save that house. She found Mr. Ross, an African American house mover. I don't know how he got into that business, but he could move a mountain. They came and jacked that house up, put it on these long steel beams, hooked them onto rollers, and rolled it two blocks down the street. The whole neighborhood stayed up to see it. My oldest brother slept in the house that night with a glass of water on the dresser. They rolled it down two blocks and set it on a new foundation and it never even tilted the water. And that was our new location. Same house. The house is still there at 2903 South 6th Street and it's still in my family.

People from the racetrack and out of towners called our neighborhood "The Hill." They were referring to that six square blocks of African American

families, probably 30 or 40 families. Everybody had eight or nine kids and we all got along. Like they say, it takes a village to raise a kid. I guess that was our little village. Other parents could correct you back then Anybody could whoop you.

The Hill was surrounded by an all-white neighborhood. We all played together after school was over. No problems whatsoever. My brothers went fishing and hunting with all the guys across the street. They were our guardians. We were surrounded by them and they kind of looked out for us. We didn't realize we didn't have anything. Everyone in the neighborhood knew each other. They knew the history of the other families. They knew what your dad did, what your mom did, where you worked, who went with who.

We came from big families. Eleven in mine. Our mothers never worked outside of the home. Our fathers worked. My mother took work stretching lace curtains for people, and my dad worked on the railroad. Most of the older people in the neighborhood worked at the L&N right there over on 3rd Street, and a lot of people came to Louisville and settled in South Louisville because of the railroad and jobs at International Harvester, American Air Filter, and American Standard. That's where I retired from. Those were good job for the people of South Louisville.

Everybody looked out for the kids; they just wanted all the kids to do good. There was a lot of support there. Dropping out of school was a no-no. You had to go to school—and if not, join the service. And if you didn't want to do that after you graduated, go to college. But do *something*. So that was instilled in everyone.

When you got old enough to be on your own, you had to go. When you grew up, you couldn't stay at the house forever. They'd break your plate. You didn't have anywhere to eat, so you had to go. There was no welfare; we weren't even aware of that then. It was the parents. It was the parents that instilled in you that you had to go to school and you had to do something, and the kids that came out the neighborhood did big stuff. It's unbelievable the talent that came out of those six blocks. Everybody turned out to be someone: principals and teachers, my brother Kenneth had a career in the Air Force, the Houston family worked at the post office and one of the brothers was head of the Housing Authority here. My cousin was a real estate developer. My sister ended up being a French teacher and taught out at Lincoln Institute. This professor wanted to take her to Haiti, but Mom didn't want to let her go. That would've been the opportunity of a lifetime. She would never have looked back.

Dr. Joseph McMillan lived three doors down the street from me. He couldn't go to the University of Louisville because they wouldn't admit him. He had to go to Municipal College, an all black college. But when he came back to Louisville, he ended up being University of Louisville's Assistant Provost for Academic and Minority Affairs. I can go on and on about the neighborhood. Look like everyone done something really successful. It was a nice neighborhood. I enjoyed it very, very much.

The Hill was always in the shadow of Churchill Downs, and we learned to follow horses at an early age.

We learned to look in the program and the *Racing Form* and find out about what they call morning works. We knew what a bullet work was, which is extremely fast. And we knew what a slow work was, which means your horse wants a distance and a slow time. You got all the information about the horses from the guys who worked on the track. They'd come back and talk about how fast their horses worked that morning, when they were going to run, and so on. If they had a horse they thought was going to win, they'd just have to tell one person before the whole neighborhood knew about it. We got a lot of tips—good ones, bad ones. We knew how to choose our horses in a race. We followed racing religiously and bet the races. From the time we were kids and could get our money together, we'd be sending it over there. We weren't able to go to the track, but we could get the money to someone who was old enough to go.

At six years old I was also placing bets for my mom with the bookie. She followed the horses in the paper. I don't know if she had favorites picked or if she worked by names or what, but she was really good at picking. I would go up to the bookie at 3rd and Winkler. Right before you go under that viaduct, there used to be a café there that faced 3rd Street. In the alley there was a back door. I'd knock on the door, this white guy would open, and I would hand him a note with the racetrack where they were running, the race, the horse's name, and my mom's 50-cent parlay written on it. You handed it to the guy, and he would close the door, come back and open the door, and he'd give you a little slip with a receipt on it. Everyone used to laugh about it. A 50-cent parlay is unheard of; you're talking horses that'll pay, maybe, $3.60 on a two dollar bet, and you're going to take part of that 50 cents and put it on another horse? What are you going to win? Four or five dollars? But she could pick the horses.

Horse racing was part of people's lives. There was excitement in the air when the racing dates at Churchill Downs were announced. And it just seemed to bring a different atmosphere to the neighborhood. We knew there would be a lot of strangers from out of town—owners, trainers, jockeys, and workers that came to the neighborhood to work with the horses and be part of Churchill Downs. And they would come over in the evenings after they were finished working. So it was an opportunity to meet a lot of different people from a lot of different places. As kids, we had a very active, exciting childhood, growing up around the horses and meeting the people who worked with them. And it was a part-time job for a lot of people in the neighborhood. The younger guys were able to learn to walk the horses, muck the stalls, and earn extra money.

People traveled with the races. A lot of them came from New Orleans. Some of them came from Lexington and Cincinnati. They'd always come back every year when the races hit Louisville and it was like a homecoming. All the guys that left to go to these other little tracks would be walking around the neighborhood again, and the buzz would be, "So-and-so is here, so-and-so just came back too."

When the racetrackers came to town they rented rooms in the neighborhood instead of staying in a hotel. That was income for the people in the neighborhood. Most of them ate in the kitchen on the track. There was a African American lady, Miss Nellie Johnson, who ran the black kitchen on the backside. She made soul food. Hearty food: bacon, eggs, sausage, gravy, biscuits, pork chops, chicken, greens. Healthy food.

They'd work on the track all day, then come over and scout the neighborhood for an evening of entertainment with the jukebox and the beer and the dancing. Some guys were looking for girlfriends, for somebody to talk to, somebody to spend time with

while they were here in a different city. It was a chance to mingle with some of the young ladies in the neighborhood. It was very exciting.

We had one little place owned by an elderly lady named Ms. Corrine. We called it The Chippy Joint. That's where we used to go and play the jukebox. We thought we were really hot stuff going in there. She'd let us come in early in the day and put us out later when the grown-ups came around. I remember Jimmy Winkfield being at The Chippy Joint when we were just little kids. He had been a jockey in the 1900s. He was the last African American to win the Kentucky Derby, which he won in both 1901 and 1902. I wasn't born until 1936, so he was an old guy when I met him. Everybody would come over to see him when he was in town.

The recognition of African Americans in the thoroughbred racing industry is fleeting at best. But there were people like Mr. Perossier, who lived to be 104 years old. He rode lead ponies, bringing the horses out onto the track. There's a lead pony that leads the parade of horses. You don't see African Americans doing that anymore. He trained horses for J. Graham Brown. He was from New Orleans. The Perossiers were really good-looking people. The girls were real fair-skinned and they had beautiful blue eyes, unusual for African American kids. Had to be mixed with French or something. That's where they got the name.

There were a lot of African American trainers and owners that came right out of South Louisville. I would say there were maybe 10-12 owners and trainers right out of the neighborhood. Carl Sitgraves was about the most well-known and he lived at 6th and Heywood. Him and his wife owned a lot of property in the neighborhood, 12 or 13 houses. He won the Junior Derby at Miles Park, the old fairgrounds in the West End, and he raced at Churchill. They weren't really

Carl Sitgraves (left) after his first win as a trainer and owner, Beulah Park, 1936

high-class horses, but they were good horses. He never really made the big time, but Mr. Sitgraves was really well-known and respected around the neighborhood. His name was Carl, but you called him Mr. Sitgraves. He was always dressed up, wore a nice hat. He was a classy guy. I don't think they ever had any kids; it was just the two of them. She was out of Alabama. Her name was Essie Sitgraves. She was a pretty smart lady and she done the hiring and kept up with the books for him. And she had a big voice in what he done.

Mr. Sitgraves won the Junior Derby with his horse Bob's Dislike. It was a small derby, but we were just so proud that he won it, and he went on to bigger and better things. There was definitely a sense of pride in the neighborhood when our neighbors were winning at the track.

Churchill Downs hasn't always been the grand racetrack that it is now. Growing up, I never looked at it like that. It was just Churchill Downs. It was just the racetrack. We never dreamed it would escalate and skyrocket like it has now. It started small and the little man had a lot to do with it. So they've made it to the top on the shoulders of the little people. All of us in the neighborhood wanted to get a piece of the action. So many of them had a little money on horses. It was good. And then there was some young guys in the neighborhood that pitched their money together and bought horses. They just thought they had a shot. That was everyone's dream out there: owning a horse.

My brother-in-law Jacob Bachelor did pretty well for himself. He had quite a few horses. Jacob started with the horses at a very young age. As a youngster, he

Sylva Mill after a win. L-R: Threodric Williams, Sylvia Arnett, Suddie Whitaker, Mildred Bachelor, Michael Bachelor, Jacob Bachelor, unknown, Harvey Williams, and Norman Bunton. Jockey unknown.

worked on the track and knew a lot about horses. He married my sister and got a job at International Harvester. He was an oiler, kept the machinery running. Plus he hauled furniture for the Green Company. He and my sister had five kids. When he started talking about getting horses she said, "This guy's gotta be crazy. Here we have five kids, I don't work, and you're going to buy a horse?" But he got it anyway. He kept it separate. The money from International Harvester was for the family. He used the money from the Green Company to take care of the horses.

It was the late '60s when Jake started training horses. He hooked up with a breeder in Frankfort, Sid Turner, and that's how he got the horses. Sid would breed them, and he would call Jake and say, "Jake, I got a good filly up here. You need to take it and see what

you can do with it." And that's how he got in it. They formed a very close relationship, and Jake took them as babies and got them to the track and raced them.

One was a filly that he named after my sister and me. My name is Sylvia. Her name was Mildred, and the horse was Sylva Mill. It won the Debutante Stakes in 1972 at Churchill Downs on Derby Day. She was a fast filly. It paid big money. We had so much money because my brother-in-law had said, "Save your money and put it on this horse. If she comes out of the gates, she's not gonna get beat." The odds were about 30-1. My brother-in-law's bet paid $17,400. He bet big. Only bet on her to win. He'd never back it up, and my sister would get so mad at him. I'll never forget, one time he sent my sister to the window. He gave her $200 to win on a horse, and she split it up:

THE HORSE THAT ALMOST RAN

Naughty Jake, who bypassed this year's Derby, nuzzles his resourceful owner.

She bet $100 to win and $100 to place. Once she got back, his money wasn't right. He said, "This is not what I got." She said, "I was playing it safe. I backed it up." He blasted her out so hard she cried. He hurt her feelings so bad. He said, "As long as you live, never change my bet. If the horse runs backwards: *win only.*"

Jacob was well-known around the track. He had an entourage that followed him around trying to figure out, "Who does Jake like?" He had a place in the grand-stand where he sat on the bleachers. He'd be there all the time. That's where you knew you could find him. They wouldn't say much to him because he was really concentrating. He could have had his own form. He

was that good. He wouldn't go to the window. He'd let the younger guys do the running for him. That was such a big deal. He'd hand them all that money and tell them to go bet $200 on a horse. All the kids hung around him because they would get their little pennies together. Whatever he was betting, they were going to bet. Somebody would say, "Jake's betting $200 on such and such." and then everybody knows what he's betting on. Everybody on the track bets the same horse and come post time, the odds done dropped on the horse.

I had everybody at American Standard betting on my brother-in-law's horse. They'd come up and ask, "What's Jake got in today?" I'd write it on a piece of paper, give it to the guy, and he'd take it back all through the plant. I'd get off work at American Standard at 4:00 and I'm beating it to the track so I can catch the last few races. We all hung out in an area on the ground floor of Churchill Downs we called the Snake Pit. There used to be a cafeteria there with very good food. We'd go down there and hang out and get all our information there. Everybody that worked on the track knew they could come there and if they had a hot tip, they could pass it along right there. It was right up under the grandstand. I couldn't get off work fast enough to get to the track. We went to races every day when they were at Churchill. That was it. We had to go to the races.

Jake named a horse after himself: Naughty Jake. A mean horse. When we went over there he'd tell us, "Stand back. Don't get near 'cause he'll bite you." Naughty Jake ran fourth in the Derby Trial, but my brother-in-law decided not to run him in the Kentucky Derby because you had to pay a lot of money to get the horse in the race, and he wasn't sure if he would recoup that money. He didn't go out on a limb. There was an article in *Sports Illustrated* about "The Horse That Almost Ran." We always felt that if he had put him in the race, we could have had an African American trained Derby winner. That was the chance of a lifetime.

If we would have gone around the neighborhood to take up a collection to get the money, we could have gotten it. I guess he knew better than we did, but we thought, *If you finished fourth in the Derby Trial, you have a chance. Why not go for it? It's something you'll always wish for and hope for but never accomplish again.* There was an air of sadness. We were very disappointed. He had a son, Michael, that he taught to be a good trainer. But Michael died tragically. He also had a son, Eric Bachelor, that owned racehorses, and Eric's a very successful businessman.

When my brother-in-law ran a horse, everybody in the neighborhood was standing in the paddock. We were just normal people, didn't really have that much, but it made you feel like a celebrity, like we'd made the big time. That's a rich man's game. It's not for poor people. But we managed to get in on the tail end of it. And we had a good time. We had a great time.

I owned a couple of race horses too, and I won a few races.

I got married in 1954. My husband was in the Marine Corps and we'd lived in California and North Carolina for twenty-something years off-and-on. We came back to Louisville for vacation one month every year. We really wanted to stay in California. That was heaven compared to Kentucky. Once we got back here, everybody in the family said, "Why do you want to go all the way to California? You only come home once a year. You moved out there and had means, so you now you want to go back? No telling when you'll come back here." So we found good jobs and we stayed.

My husband worked at Ford as the first African American security guard, and I got my job at American Standard. When you're in the service, you don't make much money. Coming out of the Marine Corps, we were used to living on meager pay, so we considered that big money. Ford was one of the best jobs around. We had more money than we'd ever had. So we could do a lot of things that we couldn't do in the Marine Corps.

I'd been hanging around the racetrack with owners, trainers, and the workers all my life. It was fascinating and I wanted to be involved in it. After my sister, Marion Johnson, her friend Joe Willis, my friend Dan Bates, my cousin Howard Amos, and my brother-in-law had success with it, I was determined that I would like to do that. My husband and I talked about it.

He said, "If you want to try it, go ahead." And that's how I got in it. The opportunity was there. And then my husband was agreeable enough to let me try. So we said, "Let's take it and see where we go." So in 1976 we started buying horses. We were daredevils.

I named one of them after my husband: Mr. Johnny. Another was Mr. Palmer. They were claimers, not stake horses. Cheap. $3,500. We hired Suddie Whitaker, a young African American trainer. He was struggling, but he knew a lot about horses. He'd been around them since he was 15 or 16 years old. He wasn't a really prominent trainer, so poor people like us gave him a chance. It was cheap labor. He didn't charge as much as the regular trainers. It costs a lot to keep a horse. I would say at least $30 a day. And then you got to feed them, shoe them, and take care of them. It was expensive, but we were all in it together. They were learning. We were all learning.

It was such an experience to be out there in the paddock with the horses. That's a tremendous step, to go from being the eleventh child of a household where my father worked at L&N Railroad and my mother stretched lace curtains, to owning a horse. It gives you a lot of prestige, you know, to walk out and you're the owner of a horse at Churchill Downs, or any track. Other people gather around and they're looking at you like, "That's an African American female, and she owns that horse." It was quite a privilege.

Racing has always been strictly for kings. It's not a little man's sport. But there are a lot of little people in there trying their hearts out, wishing for the big one. And you never know, you might get it. You just might get a horse running in the Derby. It's luck and know-how. I love horses—I just I wish I had the money to go farther. I would have been in the history books for sure: female African American owner of the Kentucky Derby winner. Wow, what an honor.

I was serious about being a trainer at one time too. I think I could have been. I think I had the ability. I wanted to be a black female trainer. There weren't any. I like the idea of breaking barriers, and the opportunity was there, being from the neighborhood and knowing all we knew. We knew what needed to be done. But when my husband and I decided to buy Mill's Lounge, the horses had to go. I let all that go.

My husband was getting ready to retire from Ford and he decided that he would like a little quiet neighborhood bar to give him something to do after he retired from two jobs. Between American Standard and Ford and some stocks we'd gotten into, we did pretty good money-wise. We had money saved up. He mentioned this to a friend of his in real estate and the guy said, "I have just what you're looking for." Mill's Lounge was for sale.

It took every dime we had. My husband was willing to take a chance. His mother had owned a restaurant on 6th Street, The Yellow Dining Room, but urban renewal wiped her out. So his family was familiar with business. I was very hesitant, but I was willing to take a chance. We made an offer and they took it, and we ended up with the club. We renamed it Syl's Lounge. Business wasn't very good at first. Things had died down. It had been a popular spot for people from Fort Knox, but that crowd was leaving. Things were changing.

This club had never had entertainment before. But my husband had friends that were musicians that were looking for a place to play. And it was a lot of African American groups that were really hungry for a place to play and expose their music. This ended up being the place for live entertainment. A little band—keyboard, guitar, and saxophone—could set up in the corner. A lot of people said, "You'll never make it," but we even had people from the East End come here because they

like jazz music. It was a mixed crowd. It was good for everyone. We never had any problem. Syl's Lounge has always been a place where compatible people would come and meet and greet. My husband ran a pretty strict place. If you created a problem, you had to go, and once word got around, people knew this was a safe place. We've tried to keep it that way. Still have no problems.

He said if anything ever happened to him I should get rid of this place. He died in '95, but I decided to try to keep it because I had fallen in love with it. And here I am. I haven't changed too much—just carpeting and new bar stools, things like that. The red lights have stayed. This year will be 29 years. I'm going to try to do 30 years. Over and out. /

Lee Wagner III

PROPRIETOR, WAGNER'S PHARMACY

I found the original note from when my grandfather bought the pharmacy from the Hagens in 1922. Hagen was the pharmacist my grandfather went to work for, and then he bought it from his widow. He borrowed $4,000 from my great-aunt and bought the business.

My grandfather was a generous friend to his neighbors and the horsemen around here. Woody Stephens came in before he passed away and talked to me about that. How he was always loyal to Wagner's because my grandfather helped him out when he had nothing. Woody was an exercise rider on the backside and worked his way up to become one of the greatest trainers of all time, a Hall of Fame horseman. But he came from nothing and when he first got started as a trainer my grandfather would loan him money for cigarettes and soap and deodorant and equipment for the barn. From that day on, he ordered his medicine here. When he was in New York, he would get my dad to ship him his medicine. He'd mail the scripts down and then we'd ship the medicine back to him. He just wanted his medicine to come from Wagner's. That's how loyal he was. He won the Derby in '84. I got to see him win with Swale.

My grandfather liked the horses, but not as much as my father did. Dad did a lot for the backside employees and horsemen too. He took care of their medicine when they couldn't pay for it. This is before the Horseman's Health and Welfare Fund. If they couldn't get a drug covered, he'd get samples from doctors to give to them. They knew it was a place where they could always come and get help. He was here seven days a week most of the time and people respected that dependability. He touched and impacted so many people. People still come in and talk about my father. It's nice to hear.

Dad saw it over and over and over again—the ups and downs of the racing industry. Jack Van Berg is a great example; Dad really had a special place in his heart for Jack. He claimed he learned everything he knew about horses from Jack and his dad Marion. So when Jack Van Berg fell on hard times, made some tough investments, and ran up a tack bill, my dad believed in him. Dad took a couple of horses for the balance and said, "When you get back on your feet…." My mother wasn't happy about that, but he and Dad remained good friends and Jack did make a comeback and he made it right. Here's a Hall of Fame trainer—he'd won the Kentucky Derby—who faced adversity and overcame it. A handshake and a man's word were good back then.

Dr. Fisher has said, "Your dad had the biggest heart. I'm not sure that he was the best businessman, but he had a big heart." But I think he *was* a really good businessman too.

Lunch counter at Wagner's original location

Like when he started selling food in the jocks' room. He said, "We're already in the kitchen on the backside, so let's cook for the jocks," and they let him do it. He wanted to be near Kenny, the silks coordinator, because we were making silks at Becker and Durski. When someone lost silks or their silks looked raggedy, they could just tell the cook, "Hey, tell Lee we need some silks for Calumet Farm or Overbrook Farm." We'd get all the tack work from the jockeys. It was a convenience thing. They knew all they had to do was make a call and we'd bring it over.

My dad was a really bright man, always looking for ways to marry the trainer and pharmacist. Looking at how medicine could work for the horses. How can it help them? How can it give them an advantage or cure them?

He added the tack shop in '65 because they were basically making all the liniments and things for the veterinarians back then. It made sense to combine the businesses. Dad wanted Wagner's to be a one stop shop for the horesmen. The pharmacy did all the compounds for veterinarians. Dad did all of Doc Harthill's liniments for years. At that time they needed a pharmacist to do that. When I was real little we'd go down there to Doc's place and my dad would mix those liniments up in all those tubs. Plummie and I would bottle up the medicine for Doc Harthill. We made some of our own stuff down there as well. I remember the smell of that place. As soon as you went in there, you got hit with all the different veterinary aromas, this unique menthol, eucalyptus, liniment type smell.

I was always with Dad from the time I was three years old. We'd make the rounds on the backside and then come open the pharmacy every morning at eight. The bookmakers Buddy Thomas and Lefty Erlanger would be there. Later John Churchman would come and sit at a table with Billy Borders. Marty Hisle, the horse dentist, would come in for lunch. I wish I could remember all the stories I heard from those guys. It was the hangout for the horsemen, and there's no doubt in my mind that that's why my dad made the lunch counter bigger in the old location, because he wanted all his friends to come in and see him more often. He ate up there with them every day.

I followed Dad around the pharmacy and the racetracks. When I was six, my dad took me out of school to watch one of his horses run. I guess he knew the horse was going to win. I placed my first bet at Churchill Downs that day. I wasn't legally old enough to bet, but they said, "Aw, he's okay. He's Lee Wagner's son. He can bet it." I remember getting in trouble at school because I come back the next day, and I've got $300 in my pocket. I'm in second grade and I'm showing all my buddies, "Look at this!" My mom was mortified. She screamed at my dad when he came home, "St. Margaret Mary principal called me into the office. I have to go in there because he's showing off $300 cash. What are you letting him do that for?" I knew how to wheel an exacta and do a trifecta by the time I was seven or eight years old.

Nowadays, people probably would be asking, "What are you doing letting your kid hang around here?" But the track didn't seem like it was unsafe. Maybe that's because Dad knew so many people. Race-trackers look after their own, and they looked after me.

Lee Wagner Jr. (left) and Leo Wagner Sr. (right)

I think that's one reason why he let me run around to different barns and all that. If you're considered part of their family, then they're going to look after you.

I'd come over to the pharmacy for work and I'd be irritating Dad and he'd tell Larry Brown or Henry McIntyre, "Take him over to the jocks' room. Get him out of my hair for a while." So I'd go over there and play ping pong with Matty Brown. He was a longtime valet and friends with my dad. He was there for four decades. He'd go to Florida in the winter time and help my dad get in with a lot of the jocks and we'd sell them all that tack. Matty was one of the big reasons we bought the tack shop by Hialeah in the '80s. I remember going down to Florida one time and hanging out with Matty for three days. He took me fishing. Who knows what my dad was doing. That whole community kind of watched me while Dad did his business.

Some people think that there's a lot of bad people on the track. It isn't like that. There might be one or two bad apples, but there's more really, really good people. The majority of the people over there are very good hearted. They care about the horses, and they care about their people. It's such a close community. They spend so much time together. It's a seven-day-a-week job. Even though you're competing against these guys, you become friends. There's a mutual respect, because you see these people getting up working hard every day too. There's that appreciation. There's not a lot of people that have that type of work ethic. Seven days a week. Those animals need them and you can count on them. That's one of the things I learned to respect the most, that dependability.

There have been so many examples of times when people needed things, had fallen on some hard times,

and other racetrackers would rally around them. It's not just one or two people. Quite a few will say, "What can I do to help?"

Eugene Roche would be one of the best examples. He got sick and couldn't work every day. He was getting older. Roche was walking those horses up into at least his late 80s. He was still hot walking them for a paycheck. When it became difficult for him to walk hots, he came to the barn less. His boss Marty knew what it meant to him. They figured out a way to get him over there and to let him continue to feel like he's a part of it and really doing something. They gave him work to do. They didn't have to do this. But they knew that without it, it would probably kill him, he probably wouldn't have had as many more good years. He had given them so many good years that they felt like that's the least they could do for him. We tried to do our part by helping with gift cards and food. He ate at Wagner's for 40-some-odd years every day they were in town. It was the ones like Roche who make Wagner's so colorful.

You talk about characters: there was a guy named Jose who was one of the best exercise riders of his time. They called him "the exercise rider to the stars." Bobby Frankel, Baffert, Zito, and all these big guys would use him. I'll never forget him coming into the pharmacy. He'd always say, "Little man! Can you get me some of those blue pills?" He thought Viagra cured everything. "Tell your daddy that cures my cold better than anything." I'd say, "No! No!" But that was just him—he was just a card. He'd say, "Tell your dad I've got a winner for him. This thing's going to win by 10 lengths." I'd tell my dad and he'd say, "He always says that shit." He just wanted to cut up. But he was a hell of a horseman.

When people say, "Describe Wagner's," I tell them, "It's full of colorful people. If you like to people

watch, you'll love it. If you like a community where you have all different types of people with a love of racing who come together to talk? There you get it." Wagner's is still a place where horsemen can go and get everything they need for their horses and get a good meal.

This is the community that helped build Churchill. That is what keeps people coming back to it. It's not just the experiences over there at the track that are so important. Anybody that ever goes to the backside, it's one of the most memorable things that they've ever done. That's their favorite thing. They went to the Derby and, sure, they had fun. But when they remember the backside they say, "I've really enjoyed this. The way the whole thing comes together." It's a different feeling than the grandstands. You can't see that everywhere, and it makes the whole racing experience more compelling.

I grew up here. I spent most of my time around here. Dad brought me in from the time I was three years old. To this day I'll be walking around here and I still get called Little Lee by these old timers. I'm 44 years old now and I still get called Little Lee. I'll never outgrow that, I guess. /

the
Thoroughbred
RECORD

ESTABLISHED FEBRUARY 5, 1875

Eugene Roche (right)

Eugene Roche Jr.

GROOM

I grew up in Tampa, Florida. I was born in 1925. I'm 91 years old. I been at the race-track about 65 years and I've rubbed some nice horses.

I worked for W. King in 1965. Dark Mirage was one of the best horses in the country. We won about 22 races in a row. She was 1-9 every time she ran. She paid $2.20 to win. Don't get any lower than that. You don't make no money. Only the big shots. They used to bet $100,000 to show. If you bet a million dollars you'll make a lot of money.

I met Smiley Adams in New York. He was one of the best trainers in the country. I worked for Smiley Adams for 19 years. I remember one time I was walking horses for him in New York, and he told me, "I'm gonna give you a good horse to rub." He gave me Master Derby, a two-year-old. I said, "What? This looks like a pony." Smiley said, "It's not a pony. It's a super-horse. I want you to make a million dollars with this horse. This is gonna be one of the best horses you ever seen. Take good care of him. Keep him nice and clean. Give him a nice blanket."

Smiley said I was one of the best grooms he ever had and he took real good care of me. I told him, "I don't need no company." So he gave me my own tack room to sleep in, bought me a bed. I had a TV and everything. I always watched my horse like a dog so nobody would bother him and stayed in the barn when they were going to race. I used to buy blankets for Master Derby.

He bit me on the arm once and put me in the hospital. We won the Preakness in 1975 with Master Derby and that's the biggest ticket I ever cashed. I bet $50 to win on him and he paid $49. Between the trainer and the jockey I got another $3,000 in stake money.

Master Derby made over $2 million. He run six furlongs in 1:15. He run a mile and sixteen in 141 and 2. Imagine how much he would've made today. I rubbed him for two years and they retired him at four. They took him to Calumet at and put him there to stud.

Then Run Dusty Run ran second to Seattle Slew in 1977 in the Belmont and the Derby, and third in the Preakness.

I've lived at the Old School Apartments for about 14 years.

I've been going to church about 41 years. We have a beautiful chapel at Churchill Downs. You ought to go see it. Services on Monday.

When Mr. Roche died in February of 2017—at 91 years old— he was likely the oldest licensed horseman in the United States. He continued coming to work in the stable area, walking hots, doing barn laundry, cleaning tack, visiting friends at Wagner's, and going to church on the backside until two months before he passed. His ashes were spread in the Kentucky Derby Winner's Circle by his friends and fellow racetrackers.

The Backside

Here's to those that work the backside,
The horses you race carry your pride.
You follow the circuit, track to track,
Busting your ass, breaking your back.

Day after day, you give it your all,
Winter, spring, summer, and fall.
Your nights are short, your days are long,
Your love for the horses, evidently strong.

More than a job, it's your way of living,
You get so little for all you are giving.
When you think that the fans don't care,
Remember, without you, they wouldn't be there!

Here's to you, the unsung hero,
Without you, no race would go.
You get up early, you stay up late,
To insure there are horses for the gate.

You work hard, night and day,
In hopes of making the cashier pay.
You work in heat, cold, and rain,
When you feel good, or are in pain.

To those who know your dedication,
You are truly an inspiration.
Most fans don't know all you do,
On behalf of them, I say, "THANK YOU

Acknowledgments

For every time we've pinched ourselves and marveled that the Louisville Story Program was able to do the first deep-dive documentary project on the backside at Churchill Downs, a familiar realization has immediately followed: A project like this hard to pull off, expensive, and takes forever. That's why books like this are so rare. To even come close to accurately documenting the richness and nuance of the backside is an enormous undertaking for a small organization like LSP, and this book would never have been possible without a dedicated community of supportive individuals and institutions who believe in our mission and who understood the value of a book like this one.

First, to the authors: Thank you for your generosity and for sharing your stories with us and now with the public. Three years of being peppered with rookie questions, hounded for rewrites, photos, and just one more good story, and here it is: the book you wrote.

Thank you to the major financial supporters of this project: Louisville Metro Government, the Fund for the Arts, Mrs. Christina Lee Brown, Matthew Barzun and Brooke Brown Barzun, the Churchill Downs Foundation, Owsley Brown III, the Snowy Owl Foundation, the Lawrence L. Jones Sr. Fund, the Gilbert Foundation, Porter Watkins, the Kentucky Oral History Commission, and Judy Oetinger.

To our early friends in the racing community and on the backside who guided us into a network of community and helped us chart a path through the stable yard with introductions, tips, and support, thank you so much: Fred and Judy Look, Jim Mulvihill, Bob DeSensi, Richard Reidel, Ben Huffman, Dr. David Richardson, Dale Romans, John Asher, Carla Grego, Bill Vest, Abram Himelstein, and The Backside Learning Center.

To all of the racetrackers, equine workers, providers, and experts who helped us navigate the South End and the world of racing or spent time giving interviews that didn't make it into the book, but which were crucially important to our work and our understanding, many thanks. Very especially our thanks go to: Tom Owens, Chaplain Joseph Del Rosario, Mary Feiock, John Lee Robertson, Beto Urduño, Jesus Castanon, Greg Perez, Sue Stidham, and Nathaniel.

To Paul Goffner for allowing us to use his photo on the cover. That joy and pride and strut is some of what we hoped to capture in this book.

To our amazing book designer, Shellee Marie Jones, who once again said yes when we asked if she would make another beautiful looking book, and also when we ask for an extension. Thank you for sharing your incredible talent, and for your graciousness. You're LSP family, and we're so grateful.

To Matt Bradshaw, who arrived at precisely the right time, and helped us with some crucially important research and editing. You're a natural and a life-saver. Thank you so much.

To Cat Sar, whose good spirit, diligence, and dedication to our mission were so helpful in the early stages of this book, you have our gratitude.

We're thankful to Dr. Karen Chandler and the University of Louisville English Department for introducing us to the interns whose work was so integral to this book.

To Spalding University for their support of Louisville Story Program's mission, and for being such fantastic neighbors, we are immensely grateful.

This project would not have been possible without our Spalding University work-studies, our SummerWorks employee, and the generous support of our volunteer transcriptionists. We could not have turned the words of our contributors into text on the page without you. Thank you so much: Sarah Dyson, Leo Smith, Chloe Teets, Taylor Thompson, Ruby Martinez, Jeanette Burke, Ellen Burt, Judy Hoge, Chastedy Johnson, Jane Kennedy, Tyrell Kessinger, Maria Kirsch, Laura Kirwin, Jason Linden, and Liana Rogers.

To our volunteer translators and editors, thank you for the generous donation of your time and immense talent: Lynn Pohl, Bob Manning, Christine Gosney, Jim Miller, Elizabeth Kuhn, Blanca Ruiz, Connie Dorval, and Rebecca Richart.

To Clarke Otte, Linda Doane, Pat McDonogh of the *Courier-Journal*, and Ben Freedman for the amazing photography they donated to this project. Your talents have given this book the visual feel that we hoped to capture from the very start. Thank you so much.

To Kertis Creative for their continued, generous, and immensely significant support of LSP. Thanks for all that you do to present our work to the public. We're so fortunate to have you in the family.

To the Kentucky Derby Museum for offering to host the book launch celebration at a significantly discounted rate, and for making some valuable connections.

To the Community Foundation of Louisville for their ongoing engagement with and support of our work.

To Taylor Made Sales Agency and Churchill Downs for donating such nice rewards for our Kickstarter campaign.

Thank you to those who donated photographs which were so important to the feel of the book: Mike Bunnell, Mary Anne Huffman, Bill Landes, Lori Liter, Carla and Andy Lucas.

To everyone who backed the project on Kickstarter, especially Allen Bush and Rose Cooper, Kristen Lucas, Stephen Reily and Emily Bingham, Nina Bonnie, Tony Sivori and Rebecca DeSensi Sivori, Mimi Zinniel, Ashbrook Farm, Judy and Fred Look, Bob and Bo Manning, Mary and Ted Nixon, Old Stone Press, Cambus-Kenneth Farm, Elizabeth Matera, Tom and Jenny Sawyer, Beth Bissmeyer, Ann Coffey and Valle Jones, Jennie Jean Davidson, Mary Grissom, Karen Koch, Keith Look and Carlotta Kustes, David López, Lois and Jim Luckett, Christine M. Naseman, Andrew and Nancy Owen, Ellen Sears, and Bob Strobo.

To John Jeremiah Sullivan for the good words. Thank you.

Thanks to Savannah Barrett for her grace, guidance, and support.

Our most sincere thanks to the reader. All of this is for you.

—Joe Manning, Elizabeth Sawyer, and Darcy Thompson
Louisville Story Program